Classical Liberalism
by Country
Vol. I: Australia, India,
South Africa, China, North and
South Korea, and Lebanon

Classical Liberalism
by Country
Vol. I: Australia, India, South Africa, China, North and South Korea, and Lebanon

Edited by
Daniel B. Klein,
Jason Briggeman &
Jane Shaw Stroup

CL Press
A Fraser Institute Project
Vancouver

CL Press

Published by CL PRESS
A project of the Fraser Institute
1770 Burrard Street, 4th Floor
Vancouver, BC V6J 3G7 Canada
www.clpress.net

Classical Liberalism by Country
Vol. I: Australia, India, South Africa, China, North and South Korea, and Lebanon
Edited by Daniel B. Klein, Jason Briggeman, and Jane Shaw Stroup

© 2023 by CL Press

ISBN: 978-1-957698-05-2

Cover design by John Stephens

Contents

Introduction

Daniel B. Klein

Econ Journal Watch is a classical-liberal journal of commentary on the doings of economists, including their judgments, research, character, methods, practices, and institutions. EJW has opened its pages to commentary on other fields, besides economics.

Character includes ideological character. EJW embarked on a series treating classical liberalism by country, beginning with a June 2014 call for papers, and publishing the first six pieces (on Australia, Spain, Poland, Lebanon, the ex-Yugoslav nations, and the Czech Republic) in the May 2015 issue. We anticipate that through EJW's 2023 issues, the series will have 24 papers. Those papers are being collected here in three volumes, with the present Introduction appearing only in the first volume:

Volume 1	Volume 2	Volume 3
Introduction	Mexico	Iceland
Australia	Guatemala	Finland
India	Ecuador	Denmark
South Africa	Peru	Spain
China	Colombia	Italy
North and South Korea	Venezuela	Czech Republic
Lebanon	Brazil	Poland
		Ex-Yugoslav nations
		Ukraine
		Romania
		Bulgaria

The chapters all began as articles at EJW, of which I am chief editor. Refereeing of the articles was copious—on many of the papers there were five or more referees. We canvassed widely for feedback. The original articles are listed in the references list below.

The volumes are published by CL Press, which Erik Matson and I co-direct. Both EJW and CL Press are projects of the Fraser Institute, of Vancouver, Canada.

Jason Briggeman, the Managing Editor of EJW, has been and continues to be my chief partner on the entire project—also in the republication, as he has handled all of the layout, typesetting, and formatting for these three CL Press volumes. Jane Shaw Stroup, EJW Editorial Advisor, also copy-edited most of original articles. Thus, the production and editing of the three volumes has been the joint work chiefly of Jane, Jason, and myself. Also vital to the overall project has been Lawrence H. White, the EJW Co-editor to whom I have turned for second editorial review and approval of most of these articles; also, as host of the EJW Audio Podcast series, Larry has thus far interviewed authors of 15 of the articles.

For the volumes, in 2022 we asked authors whether they would like to add a brief postscript, as some of the pieces appeared as long ago as 2015. Ten of the pieces have postscripts. Otherwise, the articles are republished basically as originally published: We asked the authors whether any small corrections were needed, and some of the authors instructed us to make a few changes.

Within each volume, the abstract of a chapter appears at the front, where all of the abstracts for the chapters in that volume are gathered. Author bios for each volume are collected at the end of the volume.

In this brief introduction, I do not offer chapter-by-chapter summarization. My aims here are limited to describing the project itself, clarifying its nature, and reflecting on some of the broader things I have learned from it.

About the project and its progress

The project focuses on classical liberalism, along the lines of the Smithian tradition, which, upon certain presuppositions discussed below, is predisposed against the governmentalization of social affairs. Adam Smith (1976/1776, 664) propounded a presumption in favor of "allowing every man to pursue his own interest his own way, upon the liberal plan of equality, liberty and justice." Chapters often state that such liberalism is what they will henceforth mean by "liberalism," and I do the same now.

For an author who takes up the call to write about liberalism in a country, the task is both historical and current. EJW requested that authors consider paying special attention to economic discourse, and thus to political economists, but that request was a mild one.

In the historiographical aspect of the chapters, there is a balance between intellectual history and social/political history. We requested due notice to intellectual figures, but also gave free rein to recounting and interpreting political history. Some of the chapters offer rich narratives of the fortunes of liberal politics through many generations. Since the work of intellectuals is highly conditioned by the political circumstances of their discourse, it is apt to learn the political history to understand the intellectual history.

It would be difficult to tackle England, Scotland, France, the United States, Germany, and so on, whose liberal traditions have so much to tell of. For Spain, we are grateful for a brief overview. There is a lengthy chapter on Italy, but the chapter's story begins with the 1860s.

The stories end in a recent year—when the original article appeared in EJW. All of the papers include a survey of the country's then-current liberal figures, organizations, outlets, and activities.

Within such broad parameters, and with abundant feedback from editors and referees, each author developed the paper as he or she saw fit. The chapters vary considerably in length and emphasis. Some chapters have maps and photos while others do not. Some of the countries simply do not have a rich liberal tradition to tell of. As for the authors, their characters vary. Some are young scholars who seized the opportunity to learn of the liberal heritage of their own country. Others are mature scholars who have otherwise published on some of the figures or events treated in their chapter. And many are liberal practitioners—liberal leaders—with personal experience in liberal activities of recent decades. Some of these practitioner-leaders are on the young side and look ahead, while some are seasoned and have much experience to look back on. The piece on Lebanon is based around a survey, and, like many of the chapters, describes the country's challenges generally, from a liberal perspective.

In making these volumes, we decided to include *all* papers published in the EJW series, motley as they are. Liberal principles depend on circumstances, but everywhere humans are humans, each an individual organism, with knowledge and control of very limited reach and effectiveness. The voluntary/coercive distinction depends somewhat on circumstances, but the case against coercion and against the governmentalization of social affairs is quite universal and quite timeless. As Milton Friedman said, we all spend more effectively when we spend our own money on our own concerns than when we spend other people's money on other people's concerns. And, everywhere, voluntary association presumptively generates mutual gains. It inspires and rewards innovation, making what Deirdre McCloskey calls the Great Enrichment and sustaining greater "multiplication of the species," as Smith put it repeatedly. So why not allow every person to pursue her own interest her own way, upon the liberal plan of equality, liberty, and justice?

C. S. Lewis wrote:

> As Dr. Johnson said, 'People need to be reminded more often than they need to be instructed.' The real job of every moral teacher is to keep on bringing us back, time after time, to the old simple principles which we are all so anxious not to see... (2002, 74)

Everywhere, the call of wisdom and virtue points in the liberal direction. Each of the chapters nurtures an aspiration toward greater liberty, contextualized to a country and its heritage.

Some insights from the project

From the age of 17 or so I have swum in libertarian and classical-liberal waters, in the United States. In 2015, when this project published its first pieces, I was 53 years old. But learning continues. The experience of this project has impressed upon me certain things that I had not seen so clearly, or even at all.

One insight, analogous to the brain drain, is the liberal drain. Liberals are apt to emigrate to more liberal pastures. It makes perfect sense, especially to a liberal, as liberals believe that liberal norms and institutions make a society more desirable. It was not something I had reflected on before, but the project has impressed upon me its importance. The authors of one chapter title their piece: "Venezuela: Without Liberals, There Is No Liberalism." The liberal drain is a very significant challenge to countries mired in anti-liberalism, such as Venezuela. Reading the chapters, one finds that some of the protagonists are ex-pats, working in the United Kingdom, the United States, and elsewhere. Such ex-pats can still speak to their country of origin and help move it in liberal directions, but distance sets in, making the ex-pat less in touch, less knowledgeable, less influential, and less inclined. If there is any upside to the First World's late sharp turn against liberalism and liberality, and toward the greater governmentalization of social affairs, it might be the mitigation of the liberal drain. The more that the First World turns itself into the Second and Third Worlds, the less will people, including liberals, seek to emigrate to the erstwhile First World.

At a deeper level, the project has impressed upon me certain things about the nature of Smithian liberalism, its presuppositions and preconditions, its paradoxes, its challenges and prospects. I cannot say that the project has made me more optimistic, but hope springs eternal.

At the center of Smithian liberalism is a presumption toward "allowing every man," as quoted above, and the corresponding presumption against the governmentalization of social affairs. Adam Smith suggested that *The Wealth of Nations* tills the field of "the science of a legislator"; the book teaches understandings and precepts for good policymaking, the main lesson being a presumption of liberty.

That is all well and good. Something it takes as given is "a legislator." What about the determination of who the legislator shall be? Suppose the determination is electoral in some manner. Is it part of Smithian liberalism to concern itself in partisan politics? After all, some would-be legislators are more amenable to Smith's precepts than other would-be legislators. Indeed, some violently oppose free markets, free enterprise, free speech, and other liberal principles that check the governmentalization of social affairs. Some lack understanding of the rule of law.

Practical politics is always a matter of lesser and greater evil. Surely, it is part of civic virtue to advance the lesser evil against the greater evil. Civic virtue may also call for trying to make at least one of the evils less evil, and, to do that, one must caucus or coalesce with the party.

But the more that the liberal acts to advance a lesser evil, and thereby involve himself in partisan politics, the more he must trim and compromise his liberal druthers. He tempers his call for liberty and his condemnations of governmentalization. Rolling back governmentalization is an endeavor that must involve government action, including the cooperation of politicians and administrative operatives throughout the apparatus. The liberal must govern to liberalize. The good career of the good liberal is complicated, and we must contemplate complications if we are to judge liberals.

At the first level, we have appreciation and genuine favor for liberal policy. But that level presupposed a legislator, so we then moved to a second level, the battle among evils in partisan politics. But that too rests on an important presupposition, namely, a stable, functional political order, a set of social conventions, in which things such as the processes of electoral politics proceed. That is not something to presuppose throughout countries today, even less over centuries past.

The third level is the matter of stable polity, with half-way honest and functional political institutions. The third level is concisely framed in David Hume's memorable words: "**liberty** is the perfection of civil society; but still **authority** must be acknowledged essential to its very existence" (1987, 40, emphasis added). Authority is a precondition of liberal authority. A polity is a precondition of a liberal polity. And "a polity" means more than simply the cartological designation of a geographic area on a map. The example of electoral procedure is but synecdoche of what is at stake here: A wide set of conventions and institutions for stable, half-way honest politics, including the process of law-making, the legal system soup-to-nuts, a half-way responsible and independent media, public administration not terribly cynical and grafty, and so on—as well as honest elections. Some measure of all such things is necessary for liberalism to mean something. And none is to be taken for granted. Sometimes the history of a country reads like an account of struggles from one Machiavellian moment to the next.

When reading the chapters on Latin American countries, Eastern European countries, China, Korea, India, South Africa, and Lebanon, ask yourself: Who exactly was the liberal protagonist addressing? And who exactly was the agent envisioned to reform policy in the directions advised? Meaningful discourse depends on a degree of coherence in the discourser's implied reader. Such coherence depends on a cultural ecology, a sociological topography of competing and countervailing judgments, a functional "central zone," as Edward Shils (1972) called it, or at least aspirations of such. Without virtues such as liberality, the "commanding heights" of culture are laid low. When liberals broadcast, "Let the Market Decide!," whom are they talking to? Who is doing the letting?

We thus have three levels for liberal civic virtue:

1. Appreciation of liberal policy as the alternative to governmentalization.
2. The art of liberal politics, angling for less-evil governors.
3. Having a stable, half-way functional, half-way honest polity.

Levels two and three each mull over something presupposed at its preceding level. In reading the chapters of all three volumes, we find that the third level is in play—in doubt—as we look back on the history at least at some point, except perhaps only in the chapters on Denmark and on Australia. That is how pervasively important the third level is.

The chapters in this project speak of protagonists mostly of the 19th, 20th, and 21st centuries. Those protagonists were influenced by earlier thinkers of international fame. The chapters testify to Frédéric Bastiat being one of the more influential figures, with Jean-Baptiste Say also often mentioned. Their teachings, however, remain quite focused on the first level. In my view, it was 18th century thinkers, who had a better sense of all three levels of liberal civic virtue, such as Montesquieu, Hume, Smith, and Edmund Burke. One of the reasons that liberalism has not fared better is that it has not contemplated the second and third levels as well as it might have. I advise against looking to replace liberalism with something else, but rather to fulfill and resume the sensibilities of such 18th-century figures, and preserve the liberal christening. Modifying with "conservative" would yield conservative liberalism.

When reading the chapters, ponder how the protagonists were, if only tacitly, constrained and affected by levels two and three.

A few of the chapters conclude with the sentiment that the future of liberalism is unwritten. Get writing, but contemplate always, for without an upward vitality we will in time find ourselves slipping downward.

References: Original articles now republished in the volumes

Berg, Chris. Classical Liberalism in Australian Economics. *Econ Journal Watch* 12(2): 192–220.

Berlanza, Lucas. 2020. Liberalism in Brazil. *Econ Journal Watch* 17(2): 405–441.

Bunyk, Mykola, and Leonid Krasnozhon. 2018. Liberalism in Ukraine. *Econ Journal Watch* 15(1): 83–104.

Choi, Young Back, and Yong J. Yoon. 2016. Liberalism in Korea. *Econ Journal Watch* 13(1): 100–128.

Faria, Hugo J., and Leonor Filardo. 2015. Venezuela: Without Liberals, There Is No Liberalism. *Econ Journal Watch* 12(3): 375–399.

Feng, Xingyuan, Weisen Li, and Evan W. Osborne. 2017. Classical Liberalism in China: Some History and Prospects. *Econ Journal Watch* 14(2): 218–240.

Fradejas, Fernando Hernández. 2015. Liberal Economics in Spain. *Econ Journal Watch* 12(2): 221–232.

Gissurarson, Hannes H. 2017. Liberalism in Iceland in the Nineteenth and Twentieth Centuries. *Econ Journal Watch* 14(2): 241–273.

Grandell, Jens. 2021. Classical Liberalism in Finland in the Nineteenth Century. *Econ Journal Watch* 18(2): 235–256.

Grandell, Jens. 2022. Classical Liberalism in Finland in the Twentieth Century. *Econ Journal Watch* 19(2): 296–319.

Kuchař, Pavel. 2016. Liberalism in Mexican Economic Thought, Past and Present. *Econ Journal Watch* 13(1): 129–167.

Kurrild-Klitgaard, Peter. 2015. Classical Liberalism and Modern Political Economy in Denmark. *Econ Journal Watch* 12(3): 400–431.

Machaj, Mateusz. 2015. Liberal Economics in Poland. *Econ Journal Watch* 12(2): 233–241.

Manish, G. P., Shruti Rajagopalan, Daniel Sutter, and Lawrence H. White. 2015. Liberalism in India. *Econ Journal Watch* 12(3): 432–459

Mardini, Patrick. 2015. The Endangered Classical Liberal Tradition in Lebanon: A General Description and Survey Results. *Econ Journal Watch* 12(2): 242–259.

Marroquín, Andrés, and Fritz Thomas. 2015. Classical Liberalism in Guatemala. *Econ Journal Watch* 12(3): 460–478.

Mingardi, Alberto. 2017. Classical Liberalism in Italian Economic Thought, from the Time of Unification. *Econ Journal Watch* 14(1): 22–54.

Prokopijević, Miroslav, and Slaviša Tasić. 2015. Classical Liberal Economics in the Ex-Yugoslav Nations. *Econ Journal Watch* 12(2): 260–273.

Rodríguez, Sebastián, and Gilberto Ramírez. 2022. Liberalism in Colombia. *Econ Journal Watch* 19(1): 142–165.

Romero, Pedro, Fergus Hodgson, and María Paz Gómez. 2018. Liberalism in Ecuador. *Econ Journal Watch* 15(1): 105–128.

Saenz-Armstrong, Patricia. 2018. Economic Liberalism in Peru. *Econ Journal Watch* 15(2): 179–200.

Šíma, Josef, and Tomáš Nikodym. 2015. Classical Liberalism in the Czech Republic. *Econ Journal Watch* 12(2): 274–292.

Van Staden, Martin. 2019. The Liberal Tradition in South Africa, 1910–2019. *Econ Journal Watch* 16(2): 258–341.

Other references

Hume, David. 1987. *Essays, Moral, Political, and Literary*, ed. E. F. Miller. Indianapolis: Liberty Fund.

Lewis, C. S. 2002. *The Complete C. S. Lewis Signature Classics*. New York: Harper One.

Shils, Edward. 1972. *The Constitution of Society*. Chicago: University of Chicago Press.

Smith, Adam. 1976 [1776]. *An Inquiry into the Nature and Causes of the Wealth of Nations*, ed. R. H. Campbell, A. S. Skinner, and W. B. Todd. Oxford: Oxford University Press.

Chapter Abstracts

Chapter 1: Chris Berg, "Classical Liberalism in Australian Economics"
Classical liberalism, the tradition of free markets and individual liberty, has an outsider status in the Australian economics profession. This paper surveys the origin of Australian classical liberal economics in the nineteenth century, its sharp decline in the first half of the twentieth century, and its revival and growth in recent decades. Despite a period of successful market-oriented economic reform in the 1980s and 1990s, surveys suggest that classical liberalism is a minority viewpoint among Australian economists. The classical liberal tradition is sustained only by a small number of institutions and individuals. To the extent that it is influential, it is influential thanks to a political culture that prioritises public engagement. Classical liberal economists have a high degree of participation in political and economic debate outside the academy.

Chapter 2: G. P. Manish, Shruti Rajagopalan, Daniel Sutter, and Lawrence H. White, "Liberalism in India"
We give an overview of classical liberal ideas and their proponents in India over the last century. The liberal movement in India, especially during the postcolonial era, was defined by the socialist ideas it opposed. We detail the different stages of central planning in India and the liberal opposition to the planning apparatus. The liberal movement consisted of three components. First, dissent from the ideology of planning emanated from the halls of academia. This dissent was led in the 1950s almost singlehandedly by B. R. Shenoy, who was followed in later decades by other expatriate academics. Second, there has been an anti-planning movement in politics and civil society. And third, liberal voices have emerged recently in the media.

Chapter 3: Martin van Staden, "The Liberal Tradition in South Africa, 1910–2019"

Race looms large in the politics of many countries, but perhaps nowhere more so than in South Africa. Liberals of both the classical and left varieties joined in their opposition to Apartheid, a political system that discriminated along racial lines. The historical account of this paper focuses especially on the classical liberal tradition and begins primarily in 1910, when the South African colonies were united into a polity with their own central Parliament, though at that time they were still a dominion of the United Kingdom. The first half of the paper provides a unified historical narrative describing the role of liberals, while the second half is more episodic, treating persons, organizations, and liberals in politics. The bulk of classical liberals today are found in a small number of independent think tanks and to a limited extent in the second-largest political party in South Africa.

Chapter 4: Xingyuan Feng, Weisen Li, and Evan W. Osborne, "Classical Liberalism in China: Some History and Prospects"

We explore (classical) liberal thought in China. In China's long recorded history, some ideas similar to subsequent Western liberal thinking have periodically appeared. Starting in the late nineteenth century, translated Western works on liberalism became available. Currently, because of political intrigue, economic liberal themes are rare in official academic or political settings, but even now much liberal thinking is freely available, networks of liberal aficionados have existed, and their activities and ideas have been accessible to the public, and they remain a resource available to be drawn upon. The influence of many of these ideas is still relatively weak, and there are concerns about growing restrictions on politically threatening views. But economists most influenced by liberalism have in recent decades had some role in public opinion, though less so in shaping public policy. Given the huge tasks ahead in Chinese reform, liberals need to strengthen these networks, and to gain support from entrepreneurs in particular. This is especially true due to significant changes, especially in the international situation, that have occurred since this article originally appeared. These changes are discussed in the postscript.

Chapter 5: Young Back Choi and Yong J. Yoon, "Liberalism in Korea"
We describe the place of classical liberalism in Korea's past and present. Korea first glimpsed classical liberalism in the mid-18th century, and liberalism experienced a resurgence there in the late 20th century. But Korea's history has been mostly bereft of liberalism, even after the country became democratic and economically productive. Its history began with rigid social stratification undergirded by the Confucian ideology; that was followed by failed attempts to reform and a period of colonization by Japan. Korea was liberated from Japan's control at the end of WWII, but divided into North and South. A liberal democracy was formed in South Korea in the face of communist threats, followed by a period of authoritarian rule, then a transition to democracy, and then finally some awakening of classical liberalism. Classical liberal economists still constitute a small minority of the Korean economic profession, but they have been active in educating the public and have achieved a degree of success.

Chapter 6: Patrick Mardini, "The Endangered Classical Liberal Tradition in Lebanon: A General Description and Survey Results"
Classical liberal analysis has dwindled in Lebanon after a long and vibrant tradition of *laisser faire* economic policy that lasted for many centuries, peaking in the period 1943 to 1975. Today, a sectarian-political regime, clientelistic public spending, clientelistic public employment, political patronage of public institutions, and statutory monopoly schemes are deep-rooted and have replaced the rationale of private initiative and economic freedom. A survey I devised to gauge the attitudes of Lebanese economics professors shows that some elements of classical liberalism still exist. The number of survey respondents is small but the great majority of respondents favor reducing clientelism, even clientelism that helps their own sects. However, they still believe that economic problems can be resolved throughout additional government spending. Most support liberal propositions on competition and market liberalization, but their views tend to be against liberalization when it comes to public moral laws and immigration.

Classical Liberalism
by Country
Vol. I: Australia, India, South Africa, China, North and South Korea, and Lebanon

This chapter first appeared as an Econ Journal Watch article in May 2015.
It has not been revised.

Classical Liberalism in Australian Economics

Chris Berg[1]

Classical liberalism is not a dominant tradition in Australian economics. Nonetheless, Australia has an important and underappreciated strand of classical liberal thought that stretches from the nineteenth century until today. This paper emphasises the most prominent and important classical liberals, movements, and organisations, as well as their relationship to the economics profession at large, since colonisation. Of course no survey can include every popular expositor of classical liberalism nor every academic economist who shares a philosophical disposition towards free markets and small government. Furthermore, a survey of this tradition must include not only academic economists and theoretical innovators but public intellectuals and popularisers.

Australia was colonised at the tail end of the Enlightenment. The establishment of New South Wales in 1788 as a penal colony run by the military sparked a constitutional and philosophical debate about the legitimate basis of government in Australia, a debate that to a great extent proceeded on Lockean precepts (Gascoigne 2002). Australian libraries were full of works by Scottish Enlightenment authors. Every known Australian library in the 1830s held Adam Smith's *Wealth of Nations* (Dixon 1986).

During the first half century of the Australian colonies, economics education was given privately or through the system of Mechanics Institutes that sought to raise the education of the working class. There were no formal academies of learning in Australia until the establishment of the University of

---

1. I would like to thank Stephen Kirchner, John Hyde, Richard Allsop, Alan Moran, Mikayla Novak, Sinclair Davidson, Wolfgang Kasper, and Greg Melleuish.

Sydney in 1850 and the University of Melbourne in 1853. The first Australian economics publication, James Aikenhead's *Principles of Political Economy* (1856), came out of a series of lectures to a Launceston Mechanics Institute. Aikenhead (1815–1887) was firmly in the Smithian tradition. His lectures were not highly original—J. A. La Nauze (1949, 16) dismissed them as "a feeble rehash of [John Ramsay] McCulloch"—but they were certainly liberal. Aikenhead argued that "security of property, freedom of industry, and moderation in the public expenditure are the…certain means by which the various powers and resources of human talent and ingenuity may be called into action, and society made continually to advance in the career of wealth and civilisation" (1856, 40).

Australian politics in the second half of the nineteenth century was dominated by the debate between free trade and protection. Six separate British colonies were established on the Australian continent—New South Wales, Victoria, Queensland, South Australia, Tasmania, and Western Australia. Under colonial rule, the colonies had their trade policy set by the British Colonial Office. It was only after the end of imperial preference in the 1840s and the granting of self-government to the larger colonies that the trade debate began in earnest. The question was how the colonies should trade among each other and with the wider world. Free Trade Associations were formed, and the debate was waged through pamphlets and the press. The writings were peppered with references to Adam Smith, John Stuart Mill, and the British anti-Corn Law activists Richard Cobden and John Bright. There are even two towns in Victoria named Cobden and Bright.

Not all free traders were liberals. Within the labour movement there were free traders who saw protection as a tax imposed by manufacturers on the working class (see, e.g., Pearce 1903). Other free traders were social reformers, like the New South Wales politician B. R. Wise, who preached free trade and industrial regulation. Nevertheless the dominance of the free trade debate ensured that the liberal tradition remained at centre stage in colonial politics.

Except for a brief period in the 1850s, the New South Wales newspaper *Empire* ran an aggressively pro-free trade line. Likewise the *Sydney Morning Herald* was a free trade newspaper. Protectionism was advocated by the Victorian *Age* and its proprietor David Syme. Like many Australian protectionists, Syme had been greatly influenced by John Stuart Mill's argument in his *Principles of Political Economy* (Mill 1848) that industries in young

4

countries might require temporary protection from established international competitors, an argument that was known as the infant industry argument. Given Mill's outsized profile in the English speaking world, his infant industry argument became "a familiar trump card for the protectionists" in the Australian debate (La Nauze 1949, 15).

The divide between the *Sydney Morning Herald* and the *Age* reflected the victory of free trade in New South Wales and the victory of protection in Victoria. But as Gregory Melleuish (2009) notes, while free traders had political success in Sydney, it was in Melbourne that the laissez-faire intellectual tradition thrived. In Melbourne "free trade liberals did not have to concern themselves with the realities of wielding political power that produced the more strident ideological expression of this form of liberalism" (Melleuish 2009, 580).

William Edward Hearn (1826–1888) was Australia's first academic economist and author of the country's first economics textbook. Hearn was a professor of Greek at the College of Galway when he was chosen by a London committee in 1854 to be the University of Melbourne's first professor of modern history and literature, political economy and logic—one of just four professors when the university began classes in 1855. At that time population of Australia was only 400,000. Over the next half century it rose to nearly four million in 1901.

Hearn is best remembered for his proto-marginalist *Plutology: Or, the Theory of the Efforts to Satisfy Human Wants* (1864). *Plutology* is an a priori theoretical treatise on wealth and value that begins by analysing the nature of human wants and then travels through the nature of labour, capital, innovation, exchange, cooperation, politics, and poverty. Hearn was much taken by the Spencerian idea that society evolves from simplicity to complexity. The peculiar title was chosen because Hearn felt that the traditional phrase 'political economy' was more appropriate to describe the art of governance rather than the science of wealth creation. Alfred Marshall described *Plutology* as "simple and profound," and he recommended it to students as an introductory text (Moore 2002). *Plutology* was a standard textbook for Australian economics for at least a generation. Hearn, like many other Australians working on economic subjects even into the early twentieth century, was much influenced by Frédéric Bastiat. Indeed, the French economist had a disproportionate influence on nineteenth century Australian debate (Groenewegen and McFarlane 1990, 238).

Hearn's successor John Elkington (1841–1922) has a poor reputation today. He is blamed for "retard[ing] the progress" of Australian economics through his indolence and "emotional instability" (Moore 2007, 96). But Elkington managed to keep the University of Melbourne in the free trade rather than protectionist camp—no small achievement in the midst of Victoria's protectionist political environment. The English Fabian Beatrice Webb, passing through the University of Melbourne as part of an Australian tour in 1898, wrote that "Economics are represented by a shady old man...he is an old fashioned individualist" (Webb and Webb 1965, 88). He retired from the university in 1913. Both Hearn and Elkington had a substantial influence on the Victorian law profession, most of whom they had taught. As a consequence Melbourne University was regarded as a "breeding ground for free traders" (Goodwin 1966, 15).

The University of Sydney was founded in 1850, three years earlier than the University of Melbourne, but unlike its southern counterpart did not have a dedicated professor of economics. Nevertheless, its professor of classics and logic, John Woolley (1816–1866), and its professor of mathematics, Morris Pell (1827–1879), were both liberals with an interest in economics. For Woolley, the role of political economy was the preservation of liberty and the promotion of social harmony. Pell vehemently opposed the practice of the New South Wales government of subsidising railway construction (Groenewegen and McFarlane 1990, 49–51). Both Sydney professors had a marked influence on William Stanley Jevons, who spent the years between 1854 and 1859 in New South Wales working as the chief gold assayer of the new Royal Sydney Mint. The "basic premises" (White 1982) of what was to become Jevons's *Theory of Political Economy* (1871) were formulated in Sydney.

One student of W. E. Hearn was to become the dominant free trader among Australian intellectuals at the turn of the century: Bruce Smith (1851–1937). Smith's family emigrated from England to Melbourne in 1853. Smith trained as a lawyer under Hearn and was admitted to the Victorian bar. He moved to New South Wales to take a seat briefly in the Legislative Assembly before returning to Victoria to set up the Victorian Employers' Union. Smith believed that the growing power of trade unions needed a countervailing force. He later established the NSW Employers Union. As Melleuish (2005) writes, Smith was opposed to compulsion, not to collective action.

In 1887, Smith published the most significant Australian liberal political work, *Liberty and Liberalism*. This book was a defence of "original," "true" liberalism—the liberalism of Adam Smith—against "new," or "spurious" liberalism, pushed by social reformers and protectionists such as Syme. In Bruce Smith's view, a state should not tax, limit the liberty of, or acquire the property of any of its citizens except for the purpose of "securing equal freedom to all citizens." Smith added that property could only be acquired by government conditional on the owner being fully compensated (Smith 2005/1887, 299). Having been elected to a federal seat in south-east Sydney in the first federal election as a representative of the Free Trade Party, Smith distinguished himself as a voice against the White Australia Policy, a discriminatory immigration policy favoured by both free trade and Labor politicians at the turn of the century. His stance was unfortunately rare, even among purported free traders. The parliamentary leader of the Free Trade Party, the future Prime Minister George Reid, claimed to be the originator of the White Australia Policy (Kemp 2011).

Edward William Foxall (1857–1926) was a classical liberal thinker and politician active at the turn of the twentieth century. Like many classical liberals of the time, Foxall was an advocate of Henry George's proposed single tax on land. Georgists were found both within the labour movement—who were attracted to land nationalisation—and among classical liberals. For George, free trade was as important as land taxation, and his arguments were readily adaptable to Australian conditions. Foxall published two books: the first, *The Claims of 'Capital'* (1895), written at the height of the Depression of the 1890s, and *Colorphobia* (1903), an excoriating attack on the White Australia Policy. One of the first acts of the Australian parliament after federation in 1901 was the Immigration Restriction Act effectively prohibiting migration by those with non-white backgrounds. The policy was only formally repealed in the mid-1960s. Despite the attention given by Australian historians to the White Australia Policy, Foxall has been largely neglected (Kemp 2011). Unfortunate similar neglect has met Edward Pulsford (1844–1919), a New South Wales free-trade economist also opposed to the White Australia Policy (see Pulsford 1905; Hawkins 2007).

Another notable late nineteenth-century liberal was the German-born economist Max Hirsch (1853–1909). Hirsch came to Australia at the age of 37, having spent the two previous decades as a commercial traveller.

Once he settled in Melbourne he dedicated his energy to political activism and economic reform. Also a Georgist, Hirsch's most significant book was *Democracy Versus Socialism* (1901), which was dedicated to Henry George. *Democracy Versus Socialism* was an extended defence of free trade, laissez faire economics, political liberalism, the single tax, and natural law, and a critique of socialism.

The Depression of the 1890s delivered a blow to Australian classical liberalism. This "great scar" (Blainey 1980, 331) sparked the growth of the labour movement and pushed the colonies towards federation. When federation finally occurred in 1901, the free trade question was largely resolved. Section 92 of the Australian Constitution prohibits barriers to interstate trade. However, the intellectual environment of the time favoured protection with the outside world. It was in this period that the basic elements of what Paul Kelly (1992) influentially described as the "Australian Settlement" were constructed: centralised wage fixing and arbitration, state paternalism, discriminatory immigration policy, a close reliance on the benevolence of British imperial policy, and 'protection-all-round.' In the following decades, Australia's classical liberal heritage was virtually wiped out.

Faced with the abandonment of its raison d'être, in 1906 the Free Trade Party was reconceived as the Anti-Socialist Party, a step which facilitated its eventual 1909 merger with the liberal Protectionist Party (the "spurious" liberals Bruce Smith had been so concerned about) to form a united front against the growing Labor Party. The resulting union was to become in 1945 the modern Liberal Party of Australia.

The wilderness years

Even into the 1920s and 1930s the Australian economics profession was a small community, a "fledgling, scattered university discipline," as Alex Millmow (2010, 46) writes. It was only until after the First World War that formal economics training began in Australia in earnest. Between 1912 and 1930, the universities of Sydney, Melbourne, Tasmania, Queensland, Western Australia, and Adelaide formed chairs in economics. Economics was seen as a practical discipline focused on public policy and statistical collection. The most prominent economists tended to have been in and out of official government positions as statisticians and advisors. L. F. Giblin described the economists that dominated the debates of the Great Depression as

> ...a peculiar tribe. Rarely are they nourished by the pure milk of the word. Mostly they have been advisors to governments for many years... They are frequently more practical and realistic than the business man... The word of complaint or abuse is 'academic'; but in truth they are the least academic of God's creatures. (Giblin 1943, 216)

The situation was fertile ground for the adoption of Keynesianism (Markwell 2000). Australian economic historians are proud to note that some aspects of John Maynard Keynes's thought were perhaps anticipated by Australian economists, such as the multiplier (Coleman et al. 2006, ch. 5).

One classical liberal holdout was Edward Shann (1884–1935), one of the truly dominant figures of Australian economics in the first half of the century, but whose legacy fits poorly within the Keynesian mainstream. Shann was born in Hobart and studied history under Elkington at the University of Melbourne. As Melleuish (2009, 580) writes, along with the historian W. K. Hancock and Bruce Smith, Shann "can be seen as constituting a free trade counterpoise to the more protectionist and statist conception of democracy that emerged out of late-nineteenth and early-twentieth century Victoria." Shann is best known for his magisterial *Economic History of Australia* (1930a), still one of the best expositions of Australian economic institutions and policies in the nineteenth and early twentieth century. For Shann, the story of Australia's economic history was the story of the debate over free trade and protection—an interpretation which has been dominant among Australian classical liberals since. Furthermore, the origin of the Australian colonies in communistic military-run despotism had set the tone for Australian politics with its reliance on state action, subsidy, and paternalism, which continued through to federation.

During the early years of the Great Depression, Shann was one of the strongest voices in favour of wage flexibility and against countercyclical fiscal policy. His involvement in the development of the Premiers' Plan—the Australian government response to the Great Depression—gave it much of its classical liberal edge. As he wrote in his collection of essays *Bond or Free?*: "This is no time for additional public works. One of our main troubles is an interest bill...on public works that do not earn interest" (Shann 1930b, 54–

55). Shann's contribution to liberalism was tragically cut short in 1935 when he died falling from an office window, an event that is still shrouded in some mystery (Millmow 2005).

Shann's *Economic History of Australia* was one of three books published at the outset of the Great Depression that have been held in high esteem by Australian classical liberals. Another was *Australia* (1931), an eccentric and lively profile of Australian culture, politics, and political economy by the historian W. K. Hancock (1898–1988).[2] The third was *State Socialism in Victoria* (1932) by Frederic Eggleston (1875–1954). Eggleston was a former minister in the Victorian state government, and his book was a study of the serious deficiencies of state-owned enterprises in that state. Nevertheless, Eggleston was more disenchanted socialist than classical liberal.

These few exceptions notwithstanding, the Australian economics profession coming out of the depression and Second World War was firmly in the Keynesian mould. As far as there was an 'official' position from the professional economics community on classical liberal economics, it was summarised by the major interwar report on tariff protection, written by the doyens of the Australian academy:

> In Australia, where practically all shades of thought are committed to some form of Government activity in the economic sphere, whether it be wage regulation or assistance to immigration, criticism of the policy of laissez faire is unnecessary. It will be sufficient to say rather summarily that the policy of laissez-faire in any country allows the natural inequalities of capacity, and the acquired or inherent inequalities of property, to operate to the fullest extent to the diminution of welfare. (Brigden and Committee on Economic Effects of the Tariff 1929, 93)

Modern classical liberalism in Australia

After the Second World War, classical liberals were thin on the ground and the intellectual environment was hostile. Economics itself became more professionalised, and the demand for economics education at both secondary and tertiary levels grew. Within the public service, the Great Depression and

---

2. See also Hancock (1968), in which the author of *Australia* wonders "at the differences between then and now."

the experience of war enhanced the prestige of economics graduates. So while the number of economists within the bureaucracy did not grow significantly, they assumed more influence (Groenewegen and McFarlane 1990).

The slow postwar revitalisation of classical liberalism in Australia had an origin in a most unlikely organisation: the Australian Tariff Board. The Tariff Board was an independent Commonwealth government body tasked with reviewing the tariff rates on goods and providing advice to government. It was also a breeding ground for economic dissidents and a central battleground in the struggle against Australian protectionism. Just as the Board of Customs in Edinburgh had employed Adam Smith, the Australian Tariff Board employed a bevy of free traders.

One notable member of the Tariff Board was Stan Kelly, who was acquainted with all the major economists of the pre-war era, including Edward Shann (Colebatch 2012). The Kelly family's agricultural background is significant. Australian agriculture in particular suffered in consequence of the high tariffs that were intended to protect urban manufacturing interests. Traditionally, rural voters and their political wing, the Country Party, were in the free trade camp. During the 1960s, however, the Country Party under its federal leader John McEwen formed an intellectual alliance with protected manufacturers. Stan Kelly imparted his liberal outlook to his son Bert Kelly (1912–1997), a rural politician from South Australia, who sat in the Commonwealth parliament between 1958 and 1977. A vociferous opponent of Australian protectionism, Bert Kelly was a member of the Liberal Party, rather than the Country Party, and was opposed to the latter's new farming-manufacturing protectionist alliance (Reid 1969).

McEwen, as Minister for Trade and Industry in the Liberal–Country Coalition government, had ministerial responsibility for the Tariff Board. In 1962 McEwen had forced out Leslie Melville, a former advisor for the central bank and delegate to the Bretton Woods conference, from the chairmanship of the Tariff Board, as the two had clashed over Melville's preference to reduce tariffs if at all possible (Cornish 1993). In Melville's place, McEwen appointed Alf Rattigan. Rattigan had been seen as a relatively subdued career bureaucrat, but as once appointed became one of the leading advocates for tariff liberalisation, using his advisory position as a platform to advocate against protection-all-round. Such advocacy put him firmly at loggerheads with the government. The debate over tariffs at this time involved no small amount of intrigue. Rattigan would feed Bert Kelly details of tariff absurdities, which the latter would write up in his longstanding "Modest Member" column in the *Australian Financial Review*.

Also associated with the Tariff Board were a number of young economists supportive of free trade. In the early 1960s at Melbourne University and the Australian National University Max Corden developed the concept of the effective rate of protection, which was to become a significant weapon in the public armoury of the Tariff Board (Corden 2005). As with the trade debates of the nineteenth century, not every free trader during this postwar period would today be classed as a classical liberal. Nevertheless, it was out of this new trade debate that a broader political agenda of liberalisation and deregulation grew.

One small hub of free traders was formed in Melbourne's suburbs: Monash University was founded in 1958 as the result of a Federal Government plan to create a second university in Victoria, and Monash became a major postwar centre for non-Keynesian thinking in Australian economics. Monash's status as a classical liberal centre was largely due to the influence of the economist Ross Parish (Millmow 2009). Born in rural New South Wales, Parish studied agricultural economics at the University of Sydney. There he became affiliated with the Freethought society around the professor of philosophy John Anderson, along with the young philosophers David Stove and David Armstrong and the journalist-politician Peter Coleman (Hogbin 2001). Parish did his Ph.D. at the University of Chicago and in 1959 returned to Australia. After roles at the University of Sydney, the University of New England, and the United Nations Food and Agriculture Organisation, he landed at Monash University in 1973. Parish was a microeconomist in the Chicago sense. As one colleague remarked, Parish "made microeconomics a respectable area of economic analysis in Australia" (Hogbin 2001). Parish was to be a major contributor to classical liberal institutions over the next decades, including the Centre for Independent Studies and the H. R. Nicholls Society. Another significant Monash economist was Michael Porter, whose early research was in finance, taxation, and monetary policy. He was to become highly involved in the debates over financial deregulation in the late 1970s and early 1980s.

One watershed moment in the revival of Australian classical liberalism was Milton Friedman's April 1975 visit to Australia, which was sponsored by the

Sydney stockbroker Maurice Newman. Friedman arrived at an opportune time for the dissemination of his ideas on monetary policy. Support for monetarism had been growing within the conservative Coalition opposition and had taken firm root in the Reserve Bank (Guttmann 2005). Yet monetarism was counter to the bulk of Australian academic wisdom—most economists were in the Keynesian, anti-monetarist camp—and the Whitlam government was trying to tame inflation, which it believed was created by a mixture of excessive wage growth, global military expenditure, and predatory pricing by multinationals operating in Australia (Courvisanos and Millmow 2006). Friedman's tour lasted eighteen days and he spoke to the bulk of the business and financial community. His monetarist message was aggressively supported by the small number of sympathetic journalists of the day, particularly P. P. McGuinness and Maxwell Newton. Friedman also visited the Reserve Bank of Australia, where the classical liberal line was being pushed by Austin Holmes, head of the RBA's research department. Holmes, whom John Hyde (1989, 2) describes as "the antithesis of Sir Humphrey Appleby," was a great advocate within the RBA for floating the Australian dollar.

The next year, 1976, the intellectual cause of classical liberalism was further boosted by a visit to Australia by Friedrich Hayek. He was brought out by the aviator and business leader Robert Norman, the geologist Viv Forbes, the mining entrepreneur Ronald Kitching, and the Institute of Public Affairs (IPA), a classical liberal think tank (Kitching 2007). Back in 1950 the IPA had published an article by Hayek in one of the first issues of the *IPA Review*, its long-running journal (Hayek 1950). Hayek said the IPA had "played a considerable role in the development of my writings" (1976, 83).

By the 1980s the Liberal Party of Australia found within itself two intellectual groupings, the 'Dries' and the 'Wets.' The appellation 'dry' was first associated with supporters of Margaret Thatcher, to describe those who supported classical liberal economics. Their opponents were 'wet'—a disparaging term suggesting mushiness, a feeble unwillingness to conduct necessary reform (Hyde 2002). The development of the Dries as a political movement came in large part thanks to the efforts of academic free-market economists. One of those economists was Wolfgang Kasper, a German-born economist who had worked for the German Council of Economic Advisors and the Malaysian Ministry of Finance, and who came to the Australian National University in 1973. Kasper moved in the late 1970s to the Chair of Economics at the University of New South Wales economics department at Defence Force Academy in Canberra, where he began writing a series of essays contrasting the "mercantilist" path on which Australia's economy was travelling and an alternative "libertarian" path of lower taxes and deregulation all around (Kasper 2011). The Shell Company, which was considering new investments in Australia, invited Kasper to produce a consultancy report on Australia's economic potential. Kasper brought in four other classical liberal academics to join him: Richard Blandy of Flinders University in South Australia, John Freebairn of La Trobe University, Douglas Hocking, formerly chief economist at Shell Australia but then at Monash University, and Robert O'Neill, the head of the Strategic and Defence Studies Centre at the Australian National University. The resulting publication—*Australia at the Crossroads: Our Choices to the Year 2000* (1980)—was the first major, comprehensive statement of liberal economics in Australia since Bruce Smith's *Liberty and Liberalism* a century earlier. *Crossroads* argued that adopting libertarian policies "would amount to a new phase in the growing up of the Australian nation, a move from adolescence protected by a 'Mother State' to full maturity and self reliance in society and industry" (Kasper et al. 1980, 212). *Crossroads* was notable for extending the liberal message beyond the narrow confines of the trade debate. For example, Kasper and his co-authors called for the application of market principles to social welfare provision, drawing on Friedmanite voucher proposals.

The publication of *Crossroads* sparked organisational development among the scattered Dries that were the heirs of Bert Kelly around the Liberal Party. The so-called Crossroads group was formed ostensibly to discuss the book but was in fact the origin of a liberal campaign strategy, bringing together representatives of party politics, industry, media, and the scattered think tanks and academics. A parliamentary club—the "Modest Members Society," after the title of Bert Kelly's *Australian Financial Review* column—was also formed, and from 1981 it provided a platform for education and policy discussion.

Organisations

In recent decades, academic classical liberal economics has clustered around two schools, those of the Australian National University in Canberra and RMIT University in Melbourne.

The most coherent school of liberal economics in Australia has been at the Australian National University, which had its peak in the late 1980s. ANU's economics was at that time divided between the research-only Institute of Advanced Studies and the teaching faculty, the Economics Department. It was in the teaching faculty that liberal economics thrived, led in this period by Geoffrey Brennan, Ian Harper, Peter Forsyth, and Mark Harrison. Brennan had been a co-author with James M. Buchanan of *The Power to Tax* (1980) and *The Reason of Rules* (1985), and was later co-editor of Buchanan's collected works. The ANU undergraduate program was firmly and explicitly Chicago-style neoclassical. It was a rigorous program, with an extremely high first-year failure rate, and the program focused on both a high standard of mathematics and public policy, which was unusual for the time (Kirchner 2014).

Another significant liberal economist at ANU was Helen Hughes (1928–2013). Born in Czechoslovakia, Hughes migrated with her family to Australia in 1939 and received her doctorate at the London School of Economics in 1954. After a long period as a senior economist and economics director at the World Bank, she was appointed the inaugural director of the National Centre for Development Studies at ANU (Shapley 2013). Hughes's research and career focused on economic development in the Pacific Island region and in Australia's indigenous communities. She was instrumental in building the case for integrating Aboriginal people into the market economy, and rejecting the welfare-led development programs and separatist policies which had contributed to the low living standards of indigenous communities in Australia's north.

In the early 1990s, however, the neoclassical cohort at ANU largely dribbled away. Harper moved to the University of Melbourne and was later appointed by the Howard Government to the Wallis Inquiry into financial regulation and the Fair Pay Commission (Australia's national tribunal which set minimum wages and awards). Under the Abbott Government, Harper chaired a review of competition policy. Hughes formally retired from ANU in 1994, and became a senior research fellow with the Centre for Independent Studies. Brennan eventually joined the ANU philosophy program.

Currently the only critical mass of classical liberal academic economists in Australia is at RMIT University in Melbourne. A major difference between the RMIT school and the ANU school of the previous generation is that

RMIT is less formally neoclassical in orientation and more explicitly Hayekian and institutional in orientation. Rather than aspiring to be a 'Chicago of the South,' the preferred model is George Mason University. The leaders of this school are Sinclair Davidson, professor of institutional economics, and Jason Potts, an evolutionary economist. Both have interests outside mainstream economics, although both are highly involved in contemporary policy debate.

Academic economics publishing in Australia has been dominated by *Economic Record*, founded in 1925. Reflecting broader trends within the economics community, the journal has had a strong Keynesian and interventionist tinge throughout its history, although it has published a range of voices. In 1994 was founded the journal *Agenda*, published by the Australian National University and currently edited by William Coleman. *Agenda* has a focus on policy analysis rather than theoretical development, and it has often featured articles by classical liberal economists.

The Australian think-tank sector is extremely small compared to that of the United States. Australia has two major free-market think tanks—the aforementioned Institute of Public Affairs, and the Centre for Independent Studies (CIS)—plus a small number of specialist bodies with various emphases on research and activism.

The Institute of Public Affairs was formed in 1943. At the time, the non-Labor political movement was in disarray following the collapse of the United Australia Party; the Liberal Party would not be formed until 1944. Originally the IPA was conceived as a publicity offshoot of the Victorian Chamber of Manufactures. A committee of Victorian business leaders was formed, including the metallurgist and paper manufacturer Herbert Gepp, the retailer G. J. Coles, and the banker Leslie McConnan, with the aim of forming a separate organisation to represent the case for free enterprise. A paper to the committee written by Gepp's economic assistant C. D. Kemp, who was appointed as the IPA's Executive Director, put the intellectual challenge as follows:

> [T]he freedom of Australian business is today gravely threatened by forces whose unswerving and rigid purpose is the entire nationalisation of industry and the establishment of socialism as the permanent form of Australian society... These forces are centred politically in the Labor Party and industrially in the Trade Unions; they are supported by an extremely powerful and growing section of public opinion. (C. D. Kemp, quoted in Bertram 1989)

The Victorian Chamber encouraged the Chambers in New South Wales, Queensland, and South Australia to form their own Institutes of Public Affairs. These were loosely affiliated, and most found less success than the Victorian body. The Victorian IPA established itself in the role of policy formulation for the interstate bodies (D. A. Kemp 1963). The New South Wales IPA eventually became the Sydney Institute, a forum for political and policy discussion.

The IPA's first major publication, *Looking Forward* (1944), envisaged Australia under a reformed private enterprise system with an emphasis on employee share ownership. Following the intellectual zeitgeist shared by the Crossroads group, the IPA then took a sharp turn in the direction of more radical classical liberalism. Throughout the 1970s and 1980s the IPA was involved in debates over macroeconomic policy, particularly on how to tame inflation and promote deregulation, privatisation, tax reform, and federalism. With a critique of Australia's bicentennial celebrations (Baker 1985), the IPA sparked what are now seen as the 'culture wars.' Melleuish (2001) argues that such culture-war campaigns illustrate a continued alliance between the "New Right," who tended to have a libertarian ethos, and the "new conservatives," who were culturally conservative and came from the anti-Labor and anti-socialist direction of Australian politics. That alliance substantively remains in Australian classical liberal institutions today.

In recent years, the IPA has been focused on industrial relations reform, regulatory policy, energy issues, climate change policy and civil liberties such as freedom of speech. As of 2014 the IPA has a membership base of around four thousand. Led by executive director John Roskam, it is the largest free market think tank in Australia and a lightning rod for opponents of classical liberalism. Notable economists involved with the IPA include Mikayla Novak and the RMIT economists Sinclair Davidson and Jason Potts. The IPA has published many Australian classical liberals, including Melleuish, the historian Geoffrey Blainey, and the law and economics scholar Suri Ratnapala.

The Centre for Independent Studies was founded in 1976 by Greg Lindsay, a New South Wales mathematics teacher, to be a forum for classical liberal economic thought. Lindsay was inspired by the libertarian revival in the United States. In its early years, CIS focused on seminars rather than publishing and building a network of classical liberal academics. One of the first papers delivered at the CIS was *Liberty, Justice and the Market* (eventually published in 1981) by the University of Wollongong philosopher Lauchlan Chipman. In an influential article by P. P. McGuinness (1978), the CIS was described as a place "where Friedman is a pinko;" the intellectual mentors of the CIS were, McGuinness wrote, the Austrians Ludwig von Mises and Friedrich Hayek. Nevertheless, the CIS had a very Friedmanite flavour. In its early years it produced critiques of rent control (Albon 1980), taxi licensing (Swan 1983), shopping-hours regulation (Hogbin 1983), government-business relationships (Hogan 1985), and agricultural regulation (Sieper 1982). In 1984 it hosted Israel Kirzner for its first annual John Bonython Lecture.

In its first decades many of the CIS's publications were written by academic economists. One notable member of the CIS board was Heinz Arndt, a German immigrant who had started his career as a socialist but was converted to the causes of free trade and anti-Keynesianism by the economic experience of the 1970s (Arndt 1985; Coleman, Cornish, and Drake 2007). The CIS has also published extensively the Australian liberal philosopher Jeremy Shearmur, a former assistant of Karl Popper's and who was based at the Australian National University.[3]

During the 1990s and 2000s the CIS was particularly influential at framing the debate over welfare policy. The work of Peter Saunders, head of the CIS's Social Foundations Program, on social inequality and poverty emphasised the importance of mutual obligation in welfare—colloquially known in Australia as 'work for the dole'—and the involvement of private charitable bodies in welfare provision. In 2013 the CIS launched a broad campaign, TARGET30, which aims to restrain Australian government spending to below 30 percent of GDP within the next decade.

Outside the two major think tanks there have been a small number of organisations which have espoused liberal economics in Australia. One of the most significant was the H. R. Nicholls Society, formed in 1986 by John Stone, the former head of the Commonwealth Treasury, Ray Evans, a free market activist employed by Western Mining Corporation, and Peter Costello, then a young lawyer who was to become Commonwealth Treasurer in the Howard government. The society was focused on deregulating Australia's heavily unionised and regulated industrial relations system. The society was

---

3. Another notable Australian link to Popper is through the economist Colin Simkin, who was a colleague of Popper's at Canterbury University College and is acknowledged in *The Open Society and Its Enemies*.

named after the journalist Henry Richard Nicholls, who edited the *Hobart Mercury* at the turn of the twentieth century and used his publication to criticise Henry Bourne Higgins, the High Court judge and President of the Commonwealth Court of Conciliation and Arbitration. Higgins was the judge who instituted the Australian basic wage in 1907, in a case that became known as the Harvester Judgement. Nicholls became an icon when Higgins convinced the Labor Commonwealth government to prosecute him for contempt of court. In 1986 the H. R. Nicholls Society was described by the then-prime minister Bob Hawke as "political troglodytes and economic lunatics" (Grattan 1986). But its workplace reform proposals were prescient; workplace relations was then, and in many ways still is, the next frontier of microeconomic reform. The society's longstanding president, Ray Evans, was an active institution builder, being a founding member of a number of similar issue-specific societies, including the Samuel Griffiths Society, a conservative legal constitutionalist group, and the Bennelong Society, which focused on indigenous issues.

Liberal economics has had champions within the political system. The Liberal Party harbours many classical liberals, and the party name was chosen by its founder Robert Menzies to recall nineteenth century liberalism. It may be partially by virtue of Menzies's decision that in Australia 'liberal' still generally means classical liberal, as it does in most of the world apart from North America.

The dissident Dries within the Liberal Party since the days of Bert Kelly have been variably influential. During the 1970s and 1980s they formed a powerful ginger group, with figures such as John Hyde, Jim Carlton, and Peter Shack. In recent years there has been a resurgence of liberal economic thought within the Liberal Party. A group of members of parliament adopted the name "Society of Modest Members" in 2011. Nevertheless, the Liberal Party's performance in government has tended towards big government conservatism (Norton 2006; Moore 2008). This has left an opportunity for 'microparties' professing classical liberal economics. The Workers' Party was formed in 1975. Later renamed the Progress Party, it had little success and disbanded by the early 1980s. The ideological heir of the Workers' Party is the Liberal Democratic Party, founded in 2001. The LDP successfully gained a senator in the 2013 federal election, David Leyonhjelm, representing New South Wales.

Australia today has 23 million inhabitants. There are few professional academic economists working on contemporary public policy controversies, and those who do are spread thinly among a large number of issue areas. Furthermore, the small policymaking community does not tend to use academic work to inform its efforts. Consequently, one feature of Australian political culture and policy formulation is the relative significance of popular newspaper opinion pieces. As a result, a particularly important domain for classical liberals is newspapers such as the national broadsheet *The Australian* and the business-oriented daily *The Australian Financial Review*. The *Australian* was founded in 1964 by Rupert Murdoch as the first national daily mainstream newspaper. The editor at large Paul Kelly told a parliamentary committee in 1991 that his paper "strongly supports economic libertarianism" (quoted in Manne 2005, 60). The *Australian* features two prominent academic economists, Judith Sloan and Henry Ergas, as well as the former CIS economist Adam Creighton. The *Australian Financial Review* was founded as a weekly in 1951. It published some of the most important representatives of the Liberal Dries, particularly Bert Kelly's Modest Member columns. A few particular editors of the *Australian Financial Review* stand out as aggressive opponents of Australia's high tariff regime: Maxwell Newton (who went on to be the first editor of the *Australian*), Max Walsh, and P. P. McGuinness.

Successes

Australian classical liberalism has had some substantial policy successes. The first walls of the Australian Settlement came down with the 1966 end of the White Australia Policy under the conservative Holt government. From the mid-1970s to the late 1990s the Australian economy was significantly reformed, and quite frequently in classical liberal directions. The process began with a 25 percent across the board cut to tariffs under the Whitlam government, a reform which was in large part driven by economists affiliated with the Tariff Board and Monash University.

The reform era began in earnest however with financial deregulation. In 1978 the Fraser government instituted an inquiry into Australia's financial system, known as the Campbell committee. That process was supported by the Treasurer John Howard, as well as by a few economists in the Treasurer's office and in the Department of the Prime Minister and Cabinet. One significant Howard advisor was John Hewson, an ambitious former Reserve Bank economist with a doctorate from Johns Hopkins University. The Campbell committee recommended wholesale deregulation of the financial sector, including the abolition of exchange, capital, and interest rate controls, and the removal of restrictions on foreign bank entry (Kasper and Stevens 1991).

It was not until the election of the Hawke government that many of the Campbell committee recommendations were implemented. In the space of just a few years, Australia floated the dollar, eliminated legacy interest controls that dated back to the Second World War, and opened up the Australian market to foreign banks. Financial deregulation precipitated a broader reform movement under the Labor government, and later under the Coalition. State-owned enterprises were corporatised and then in many cases privatised, including the Commonwealth Bank, the telecommunications monopoly Telecom, and the airline Qantas. Tariffs were reduced, turning Australia from one of the most highly protected to one of the least-protected economies in the world. With the advent of the Howard Government, industrial relations was partially deregulated. In 2000 the Commonwealth introduced a value added tax to replace a number of inefficient state and federal taxes.

The success of this reform movement in bringing about changes should not be overstated. The reforms were coupled with substantial re-regulation of the economy, albeit regulation with a different emphasis and purpose (Berg 2008). The stalling of reform momentum at the Commonwealth level can be dated with a fair degree of precision—to the 1993 Federal Election. It was in 1991 that John Hewson, now in parliament and leader of the Coalition opposition, put forward arguably the most substantial reform agenda that Australia has ever seen. The *Fightback!* package was a detailed 650-page blueprint for reform along liberal lines, the centrepiece of which was a value added tax with a 15 percent rate. Hewson had the misfortune of presenting this package in the middle of a recession, and was defeated at the 1993 election by the incumbent Labor prime minister Paul Keating. No federal election campaign since has featured as much radical policy reform, and in excruciating and explicit detail as was *Fightback!*, even while some of the policies, such as a value added tax, have been since introduced in some form. On the other side of the ledger, some of the deregulatory reforms of recent decades have been rolled back. For instance, in 2009 the Rudd government reversed some of industrial relations deregulation that had occurred under the Howard government.

Nevertheless, while reform slowed at the federal level, at the state level there was, and still is, much low-hanging fruit to be picked. A particularly noteworthy success was the Victorian movement under Premier Jeff Kennett and his Treasurer Alan Stockdale—noteworthy as much for the influence of liberal economists as the substance of the reforms. The Victorian reform movement was much influenced by the agenda spelled out by Project Victoria, a joint research program by the Institute of Public Affairs and the Tasman Institute, a small free-market think tank established by Michael Porter in the early 1990s (Teicher and van Gramberg 1999; Cahill and Beder 2005). Project Victoria outlined an agenda of privatisation, public service reform, and industrial relations reform. Stockdale, who was a member of the Crossroads group and later became Chairman of the IPA, also later credited Ray Evans with intellectual support for the Victoria reform program (Stockdale 1999).

Contemporary status

Despite a generation of reform, classical liberalism continues to be a minority viewpoint in the policy and intellectual communities.

In 2011 the Economics Society of Australia surveyed its members on their opinions about policy (Economic Society of Australia 2011). Of the 575 respondents, two-thirds had a master's degree or Ph.D. The survey demonstrated that classical liberalism is a minority view among Australian economists. The monetarist revolution of the 1970s has failed to take hold with this generation of economists: less than 40 percent of Australian economists agree that inflation is caused primarily by money supply growth. A majority—58 percent—agreed that the free flow of capital should be restricted in order to "assist the stability and soundness of the international financial system." However, there was also a plurality who agreed with the statement that "there would be less unemployment if the minimum wage was lowered"—45 percent, compared to 38 percent who disagreed. Forty-four percent of economists agreed that "the government should adopt policies to make the size distribution of income in Australia more equal than it presently is," where only 33 percent disagreed. When asked whether the government ought to "provide greater economic incentives to improve diet," 42 percent agreed while only 27 percent disagreed.

Nevertheless, until the global financial crisis of 2008 there was a rough and ready policy consensus in public economic debate. It was believed that industry assistance in the form of tariff protection was to be reduced gradually, and corporate and personal taxation ought to be reasonably low. The then-Prime Minister Kevin Rudd wrote a series of essays which contrasted his view with what he saw as the "Hayekian view that a person's worth should primarily, and unsentimentally, be determined by the market" (Rudd 2009). In a previous essay Rudd (2006) claimed the "modern Liberals, influenced by Hayek, argue that human beings are almost exclusively self-regarding." Hayek became the bête noire of the Labor government's response to the global financial crisis.

In 2004 the Commonwealth Treasury quietly held a series of internal workshops that revitalised Keynesian stimulus as a policy prescription (Taylor and Uren 2010; Uren 2014). The workshops created a plan for economic policy during a recession that emphasised, in the words of Treasury secretary Ken Henry, stimulus should "go hard, go early, go households." The cause of Keynesian stimulus was given greater impetus by the fact that the Labor government under Rudd was relatively new and feared suffering the fate of the 1929–1931 Scullin government, which had a brief and unhappy single term at the start of the Great Depression.

When the crisis hit in late 2008, it sparked a major debate over Keynesian fiscal policy. For the most part, the debate concerned the relative size and timing of stimulus packages. The Coalition opposition, first under Malcolm Turnbull and then Tony Abbott, supported a first AU$10.4 billion tranche of stimulus in October 2008 but opposed a second, larger tranche of $42 billion in February 2009. Both Turnbull and Abbott have stated that they support fiscal stimulus in principle (Taylor and Uren 2010).

The Labor government under Rudd and then later under Julia Gillard was dogged by claims that the Australian public debt was out of control as a result of those stimulus packages. The public debt was a focus in the 2013 election, which Labor lost to Tony Abbott's Coalition. Yet to the extent that the debate over fiscal stimulus was won by stimulus opponents, it was won on the grounds that the specific measures chosen by the Rudd Government in the second tranche were wasteful or poorly implemented rather than on any ground about the undesirability of Keynesian policy. The fact that Australia avoided a recession has created a strong presumption in favour of the stimulus program among policymakers. In 2010 a group of 51 Australian economists signed a letter arguing that the stimulus package prevented a "deep recession" and a "massive increase in unemployment" (Quiggin 2010). The 2011 Economics Society survey revealed that three quarters of Australian economists believe that "a substantial increase in public spending is an appropriate response to a severe recession," alongside a similar result for monetary easing.

There have only been a few professional and academic economists to cast doubt on the program of fiscal stimulus. Tony Makin of Griffith University argued the fiscal multiplier is either near zero or small and that countercyclical fiscal policies have been ineffective (Makin and Narayan 2011; Guest and Makin 2011; Makin 2009). Makin (2010) held that Australia's crisis performance was largely attributable to the monetary actions of the Reserve Bank of Australia. Further significant critiques of Keynesian stimulus from a liberal perspective were offered by Henry Ergas and Alex Robson (2009), Sinclair Davidson and Ashton de Silva (2009; 2013), and contributors to a volume edited by Stephen Kirchner (2009a). Australia has also produced a liberal textbook, *Free Market Economics: An Introduction for the General Reader* (2011) by Steven Kates at RMIT University, as a response to the activist fiscal policies brought about by the crisis. Wolfgang Kasper is lead author of a significant textbook on institutional economics (Kasper, Streit, and Boettke 2012).

State institutions, particularly the Commonwealth Treasury and the Reserve Bank of Australia, dominate the market for economics graduates and have an outsized authority on economics debate. Treasury's reputation has been eroded by a perception that it has become politicised (Davidson 2013b; Costa 2009). Treasury has made some high-profile errors in recent years (Davidson 2011), and its revenue forecasting was implicated in the Rudd and Gillard government's inability to return the Commonwealth budget to surplus. By contrast, the RBA's reputation has been buttressed by reforms in 1996 that enhanced its policy independence, reducing a longstanding belief that the central bank is the pawn of the government of the day (Bell 2004). Over the last decade it has even become common to claim that central bank independence is violated when government figures publicly question the RBA's monetary stance (Kirchner 2009b). It is instructive to compare the deference given to Australian central bankers when they appear in front of Senate Estimates hearings with the relative scepticism that the Governor of the Federal Reserve receives in U.S. Congressional hearings. In Australia, the policy pronouncements and economic forecasts of Reserve Bank governors are granted high degrees of authority in public debate.

Discussion

The best volume on the history of Australian classical liberalism is Greg Melleuish's *A Short History of Australian Liberalism* (2001). Other sources are perhaps more comprehensive, but these are also often written from a statist perspective and often hostile. The *Australian Dictionary of Biography* treats free traders poorly and characterises classical liberals as "conservatives." A typical example is the entry on Bruce Smith, which describes his classic book *Liberty and Liberalism* as "anachronistic" and his support of free trade "doctrinaire, extreme" (Rutledge 1988). The dictionary offers no entry for E. W. Foxall, even though his *Colorphobia* is one of the most powerful expressions of anti-racist liberalism at the turn of the century. Foxall's reputation was only recently revived (Kemp 2011). W. E. Hearn is somewhat better appreciated, as the first Australian academic economist. Yet the first book dedicated to his work, by Douglas B. Copland (1935), focuses more on criticising Hearn's failure to adhere to the Keynesianism of Copland's day rather than recounting Hearn's economics on its own terms (Hayek 1936). Copland's treatment of Hearn is indicative of the Australian academic attitude to the country's classical liberalism.

As I have noted, academic classical liberal economists in Australia have enjoyed clusters in four episodes: the University of Melbourne at the end of the nineteenth century, Monash University in the 1970s, the Australian National University in the 1980s, and RMIT University in first decades of the twentieth century. While the jury is of course out on RMIT, these schools did not manage to replicate themselves for more than a generation. Hearn moved into the law faculty, and while his free trade views were disseminated to the next cohort of students by his successor Elkington, this tradition at Melbourne did not survive into the twentieth century. Neither Monash University nor ANU successfully established a long term classical liberal presence. John Lodewijks (2001) points out that few Australian universities have reputations of developing 'schools' of speciality, let alone self-sustaining schools. To the extent that economics faculties have a reputation for specialising in any particular field, "often that reputation is based on one very influential researcher" (Lodewijks 2001, 5)

One possible explanation for the failure to maintain longstanding non-mainstream schools, classical liberal or otherwise, is the structure of economics postgraduate study. It has been often remarked that the Australian economics profession after the Second World War became 'Americanised,' in terms of increasing professionalism and emphasis on mathematics and also a trend for students to prefer study in the United States over the United Kingdom. Groenewegen and McFarlane argued that Australian economics had become "a minor sub-branch of the American Economic Association" (1990, 237). But Australian Ph.D.s in economics have for the most part adhered to the British model of study. Students conclude an initial specialised degree, and at postgraduate level submit a large monograph-length thesis. Unlike in the United States, where students do extensive coursework, in Australia coursework is limited. This is in part a consequence of the relatively small size of Australian economics departments and Ph.D. cohorts: it is uneconomical to dedicate the resources necessary for coursework for few students (Lodewijks 2001). It is plausible that the absence of coursework impedes the development of longer-term 'schools,' as the self-directed nature of the monograph-length thesis reduces the students' interaction with research staff and their peers. However, such institutional arrangements are changing: coursework is a growing component of Ph.D. programs, particularly in the largest universities. Also today there is an increasing tendency to recruit from the American Economics Association meetings, another practice which dilutes distinct research schools. Nevertheless, the 'Americanisation' thesis should perhaps not be overstated; as William Coleman (2014) points out, some of the most distinctively 'American' branches of economic study, such as public choice and law and economics, have found little favour in Australia (see also Pincus 2014).

Further structural features of Australian economic research of possible relevance are the dominance of public universities and the towering influence of the Australian Research Council, which provides funding for research projects and ranks universities on their "research excellence." These rankings are non-transparent and hard to reconcile with publicly available sources (Davidson 2013a).

Whatever the explanation, classical liberalism in Australia has an outsider status in the Australian economics profession. Classical liberal schools have tended to form at relatively young universities. Hearn was brought to Australia to be one of Melbourne's first professors. Monash University had only been established fifteen years when Ross Parish took an economics chair in 1973. RMIT University was only made a public university in 1992, and Sinclair Davidson joined in 1995. The exception was the ANU, which was formed after the Second World War. But there the outsider status of classical liberalism was manifest as well: it was in the ANU's teaching university, rather than the more prestigious research-only unit, that the classical liberal school was developed.

The short lives of the major schools means that academic classical liberalism has found its organisational foundation outside the academy, most notably in the two major Australian think tanks, the Institute of Public Affairs and the Centre for Independent Studies. Almost all the major classical liberal economists have developed some form of institutional connection with either or both of these organisations, whether as members of staff or academic advisors. Those affiliations furthermore give classical liberal economics a firmly policy-oriented flavour, and a high degree of engagement with public debate.

Conclusion

Blainey (1966) famously argued that Australian history has been shaped by distance. To that one could add size. The character of classical liberalism in Australian economics has been substantially determined by the country's small population. While the free trade tradition of the nineteenth century was strong, it was built on an extremely shallow base. It was not until the First World War and after that Australian universities began instituting chairs in economics. As a small and young country Australia was fertile ground for heterodox economic thought—the popular appeal of thinkers such as Henry George in the nineteenth century and monetary theories like Douglas Credit during the interwar years was substantial. In the 1930s the small corps of economic academics rapidly embraced Keynesianism. The dominance of Keynesianism and a bias towards interventionism lasted well into the 1970s.

Today classical liberalism remains outside the academic economics mainstream. It is influential insofar as it has champions in politics and the press. While Australia's size has meant that schools of economics have not become self-sustaining, that same size has given high prominence to some methods of public engagement—particularly the newspaper opinion piece—that has allowed some liberal economists to have substantial influence on policy and to help make Australia a relatively free and prosperous country.

References

Aikenhead, James. 1856. *Principles of Political Economy*. Launceston, Australia: J. S. Waddell.

Albon, Robert, ed. 1980. *Rent Control: Costs & Consequences*. Sydney: Centre for Independent Studies.

Arndt, H. W. 1985. *A Course Through Life: Memoirs of an Australian Economist*. Canberra: Australian National University.

Baker, Ken. 1985. The Bicentenary: Celebration or Apology? *IPA Review* 38(4): 175–182.

Bell, Stephen. 2004. *Australia's Money Mandarins: The Reserve Bank and the Politics of Money*. Cambridge, UK: Cambridge University Press.

Berg, Chris. 2008. *The Growth of Australia's Regulatory State: Ideology, Accountability and the Mega-Regulators*. Melbourne: Institute of Public Affairs.

Bertram, Michael. 1989. *A History of the Institute of Public Affairs*. Master's thesis, Department of Business and Economics, University of Melbourne.

Blainey, Geoffrey. 1966. *The Tyranny of Distance: How Distance Shaped Australia's History*. Melbourne: Sun Books.

Blainey, Geoffrey. 1980. *A Land Half Won*. Melbourne: Macmillan.

Brennan, Geoffrey, and James M. Buchanan. 1980. *The Power to Tax: Analytical Foundations of a Fiscal Constitution*. Cambridge, UK: Cambridge University Press.

Brennan, Geoffrey, and James M. Buchanan. 1985. *The Reason of Rules: Constitutional Political Economy*. Cambridge, UK: Cambridge University Press.

Brigden, J. B., and Committee on Economic Effects of the Tariff. 1929. *The Australian Tariff: An Economic Enquiry*. Melbourne: Melbourne University Press.

Buchanan, James M. 1999–2002. *The Collected Works of James M. Buchanan*, 20 vols., eds. Geoffrey Brennan, Hartmut Kliemt, and Robert D. Tollison. Indianapolis: Liberty Fund.

Cahill, Damien, and Sharon Beder. 2005. Neo-Liberal Think Tanks and Neo-Liberal Restructuring: Learning the Lessons from Project Victoria and the Privatisation of Victoria's Electricity Industry. *Social Alternatives* 24(1): 43–48.

Chipman, Lauchlan. 1981. *Liberty, Justice and the Market*. Sydney: Centre for Independent Studies.

Colebatch, Hal G. P. 2012. *The Modest Member: The Life and Times of Bert Kelly*. Ballan, Australia: Connor Court Publishing.

Coleman, Peter, Selwyn Cornish, and Peter Drake. 2007. *Arndt's Story: The Life of an Australian Economist*. Canberra: Australian National University E Press.

Coleman, William. 2014. Australia and New Zealand: A Young Tree Dead? In *Routledge Handbook of the History of Global Economic Thought*, ed. Vincent Barnett, 281–293. Abingdon, UK: Routledge.

Coleman, William, Selwyn Cornish, and Alf Hagger. 2006. *Giblin's Platoon: The Trials and Triumphs of the Economist in Australian Public Life*. Canberra: Australian National University E Press.

Copland, Douglas Berry. 1935. *W. E. Hearn: First Australian Economist*. Melbourne: Melbourne University Press.

Corden, Max. 2005. Effective Protection and I. *History of Economics Review* 42(Summer): 1–11.

Cornish, Selwyn. 1993. Sir Leslie Melville: An Interview. *Working Papers in Economic History* 173, Australian National University (Canberra).

Costa, Michael. 2009. Budget Honesty Now for the Generations to Come. *The Australian*, May 22.

Courvisanos, Jerry, and Alex Millmow. 2006. How Milton Friedman Came to Australia: A Case Study of Class-Based Political Business Cycles. *Journal of Australian Political Economy* 57: 112–136.

Davidson, Sinclair. 2011. Stimulusgate. *Agenda: A Journal of Policy Analysis and Reform* 18(1): 5–12.

Davidson, Sinclair. 2013a. Excellence in Research for Australia: An Audit of the Applied Economics Rankings. *Agenda: A Journal of Policy Analysis and Reform* 20(2): 5–20.

Davidson, Sinclair. 2013b. Hold Treasury to Account. *The Australian*, July 29.

Davidson, Sinclair, and Ashton de Silva. 2009. Submission to the Senate Inquiry into Stimulus Packages. Institute of Public Affairs (Sydney).

Davidson, Sinclair, and Ashton de Silva. 2013. Stimulating Savings: An Analysis of Cash Handouts in Australia and the United States. *Agenda: A Journal of Policy Analysis and Reform* 20(2): 39–57.

Dixon, Robert. 1986. *The Course of Empire: Neo-Classical Culture in New South Wales, 1788–1860*. Melbourne: Oxford University Press.

Economic Society of Australia Central Council. 2011. Policy Opinion Survey of Australian Economists 2011. Economic Society of Australia (Sydney).

Eggleston, F. W. 1932. *State Socialism in Victoria*. London: P. S. King.

Ergas, Henry, and Alex Robson. 2009. The 2008–09 Fiscal Stimulus Packages: A Cost Benefit Analysis. Working paper.

Foxall, Edward W. 1895. *The Claims of "Capital" (Involving an Enquiry into the Subjects of Currency and Banking), and, Financial Crises, Their Causes and Symptoms*. Sydney: Cunninghame.

Foxall, Edward W. 1903. *Colorphobia: An Exposure of the "White Australia" Fallacy*. Sydney: R. T. Kelly.

Gascoigne, John. 2002. *The Enlightenment and the Origins of European Australia*. Cambridge, UK: Cambridge University Press.

Giblin, L. F. 1943. Reconstruction in Australia. *Agenda: A Quarterly Journal of Reconstruction* 2: 213–225.

Goodwin, Craufurd D. W. 1966. *Economic Enquiry in Australia.* Durham, N.C.: Duke University Press.

Grattan, Michelle. 1986. Hawke Hits 'Lunacy' of New Right. *The Age* (Melbourne), August 29: 1.

Groenewegen, Peter D., and Bruce J. McFarlane. 1990. *A History of Australian Economic Thought.* London: Routledge.

Guest, Ross, and Anthony J. Makin. 2011. In the Long Run, the Multiplier Is Dead: Lessons from a Simulation. *Agenda: A Journal of Policy Analysis and Reform* 18(1): 13–21.

Guttmann, Simon. 2005. *The Rise and Fall of Monetary Targeting in Australia.* Melbourne: Australian Scholarly Publishing.

Hancock, W. K. 1931. *Australia.* New York: C. Scribner's Sons.

Hancock, W. K. 1968. Then and Now. *IPA Review* 22(3): 90–95.

Hawkins, John. 2007. Edward Pulsford (1844–1919). In *A Biographical Dictionary of Australian and New Zealand Economists*, ed. J. E. King, 229–230. Cheltenham, UK: Edward Elgar.

Hayek, Friedrich A. 1936. Review of *W. E. Hearn: First Australian Economist* by D. B. Copland. *Economica* 3(9): 101.

Hayek, Friedrich A. 1950. Full Employment, Planning and Inflation. *IPA Review* 4(6): 174–184.

Hayek, Friedrich A. 1976. Address at the 33rd Annual Meeting of The Institute of Public Affairs. *IPA Review* 30(4): 83–86.

Hearn, William Edward. 1864. *Plutology: or, The Theory of the Efforts to Satisfy Human Wants.* London: Macmillan.

Hewson, John, and Tim Fischer. 1991. *Fightback! It's Your Australia: The Way to Rebuild and Reward Australia.* Canberra: Liberal Party of Australia and National Party of Australia.

Hirsch, Max. 1901. *Democracy Versus Socialism: A Critical Examination of Socialism as a Remedy for Social Injustice and an Exposition of the Single Tax Doctrine.* London: Macmillan.

Hogan, Warren P. 1985. *Enterprise: Free, Dependent or Captor?* Sydney: Centre for Independent Studies.

Hogbin, Geoffrey R. 1983. *Free to Shop.* Sydney: Centre for Independent Studies.

Hogbin, Geoffrey R. 2001. Ross McDonald Parish, 24 December 1929–5 October 2001. *Policy* (Centre for Independent Studies) 17(4): 62–64.

Hyde, John. 1989. Foreword to *The Good Fight: Essays in Honour of Austin Steward Holmes (1924–1986)*, ed. Chris Ulyatt. Perth: Australian Institute for Public Policy.

Hyde, John. 2002. *Dry: In Defence of Economic Freedom.* Melbourne: Institute of Public Affairs.

Institute of Public Affairs. 1944. *Looking Forward: A Post-War Policy for Australian Industry.* Melbourne: Institute of Public Affairs.

Jevons, William Stanley. 1871. *The Theory of Political Economy.* London: Macmillan.

Kasper, Wolfgang. 2011. A Generation of Reform…and a Few Years of Backsliding. *Quadrant* 55(4): 49–58.

Kasper, Wolfgang, Richard Blandy, John Freebairn, Douglas Hocking, and Robert O'Neill. 1980. *Australia at the Crossroads: Our Choices to the Year 2000.* Sydney: Harcourt

Brace Jovanovich.

Kasper, Wolfgang, and Glenn Stevens. 1991. Lessons from the Australian Monetary Reforms of the 1980s: Possible Pointers for Malaysia in the 1990s? *Banker's Journal Malaysia* 65: 27–38.

Kasper, Wolfgang, Manfred E. Streit, and Peter J. Boettke. 2012. *Institutional Economics: Property, Competition, Policies*, 2nd ed. Cheltenham, UK: Edward Elgar.

Kates, Steven. 2011. *Free Market Economics: An Introduction for the General Reader*. Cheltenham, UK: Edward Elgar.

Kelly, Paul. 1992. *The End of Certainty: The Story of the 1980s*. Sydney: Allen & Unwin.

Kemp, David A. 1963. *The Institute of Public Affairs Victoria, 1942–1947*. B.A. Hons. essay, School of History and Political Science, Melbourne University.

Kemp, David A. 2011. Edward William Foxall: A Classical Liberal in a Racist Age. *Policy* (Centre for Independent Studies) 27(3): 35–43.

Kirchner, Stephen, ed. 2009a. *Fiscal Fallacies: The Failure of Activist Fiscal Policy*. Sydney: Centre for Independent Studies.

Kirchner, Stephen. 2009b. The Myth of an Independent Treasury. *Institutional-Economics.com*, May 16.

Kirchner, Stephen. 2014. Correspondence with Chris Berg.

Kirzner, Israel M. 1984. *The Role of the Entrepreneur in the Economic System*. Sydney: Centre for Independent Studies.

Kitching, Ron. 2007. The Untold Story of How Friedrich von Hayek Caught Inflation by the Balls. *BrookesNews.com*, April 23.

La Nauze, J. A. 1949. *Political Economy in Australia: Historical Studies*. Melbourne: Melbourne University Press.

Lodewijks, John. 2001. Educating Australian Economists. *Journal of Economic and Social Policy* 5(2).

Makin, Anthony J. 2009. Fiscal 'Stimulus': A Loanable Funds Critique. *Agenda: A Journal of Policy Analysis and Reform* 16(4): 25–34.

Makin, Anthony J. 2010. How Should Macroeconomic Policy Respond to Foreign Financial Crises? *Economic Papers* 29(2): 99–108.

Makin, Anthony J., and Paresh Kumar Narayan. 2011. How Potent Is Fiscal Policy in Australia? *Economic Papers* 30(3): 377–385.

Manne, Robert. 2005. *Do Not Disturb: Is the Media Failing Australia?* Melbourne: Black Inc.

Markwell, Donald J. 2000. Keynes and Australia. *Research Discussion Paper* 2000-04, Reserve Bank of Australia (Sydney).

McGuinness, P. P. 1978. Where Friedman Is a Pinko. *Australian Financial Review*, April 4: 4.

Melleuish, Gregory. 2001. *A Short History of Australian Liberalism*. Sydney: Centre for Independent Studies.

Melleuish, Gregory. 2005. Introduction to *Liberty and Liberalism*, new ed., by Bruce Smith. Sydney: Centre for Independent Studies.

Melleuish, Gregory. 2009. Bruce Smith, Edward Shann, W. K. Hancock: The Economic Critique of Democracy in Australia. *Australian Journal of Political Science* 44(4): 579–595.

Mill, John Stuart. 1848. *Principles of Political Economy*. London: John W. Parker.

Millmow, Alex. 2005. The Mystery of Edward Shann. *History of Economics Review* 42(Summer): 67–76.

Millmow, Alex. 2009. The Transition from Keynesian to Monetarist Economics in Australia: Joan Robinson's 1975 Visit to Australia. *History of Economics Review* 49(Winter): 15–31.

Millmow, Alex. 2010. *The Power of Economic Ideas: The Origins of Keynesian Macroeconomic Management in Interwar Australia, 1929–1939.* Canberra: Australian National University E Press.

Moore, Des. 2008. Status Quo Conservatism: The Coalition's Taxing and Spending Record. *IPA Review* 59(4): 37–39.

Moore, Gregory. 2002. Selling Plutology: Correspondence Relating to the Failure of Australia's First Economics Text. *History of Economics Review* 35(Winter): 63–77.

Moore, Gregory. 2007. John Simeon Elkington (1841–1922). In *A Biographical Dictionary of Australian and New Zealand Economists*, ed. J. E. King, 96–97. Cheltenham, UK: Edward Elgar.

Norton, Andrew. 2006. The Rise of Big Government Conservatism. *Policy* (Centre for Independent Studies) 22(4): 15–22.

Pearce, George Foster. 1903. Free Trade from a Labour Standpoint. In *Australia and the Fiscal Problem*, ed. G. Reid. London: Causton & Sons.

Pincus, Jonathan. 2014. Public Choice Theory Had Negligible Effect on Australian Microeconomic Policy, 1970s to 2000s. *History of Economics Review* 59(Winter): 82–93.

Popper, Karl R. 1945. *The Open Society and Its Enemies*. London: Routledge.

Pulsford, Edward. 1905. *The British Empire and the Relations of Asia and Australasia: Immigration Restrictions in Australia.* Sydney: William Brooks & Company.

Quiggin, John. 2010. Open Letter on Stimulus. *John Quiggin*, August 16.

Reid, Alan Douglas. 1969. *The Power Struggle*. Sydney: Shakespeare Head Press.

Rudd, Kevin. 2006. Howard's Brutopia. *The Monthly* (Melbourne), November.

Rudd, Kevin. 2009. The Global Financial Crisis. *The Monthly* (Melbourne), February.

Rutledge, Martha. 1988. Smith, Arthur Bruce (1851–1937). In *Australian Dictionary of Biography*, vol. 11, ed. Geoffrey Searle. Melbourne: Melbourne University Press.

Shann, E. O. G. 1930a. *An Economic History of Australia.* Cambridge, UK: Cambridge University Press.

Shann, E. O. G. 1930b. *Bond or Free?: Occasional Economic Essays.* Sydney: Angus and Robertson.

Shapley, Maggie. 2013. Hughes, Helen (1928–). *The Australian Women's Register* (National Foundation for Australian Women), February 20.

Sieper, Edward. 1982. *Rationalising Rustic Regulation.* Sydney: Centre for Independent Studies.

Smith, Bruce. 2005 [1887]. *Liberty and Liberalism: A Protest Against the Growing Tendency Toward Undue Interference by the State, with Individual Liberty, Private Enterprise, and the Rights of Property.* Sydney: Centre for Independent Studies.

Stockdale, Alan. 1999. The Politics of Privatisation in Victoria. *Privatisation International*, November.

Swan, Peter L. 1983. *On Buying a Job: The Regulation of Taxicabs in Canberra.* Sydney: Centre for Independent Studies.

Taylor, Lenore, and David Uren. 2010. *Shitstorm: Inside Labor's Darkest Days.* Melbourne:

Melbourne University Publishing.

Teicher, Julian, and Bernadine van Gramberg. 1999. 'Economic Freedom': Industrial Relations Policy Under the Kennett Government. In *The Kennett Revolution: Victorian Politics in the 1990s*, eds. Brian Costar and Nicholas Economou. Sydney: University of New South Wales Press.

Uren, David. 2014. Avoid Rigid Stimulus Packages, Says Treasury. *The Australian*, October 25.

Webb, Beatrice, and Sidney Webb. 1965. *The Webbs' Australian Diary 1898*, ed. A. G. Austin. Melbourne: I. Pitman.

White, Michael V. 1982. Jevons in Australia: A Reassessment. *Economic Record* 58(1): 32–45.

This chapter first appeared as an Econ Journal Watch article in September 2015. It has not been revised.

Liberalism in India

G. P. Manish, Shruti Rajagopalan, Daniel Sutter, and Lawrence H. White

We tell of the life of liberal ideas in India, from the nineteenth century down to today. Indian intellectuals in the nineteenth century were influenced by British and continental liberal philosophers. During the early twentieth century, however, the imagination of the Indian intelligentsia was captured by socialist ideas, which were gaining immense popularity all over the world. By the 1920s the reigning intellectual force in colonial India was socialism, in particular, the Fabian Society brand of socialism. In 1947, when India became independent, its leadership—with Jawaharlal Nehru at the helm—was committed to socialist and statist solutions working within a democratic framework.

For the next four decades, India experienced central planning, with each decade witnessing greater state control over citizens. The only liberal movement during this time was a fringe of opposition, represented in academia by the economist B. R. Shenoy. The opposition to planning in political and civil society was, mostly, led by C. Rajagopalachari. Also growing in importance were academic Indian expatriates, who lived in the United States or elsewhere but advanced liberal ideas for India. More recently, in post-liberalization India, there are many different voices in the press and civil society that support liberalism.

Intellectual currents before 1947

In India in the 19th century, prominent intellectuals like Ram Mohun Roy, Dadabhai Naoroji, and Sir Syed Ahmed Khan were influenced by British and continental liberal philosophers. Many Indian liberals wrote against the caste system and lobbied for equal rights for men and women (see Guha 2010,

33, 101, 213). Roy (1772–1833) was an advocate of "a limited government presenting a variety of checks on any abuse of its powers" (Arnot 1834). He argued for constitutional limitations constraining the British East India Company and advocated greater freedom of press, judicial independence, and elected representatives (Bayly 2007).

Liberals who supported individual rights and freedom and wanted to make them available to Indian citizens of the Empire founded the Indian National Congress Party in 1885. The party played a leading role in the independence movement, culminating in independence in 1947. Gopal Krishna Gokhale (1866–1915), who joined the party in 1889, was inspired by liberal thinkers such as Edmund Burke and John Stuart Mill. Gokhale believed in a free society with a limited role for the state in the provisioning of public goods and free education (Guha 2010, 99). He was teacher and mentor to the man who was perhaps the most important Indian leader in the early twentieth century, Mohandas Gandhi. Gandhi, however, felt that Gokhale was too liberal in his ideas and his favor for Western institutions; Gandhi believed more in village-level grassroots institutions.

Dadabhai Naoroji (1825–1917) was also a liberal thinker and "first and foremost a constitutionalist" (Doctor 1997, 28). Even though both he and Gokhale wrote extensively against the British Empire, and supported self-rule in India, their demand was for a liberal society. Given that India was dealing with social problems such as the caste system, untouchability, and the low status of women, the only legal way to deal with these concerns was to create a liberal constitution that granted political equality.[1]

In the 1920s the movement for some form of home rule or *Swaraj* gained momentum. At the All Parties Conference in 1928, Motilal Nehru, father of Jawaharlal Nehru, wrote a draft constitution calling for a democratic republic. The first proposed constitution for India written by Indians, it conceived of Dominion status for India within the Empire and was very similar to the American constitution, going so far as to outline a Bill of Rights. But with the passing of leaders like Gokhale and changing times, the once-strong liberal character of the Indian National Congress had faded.

By the late 1920s the new generation of Congress leaders was more

---

1. This critical social reform was an urgent and pressing concern. Changing these social circumstances through education and culture was considered too long a process, leaving social change through state intervention to be seen by many as the ideal solution.

inspired by socialist ideas. In particular, the British Fabian Society influenced Indian intellectuals (see Bhagwati 1993; Austin 1999; Das 2000; Guha 2007; Varma 2008; White 2010). The most prominent political leader amongst the young and upcoming socialists was Jawaharlal Nehru (1889–1964), who, while studying law in London, was enormously influenced by Fabian ideas.[2] Nehru believed that capitalism in India would weaken both political and socioeconomic equality: "Democracy and capitalism grew up together in the nineteenth century, but they were not mutually compatible. There was a basic contradiction between them, for democracy laid stress on the power for many, while capitalism gave real power to the few" (Nehru 2004/1936, 547).

The main thread joining the dislike of capitalism and the embrace of democracy was the idea that political equality in India would be meaningless without economic equality. Sidney and Beatrice Webb, the founders of the Fabian Society, emphasized this connection (Webb and Webb 1920). The ideas of the Webbs, George Bernard Shaw, and Harold Laski all left their mark on Nehru during his time at Harrow, Cambridge, and London (Nehru 2004/1936, 27). Whereas the liberal Whig philosophy of the 18th century profoundly influenced the founding and set the early course of an independent United States, the democratic-socialist philosophy of the late 19th century profoundly influenced the founding and set the early course of an independent India.

The ideology of planning gradually found its way into the heart of the burgeoning independence movement, the Indian National Congress. A Congress Socialist Party, spearheaded by Nehru and consisting of ardent socialists and planning enthusiasts, was formed within the broader fold of the Congress in 1934. More importantly, the Congress organized a National Planning Commission in 1938 to chart out in greater detail the role that state planning could play in aiding the growth of the nation. The National Planning Commission met at intervals throughout the late 1930s and early 1940s, coming up with proposals that greatly influenced the goals and the institutional structure of the planning mechanism in independent India. By the end of the Second World War, socialism was the new orthodoxy in Indian politics. This orthodoxy led to the adoption of central economic planning

2. The core of Fabian socialism was to advance the principles of socialism through gradualist and reformist means and not by violence or revolution.

when India gained independence from the British in 1947.

From the perspective of liberalism, the years since independence can be broken up into three broad periods:

- 1950–1975, featuring the liberal economist B. R. Shenoy and the emergence of a broader movement opposed to state planning;
- 1975–1990, characterized by the absence of any significant liberal opposition within Indian civil society and a shifting of the anti-planning forces to universities abroad; and
- 1990–2015, the years of economic reform, which have witnessed the re-emergence of a limited liberal movement making headway within the press and policy circles but not in academia.

The state-planning ideology comes to power

During the second half of the 19th century and the early decades of the 20th century, significant economic change rippled through the Indian economy. India became more integrated into world trade and opened up to "the influences emanating from the rapidly growing areas centering on the North Atlantic" (S. Shenoy 1971, 13). There was a deepening of the division of labor and increased commercialization in the rural economy. More output was sent to market and the cultivation of commercial crops such as cotton, jute, and oilseeds became more widespread. Pockets of modern industry began to emerge and towns and cities mushroomed, owing their existence not, as before, to the largesse of *rajas*, both petty and noble, but to the hustle and bustle of commerce. By 1947 India could boast of having the world's largest jute textile industry and the sixth-largest cotton textile industry, and of accounting for nearly half of the world's tea exports.

Yet these changes barely altered the fundamental nature of the colonial Indian economy. It remained highly agrarian, with the rural economy in many parts of the country characterized by a pre-modern institutional framework, resembling the rural economy of medieval Europe or Czarist Russia more than one of an industrialized Western nation. Indeed, most modern economic growth occurred in the interstices of that institutional framework, in pockets where market forces could emerge and operate. Nevertheless, by the late 1930s a vocal and committed movement had emerged calling for centralized economic planning and singing the praises of socialism, while blaming most of the abject poverty of the country on the evil forces of markets and capitalism.

Two momentous international events fuelled the movement toward statist ideologies and policies. The Great Depression had wreaked havoc on the international division of labor, leaving in its wake severe agrarian distress in parts of India, which occasioned bitter criticism of trade and markets. More importantly, the grand experiment with central planning in the Soviet Union had commenced. While many important Indian planning enthusiasts, including Nehru, were uneasy with some aspects of Soviet central planning, they admired the rapid industrialization that it apparently had engendered. The imagined success of state planning reinforced amongst the Indian intelligentsia the already dominant idea that a market economy is inherently unstable and unreliable, while a centrally planned economy can deliver rapid growth and development.[3]

During the 1930s and 1940s there appeared numerous plans for India's economic development. The first emerged in 1934 and was the brainchild of Sir Mokshagundam Visvesvarayya, an engineer from Mysore; its "essence [...] was industrialization," with a "proposed doubling of the national income over a period of ten years" (Hanson 1966, 30). In the 1940s came the Bombay Plan, drawn up by a group of industrialists; the People's Plan, crafted by M. N. Roy and encapsulating the position of the more radical communist Left; and the Gandhian Plan of S. N. Agarwal, which placed a greater emphasis on the preservation of the village and traditional cottage industry. Politicians debated which plan to pursue, but not the question of whether the state should engage in central planning.

With the Second World War, the planning enthusiasm spread to the colonial government as well. In 1944 the government set up a Planning and Development Department under the leadership of Sir Ardeshir Dalal, one of the signatories of the Bombay Plan. In 1945 the department issued "a Statement of Industrial Policy which foreshadowed in many ways the Industrial Policy Resolutions of 1948 and 1956" (S. Shenoy 1971, 21). More importantly, the war brought with it a host of economic controls, including price controls, distribution controls, and the large-scale rationing of many

---

3. On the influences of the Great Depression and the Soviet Union on the emergence of a socialist movement in colonial India, see Frankel (1978).

commodities. Also introduced were systems of import controls and capital issues controls, and a rudimentary system of industrial licensing, all aimed at constraining inflation and conserving scarce foreign exchange. Most of these controls outlived the war and formed the basis of the future planning apparatus.

The goals of planning in independent India

In 1947, agriculture still accounted for more than 50 percent of the national income, whereas manufacturing industries accounted for only 12.3 percent. In the industrial sector, production was heavily oriented toward consumer goods; industries such as cotton textiles, jute textiles, and vegetable oil contributed 62 percent of the total industrial output. The iron and steel and engineering industries contributed a meager 11.5 percent to industrial output (Tomlinson 1979, 33), while a capital goods sector was virtually nonexistent (Morris 1983, 642). In view of this structure of production, India was primarily an exporter of agricultural commodities and light-manufactured consumer goods, while her imports, in contrast, consisted largely of capital goods, industrial inputs, and manufactured consumer goods (Chaudhuri 1983; Roy 2006).

The supporters of planning believed that the nation's dependence on imported capital goods was the chief obstacle in the path of its economic progress. Consider, for example, the following passage from P. C. Mahalanobis, the architect of the Second Five Year Plan:

> Why do we then import machinery? Because we have not started factories to fabricate heavy machinery needed for the production of steel, cement, etc. ... [O]nce we do this, and establish a heavy machine building industry we shall be able to use our own iron ore and with our own hands produce steel; and then use the steel to produce more machinery. ... [O]ur dependence on foreign supplies will be greatly reduced. *The main obstacle to rapid industrialization thus removed*, we shall be able to increase production and employment quickly. (Mahalanobis 1961, 48, emphasis added)

An immediate goal of planning, therefore, was to diversify India's production base and to industrialize the nation rapidly. But this process of indigenization was not to be restricted to the capital and intermediate goods industries. Instead, the plan was to gradually utilize the tools and machines produced domestically to step up the domestic production of agricultural and industrial consumer goods in the future. Consumer goods that were being imported would in due course be produced at home, and the state would discourage exports of agricultural commodities and consumer goods. Instead, the supply of these goods was to be reserved for the home market.

Thus, the Indian planners were motivated primarily by the ideology of economic nationalism: a mix of central economic planning at home combined with autarkic tendencies in the realm of foreign trade.[4] The aim was to increase national output by inducing home production of consumer, intermediate, and capital goods.

The planning apparatus

After independence in 1947, the newly empowered Indian government continued to add to the controls and regulations that it had inherited from the colonial government, and it enshrined many of these inherited powers of control into law. The Planning Commission, instituted in 1950 with Prime Minister Jawaharlal Nehru at its helm, had responsibility for drafting the document that formed the entire planning system's cornerstone, namely, the Five Year Plan. The initial Five Year Plan and its successors each contained a detailed list of the investment expenditures to be incurred by the public and private sectors and the sectoral allocation of these investments. Linked to these expenditures on various projects was a list of targets to be achieved by various industries.

The Industrial Policy Resolutions (IPRs) of 1948 and 1956 divided industries into three broad categories. The first category included industries in which either the state would have a total monopoly or only the state could undertake any new investment. Existing private firms in these industries could continue to operate and expand, but no new private firms could enter. The second category included industries in which the state would gradually establish new units, while permitting new private firms to enter as well. The third category contained the industries that would be the private sector's responsibility. The state, however, could enter these industries if it wished to do so.

---

4. On economic nationalism, see Heilperin (2010/1949).

Political constraints stopped the government from nationalizing all industry. Instead, it chose to control and regulate the private sector to ensure that private production and investment conformed to the priorities listed in the Five Year Plan. Indeed, as noted by Jagdish Bhagwati and Padma Desai (1970, 231), private-sector investment was "directed by the state, by physical controls operated primarily through an exhaustive licensing system combined with a detailed setting of 'targets' by the Planning Commission."

Key to the system of control was the 1951 Industries (Development and Regulation) Act, which instituted the highly restrictive industrial licensing regime requiring all private industrial undertakings to register with the central government. Several other laws along the same lines were instituted rapidly. The 1955 Essential Commodities Act gave the central government the authority to control the production, distribution, and pricing of commodities that it deemed "essential." The Companies Act of 1956 constituted "one of the most detailed and stringent codes of business legislation to be found anywhere in the world" (Hanson 1966, 486). The Capital Issues Control Act of 1956 gave the government the power to control the issue of capital by joint-stock companies. Also, a vast apparatus of import and export controls was carried over from pre-independence days.

The liberal opponents of planning: 1950–1975

The period from 1950 to 1975 witnessed significant and articulate opposition to planning, from the economist B. R. Shenoy within Indian academia and from the emergence of a broader movement opposed to planning in the civil society. This was a time when, within India and all over the world, intellectuals and politicians were convinced that centralized resource allocation was the way forward. Within academia in India, Shenoy kept the liberal flame alight. In politics and civil society, there were a handful of others.

B. R. Shenoy

Described as "a hero and a saint" by Peter Bauer (1998, 1), B. R. Shenoy almost singlehandedly spearheaded the academic intellectual resistance to the juggernaut of planning and interventionism. His was a lonely mission; at the time of his death in 1978, he was perhaps "the only liberal economist between Athens and Tokyo" (S. Shenoy 2003, 2). But it was precisely this courageous resistance to the *zeitgeist* and the unflinching faith in his own ideas that drew such admiration from Bauer. Shenoy was a heroic figure because he "publicly resisted fashionable fads and fancies, however influentially canvassed and widely accepted," and he was saintly because "he remained unmoved, even serene, in the face of neglect, disparagement, even abuse" (Bauer 1998, 1).[5]

Shenoy's criticism of Indian planning began with his famous "Note of Dissent" (Shenoy 1955) from the draft of the Second Five Year Plan. One of twenty economists on the government advisory panel, he was the sole dissenter (Bauer 1998, 1). His views also cut against those of international luminaries such as Oscar Lange, Nicholas Kaldor, Joan Robinson, Gunnar Myrdal, and Ragnar Frisch, who were all enthusiastic supporters of the Indian experiment with planning (ibid., 2). Moreover, Shenoy's dissidence miffed and angered those in power at home. According to Shenoy's daughter, Nehru "got very upset" (S. Shenoy 2003, 2) over Shenoy's criticism of what was to become the signature document of Indian planning.

Shenoy followed his "Dissent" with a string of works that attacked the Indian experiment with planning (e.g., Shenoy 1958; 1963; 1968; 1974).[5] Unlike other contemporary critics, such as P. N. Vakil and P. R. Brahmanand, Shenoy did not merely criticize specific goals of the plans. Shenoy's criticism was radical; he opposed the idea of central planning, root and branch, and the rising tide of statist control.[6]

The fundamental weakness of a planned economy, according to Shenoy, is "a divorce between production and consumer needs" (1966, 3), in sharp contrast to a market-based economy, where consumers reign supreme. On the consumer sovereignty that characterizes a free market, Shenoy wrote:

> Ordinarily, in free societies, production would get adjusted to meet the

---

5. *See* Balakrishnan (2011) and Prakash (2013) for brief overviews of Shenoy's economic thought.

6. In this radical opposition, Shenoy was highly influenced by F. A. Hayek and other economists working in the Austrian tradition. Shenoy was a graduate student at the London School of Economics when Hayek delivered the lectures that formed the basis of *Prices and Production* (Hayek 1931). Shenoy was so smitten with the Austrian tradition that, according to his daughter, "after studying Austrian theory, he said he was immunized against every other framework" (S. Shenoy 2003, 2).

changing needs of consumers, this adjustment being effected by the pricing
system. Prices of commodities in larger demand would rise and
entrepreneurs would increase the output of such commodities under the
inducement of higher returns on the capital invested, which higher prices
would bring. (Shenoy 1966, 2–3)

Under the regime of centralized planning then prevailing in India, however,
"production is directed, or indirectly controlled, by the Planning Commission." Constrained and hobbled by the controls wielded by the planning
authorities, "entrepreneurs have not been free to orient production to satisfy
consumer demands" (ibid.).

In a world where there is a divergence between production and consumer
preferences, "we can no longer depend on the statistics of national product
for a measure of overall economic progress," where the latter term means
"a rise in the level of living of the masses" (Shenoy 1966, 4). Planning in
India had been characterized by significant increases in the production of
various capital goods; the heavy and basic industries had apparently flourished
since independence. Yet these significant investments had failed to flow into
consumer goods. Instead, they had given rise to "idle production capabilities
and idle stocks," activities that, while they do "drive up the curve of economic
development in the same way as [...] effective capital formation and increased
consumption," nevertheless do not "add to the well-being of the people"
(ibid., 7). Indeed, such production had led to a scenario where, in the midst
of towering dams and rising factories, "the masses of the people" were "ill
clad and underfed." Shenoy concluded that the spectacle was not economic
development, but "show-window economic activity and at best sectoral
development" (ibid., 2).

Shenoy determined that taking a look at the "consumer goods content
of the national product" would provide a much better picture of economic
well-being (1966, 4). The statistics showed that planning had not significantly
increased the per capita availability of food. The per capita availability of
cereals had averaged 13.9 ounces per day for the period 1958–1965, which was
more or less on par with the figures for the period 1931–1938, which stood
at 14.2 ounces per day—and this despite much higher imports of cereals in
the 1958–1965 period (Shenoy 1966, 8). Shenoy notes also that the output
of other mass consumer goods such as cotton cloth, matches, and soap

witnessed only modest increases from 1951 to 1965 (ibid., 8, 16).[7]

Moreover, much of whatever increase in national income there had been had "accrued to a thin upper crust of the privileged sections of the people" (Shenoy 1966, 7). Thus, the output of consumer goods used by the comparatively well-off sections of society, "a fraction of the population," rose sharply and at a much higher pace than the mass consumer goods. The output of electric lamps, for instance, increased 3.9 times, that of electric fans rose by a multiple of 6.4, radios by a multiple of 9.5, and rayon yarn by a multiple of 34. All these goods, however, were largely "curios to the masses" (ibid., 16).

What, then, was the remedy? According to Shenoy, a rapid lift in the "precarious standard of living of the common man" could be achieved only by bringing an end to "the policies of economic interventionism" (1966, 20). "A decisive shift from interventionism—misplaced 'planning'—to the free market and the free pricing system is the first basic reform which the Indian economic situation urgently calls for" (ibid., 23). Production and the allocation of resources should be left to private entrepreneurs, with the consumer being in "supreme charge of affairs," acting "through the shopping referendum" (ibid., 20–21). Liberal arrangements would better ensure that resources were allocated, not according to the whims and dictates of those in power, but according to the preferences of consumers. And it would also imply an end to the "queer bundle of economic oddities of rising incomes, food shortages and declining per capita availability of cloth; mounting foreign aid and mounting investments; shift of resources from sectors where the output is phenomenal to sectors where it is meagre; mounting unemployment; continued mass poverty and growing opulence of the few; and intractable balance of payments deficits with inability to meet the amortisation payments on external debt" (ibid., 21). "It takes a Planning Commission to produce these oddities," Shenoy quipped.

In his later years, B. R. Shenoy was joined in criticizing central planning and extolling free markets by his daughter, Sudha Shenoy. The younger Shenoy wrote a remarkable pamphlet for the Institute of Economic Affairs in 1971, in which she presented her father's case against planning in detail and also tackled various objections raised by the supporters of planning.

---

7. Manish (2011; 2013; 2014) presents, along the lines suggested by Shenoy, a more detailed analysis of Indian economic development under central planning.

Nevertheless, in India in the 1940s and 1950s, no one in academic circles other than Shenoy fought against statism and central planning. There was, however, a growing liberal movement in politics and civil society.

C. Rajagopalachari

Chakravarti Rajagopalachari (1878–1972) was the most important figure in liberalism in post-colonial India. Popularly known as Rajaji, he was a towering figure along with Gandhi, Nehru, and Jinnah in the independence movement. He was Governor General of India—the only Indian to ever hold the position—from June 1948 to January 1950, during the drafting of the Constitution of India. Rajaji was part of Nehru's cabinet immediately after Sardar Patel's death, but he resigned in 1951 in part over strong objections to the government's preference for Soviet-style planning.

In 1952 Rajaji entered politics in Madras, and his chief target for opposition was the Communist Party of India. As Chief Minister of Madras, one of his first executive orders was abolishing price controls on food grains, controls that had been introduced as a temporary wartime measure in 1938. The opposition predicted food shortage and starvation, but instead Madras witnessed an increase in supply of food grains and a fall in price. After the tenure as Chief Minister of Madras, Rajaji resigned in 1954, intent on retiring from politics. In 1955 he received the Bharat Ratna, the highest Indian civilian award.

As the government's planning efforts increased in both size and scope, no politician of stature was willing to oppose Nehru's policies. Minoo Masani, another liberal politician (who is further discussed below), implored many leaders to head the opposition against Nehru and his brand of socialism. When no one stepped up to the task, Rajaji came out of retirement and became the face of political dissent. In 1959, he formed the Swatantra ("Freedom") Party to provide opposition to Congress. Its founders formulated 21 principles emphasizing a goal of protecting individual liberty and limiting government.[8] With Swatantra, as Khasa Subba Rao put it, Rajaji aimed at saving individuals from "the soul-crushing oppression of the

---

8. See "Statement of Principles of the Swantantra Party," *Economic Weekly*, July 1959, page 894.

Leviathan State disguised in Socialistic raiment" (quoted in P. Vaman Rao 2001, 146).

In addition to a strong political opposition, Rajaji also provided a strong intellectual opposition to socialism. In 1956 he started *Swarajya*, an English-language weekly magazine, for which he wrote a weekly column discussing current economic and social policy in the context of individual freedom and economic liberty. He is credited with labeling Nehruvian socialism as a "permit–quota–license raj," a new kind of oppression following on the heels of the British Raj. Rajaji's weekly columns informed the public of infringements on property rights, expanding controls on prices and quantities, the backwardness of India's agricultural policy, and rule uncertainty arising from frequent amendment of the Constitution.[9]

Minoo Masani

Another founding member of the Swatantra Party was Minocher Rustom (Minoo) Masani. Masani's intellectual trajectory was quite different from Rajaji's. Like Jawaharlal Nehru and V. K. Krishna Menon, Masani was a student of Harold Laski at the London School of Economics, where he studied law. In 1927, he went to Moscow for the tenth anniversary celebration of the Bolshevik revolution, and he returned an ardent fan of the Soviet communists (Masani 1936).

In 1928, Masani joined the Congress Socialist Party within the Indian National Congress Party. He was close to other socialists in the independence movement like Jayaprakash Narayan, Ram Manohar Lohia, Ashok Mehta, Achyut Patwardhan, and Yusuf Meherally. But during the late 1930s, largely because of Stalin's totalitarianism, Masani started questioning Communist ideas.

Masani's movement specifically to liberalism began with conversations and debates with Mahatma Gandhi.

> Two fundamentals I accepted from Gandhi's thought—first, that the end does not justify the means, and that no decent social order can evolve through the use of force or fraud; and that in the second half of the twentieth century, the omnivorous state is in danger of becoming the

---

9. For a representative collection of these ideas, see Rajagopalachari (1961).

biggest single threat to human liberty. No school or thought or system of government offends against these two beliefs as violently as totalitarian socialism. (Masani 1956, 36)

By 1940, Masani was very critical of socialism, communism, and Marxism. He wrote a detailed critique, *Socialism Reconsidered* (1944). He attacked the methods used by communists and socialists, like abolition of private property, as never leading to an equal society. Though critical of socialist methods, Masani supported ideals of a "free" and "equal" society. In the 1940s, he began to formulate ideas on a mixed economy. In 1952, Masani founded *Freedom First—The Liberal Monthly*, where he often criticized policies of the incumbent government. And in 1965, along with B. R. Shenoy, Khushwant Singh, and other writers, Masani founded the Indian Liberal Group (ILG), an organization that put forward criticism of government policy, especially on matters of free speech.[10]

Masani was a member of the Indian Legislative Assembly, which, after independence, became the Constituent Assembly of India. He was a Member of Parliament from 1957 to 1971, initially as an independent, and later as a member of Swatantra Party. In parliamentary debates as well as through his writing in popular outlets and *Swarajya* magazine, he opposed socialist policies, especially the more aggressive forms of socialism pursued by Indira Gandhi. Some of his famous contributions to parliamentary debates took place during 1967–1970 in the Lok Sabha, when Gandhi attempted a spate of nationalizations, and Masani provided economic and moral arguments against them.

In 1971, Indira Gandhi's command-and-control socialism, armed with her *Garibi Hatao desh bachavo* slogan ("Abolish poverty, rescue the country"), helped the Indian National Congress Party win by large margins, and every opposition party, including the Swatantra Party, faced huge electoral losses. Masani took personal responsibility for the political and intellectual loss of liberal ideas and retired from active politics in 1971. He continued to actively write and edit *Freedom First*. During the Emergency declared by Gandhi, lasting 21 months from 1975 to 1977, *Freedom First* was subjected to censorship. Rather than submit, the magazine shut down for six months while Masani

---

10. ILG underwent a revival in the year 2000 with a new organizational constitution and call for membership from the youth of India.

fought censorship in court. Except for that brief period during the Emergency, *Freedom First* has been in print for over 60 years and has printed 540 issues. Masani continued to engage with liberals and debate with socialists, outside the realm of active politics, until his death in 1998 at the age of 93.

Khasa Subba Rao

In addition to the political movement started by the Swatantra Party, popular publications were crucial to advancing liberal ideas. Khasa Subba Rao was perhaps the most important intellectual figure in presenting the liberal critique of socialist policies. Subba Rao was a writer, journalist, and editor. He started his career with the newspaper *Swarajya*, and he worked at smaller publications like *Free Press Journal* and *Liberty*. He joined *The Indian Express*, then gaining popularity as a national daily, and was involved in reporting and writing about the freedom struggle, even facing imprisonment during the Quit India movement.

In 1946, Subba Rao started his own weekly publication called *Swatantra*, a venture that lasted ten years. Important leaders like Rajaji contributed to *Swatantra* during this time. In 1956, Subba Rao launched a new weekly, *Swarajya* magazine. This magazine had much greater readership and more success, even after Subba Rao's death in 1961.[11] With the closure of *Swarajya* in 1978, the Indian liberal movement lost its megaphone and voice, and liberals were sidelined.

A. D. Shroff

Ardeshir Darabshaw Shroff (1899–1965) advanced liberalism within the world of business. An astute student, he went to the London School of Economics to study finance. He too was exposed to the Fabianism of Laski, Shaw, and the Webbs, but he did not take to socialism. He returned to India to work as a stockbroker. Shroff quickly climbed business circles in Mumbai. The 1930s witnessed the rise of a new wave of socialists in India with Nehru at the crest. Shroff strongly believed in private enterprise, but was appointed in 1938 as a member of the Planning Committee of the Indian National

---

11. Subba Rao was well eulogized (Ranganathan 1961) in *The Indian Libertarian*, a fortnightly journal first published in 1957 by R. B. Lotvala and edited by Kusum R. Lotvala.

Congress. Along with a number of leading industrialists, Shroff contributed to the "Bombay Plan," which recommended a middle path instead of full state socialism (Thakurdas 1945).

Post-independence, Shroff continued to be prominent in business circles in Mumbai but also chaired several important government committees, notably ones on banking and finance. In the 1950s, Nehru's vision for socialism and more controls in every aspect of the economy became apparent, leading up to a nationalization of many sectors. Shroff felt that the only way to combat statism was to educate citizens on the importance of private enterprise in ordering society. In 1956, he started the Forum of Free Enterprise, mainly as an education and outreach organization. Shroff wanted to distance the Forum from politics and focus on educational outreach. The Forum actively published booklets on policy issues and free enterprise into the 1970s, and then sporadically until 2010. The Forum published critical analysis of the government's Five Year Plans and of every budget. Nani Palkhivala, a senior lawyer and supporter of the Forum (and who is discussed below), gave a speech analyzing the Central Budget every year using the outreach platform of the Forum. Shroff wrote several pamphlets between 1956 and 1965, developing two parallel critiques of socialist planning in India. The first was that its outcomes were inefficient: that scarce resources would be more efficiently developed and directed in the private sector. The second was that the means used to implement socialism—government control of the means of production—chipped away at constitutional principles.[12]

Nani Palkhivala

An exceptional figure associated with the classical liberal movement, but with an important identity outside of the movement, was Nani A. Palkhivala (1920–2002). Best known as senior advocate at the Supreme Court of India, Palkhivala had a towering reputation during his active decades. Palkhivala authored one of the earliest and most comprehensive interpretation and

12. In one such pamphlet, Shroff described the political state of affairs in India: "With a characteristic schizophrenia, both totalitarian and democratic Socialists, have talked one way and acted another. While they accept Freedom and Democracy in theory, in actual practice Socialist pattern is being identified with 'an all-powerful State, with heavy-handed bureaucracy, and regimentation'" (1956, 12).

critiques of Indian tax law. Palkhivala wrote *The Law and Practice of Income Tax* in 1950, which remains a canonical legal text (10th ed., Datar et al. 2013). He was the lead counsel in several cases that have shaped the Indian Constitution and the Indian Supreme Court. Palkhivala was an advocate of free markets, especially in challenging socialist legislation in court and in defending limited, responsible government (see Palkhivala 1984b). After the Second Five Year Plan was announced, Palkhivala began efforts to decode the tax law for the public. For many years thereafter he gave a post-budget lecture on tax law, aimed at the layman. Palkhivala had such a gift that these annual lectures gained immense popularity. In later years, the lecture was held in the Brabourne cricket stadium and would be attended by lawyers, judges, tax experts, accountants, journalists, and thousands of individuals attempting to understand how the budget and taxes affected their daily lives.

Palkhivala was a critic as well as an interpreter of tax law in India. In his first lecture for the Forum of Free Enterprise, in 1957, he characterized the wealth tax as expropriationist. In 1965, Palkhivala gave a notable talk in Madras with the title "The Ideology of Taxation" (Palkhivala 1984a). He criticized the Indian tax system for its uncertainty, unpredictability, complexity, arbitrary provisions, and excess burdens—each aspect a violation of one of five cardinal rules for taxation.

The Constitution of India was frequently amended during 1950–1978, the peak era of socialism, to accommodate policies to salvage the Five Year Plans. Such constitutional amendments enabled the planners to retroactively give effect to plan objectives after instances where the Indian judiciary had struck down a policy for violating constitutional principles. The amendments were substantive infringements on individual rights and important aspects of liberal governance like federalism and separation of powers (see Rajagopalan 2015). Palkhivala (1974) described this amendment process as the systematic defiling and defacing of the Indian Constitution.

As a senior advocate in the Indian Supreme Court, Palkhivala argued some of the most important cases affecting the constitution and the rule of law in India. In one case, he argued against bank nationalization. Another case concerned the Twenty-Fourth Amendment, which gave Parliament supremacy in amending the Constitution. Palkhivala challenged the constitutional validity of the amendment (among others) in the Supreme Court. Palkhivala was lead counsel in one of the most important cases in Indian history, *Kesavananda Bharati v. State of Kerala* (1973) on the question of the amendability of the Constitution.

Throughout Indira Gandhi's tenure as Prime Minister, Palkhivala was a mainstay in important cases, which often were a matter of socialist abuse

of constitutional rules. After Gandhi's declaration of the Emergency,[13] Parlia-

13. Indira Gandhi's power was threatened due to a series of events beginning with the 1971 election. Raj Narain, a politician who lost to Gandhi in the 1971 Parliamentary election, filed a petition alleging that she had won the election through corrupt practices and had used government officials and official machinery in her campaign. On June 12, 1975, the Allahabad High Court found Gandhi guilty and her election to Parliament was declared null and void. While her appeal was pending in the Supreme Court and she was under pressure to resign, Gandhi issued an Ordinance on June 25, 1975, declaring a state of internal emergency in India. This declaration allowed the Prime Minister to suspend elections and civil liberties. Gandhi

ment attempted to rewrite the Constitution with the Forty-Second Amendment to remove all binding constitutional constraints. Palkhivala again argued successfully, in the landmark case *Minerva Mills Ltd. v. Union of India* (1980), that Parliament's power to amend the Constitution was limited.

Situated abroad: Jagdish Bhagwati and T. N. Srinivasan

We have seen that statism dominated Indian economic thought after independence. The liberal, anti-planning movement described above had, by the mid-1970s, very little to show for itself in terms of policy reform. From 1975 and the Emergency, the years under Indira Gandhi were characterized by the almost complete disappearance of liberal ideas within India. But opposition to statism in India came from figures at institutions abroad.[14]

By the mid-1960s, the inefficiency, poor growth results, and corruption of the heavily interventionist system could no longer be ignored and covered up, and a new generation of liberal researchers examined the evidence. Jagdish Bhagwati was the most prominent of the young economists to criticize the poor results of the system's protectionism, central industrial planning, and the associated 'permit–quota–license raj.'

By his own account, Bhagwati first began to experience an "intellectual conversion" around 1962 in favor of free trade and against the protectionist policy of import substitution (Bhagwati 2001). In reviewing Bhagwati's 1966 book *The Economics of Underdeveloped Countries*, P. T. Bauer (1971, 525–526) detected in it the standard views that "state control of the direction and composition of economic activity is indispensable for development" and that "foreign aid is essential" for rapid development. But in 1969, Bhagwati reviewed a book by B. R. Shenoy, giving Shenoy credit for being "among the few economists to notice and condemn the inefficiency of the import control regime and the wastefulness of the detailed control of industrial licensing and production, when in fact it was fashionable and personally rewarding to do

---

ruled by decree for the next three years.

14. Not all Indian economists trained abroad opposed statist policies. An important figure is Amartya Sen, recipient of the Nobel Prize in Economics in 1998 and perhaps India's most famous economist. In his early years, Sen explicitly advocated socialism as a viable alternative to capitalism (see Sen 1959). However in later years, though Sen remains politically aligned with leftist policies in India, his focus has shifted away from socialism (Briggeman 2013).

otherwise" (Bhagwati 1969, 636). Bhagwati did however remain dismissive toward Shenoy's "strong ideology of the Friedmannite variety" and "his antipathy to planning *per se*" (ibid., 635, 636).[15] Bhagwati still favored a "form of planning where key, efficient decisions are taken in selected areas and the rest is left largely to the market" (ibid., 637).

Bhagwati's empirical critique of the detailed planning and licensing regime, especially in books co-authored with his wife Padma Desai (1970) and with T. N. Srinivasan (1975), was influential in persuading many younger Indian economists to turn from dirigisme toward liberalization.[16] Deepak Lal (2008) writes that these works "marked the beginning of the end of the planning syndrome that had held Indian economists in thrall for nearly a century."[17] Bhagwati has noted that, by the time Congress Party leader Rajiv Gandhi sought deregulatory advice in the 1980s, he was able to talk to "a lot of people like myself who were keen on reforms" (Bhagwati 2001).

Bhagwati moved to MIT in 1968 and later to Columbia, and Srinivasan relocated to Yale in 1980. Yet they became important and enthusiastic supporters of India's liberalizations. One critic of "neoliberal" reform in India offers this assessment of their importance:

> Among the large number of eminent Indian émigré economists, Jagdish Bhagwati and T. N. Srinivasan have been prominent and forceful in their defence of the liberalizing reforms. Bhagwati in, for example, his Radhakrishnan Lectures...published as *India in Transition: Freeing the Economy* (Bhagwati 1993); Srinivasan in, for example, Srinivasan (1991a, 1991b,

---

15. In an interview decades later, Bhagwati remarked: "When I first came back from Oxford, we all were supporters of the [import-substitution] policy. ... I don't know anyone whom we respected who was against import substitution in those days. B. R. Shenoy was a vocal opponent but we (wrongly) put him down as a libertarian and an ideologue" (Bhagwati 2001; parentheses around "wrongly" as in original).

16. Another liberal economist of the time worthy of mention is V. K. Ramaswami, co-author with Bhagwati of a well known theoretical paper defending free trade (1963).

17. Indeed, in the words of economist Deena Khatkhate (1994, 1098), "The pioneering work of Bhagwati and Desai in the late 1960s (Bhagwati and Desai 1970) provided the first intellectually coherent analytic framework for assessing Indian planning and industrialization strategies." And she goes on to note that Bhagwati "is regarded widely as the intellectual forerunner, the theoretician, of the ongoing reforms (of the early 1990s). The Finance Minister [Manmohan Singh], spearheading the reforms, has declared that India's misfortune was to wait so long to implement what Bhagwati had urged with clarity and foresight two decades earlier" (Khatkhate 1994, 1099).

> 1993); and the two together, in deadly combination, in...*India's Economic Reforms*, [which] was commissioned for the Ministry of Finance by Manmohan Singh (Bhagwati and Srinivasan 1993).... In it, they congratulate the Rao government on the boldness of its reforms and urge it 'to extend them boldly in several new directions,' with all speed. (Byres 2014, 45 n.6)

Bhagwati and Srinivasan were joined in their push for reforms, especially after the turn of the century, by Arvind Panagariya. In his influential book *India: The Emerging Giant*, Panagariya (2008) extends the Bhagwati and Srinivasan critique of the failures of Indian planning and lays out a roadmap for reforms in different sectors of the economy. Especially liberal is his call for greater freedom in the realm of foreign trade as well as the removal of controls over many sectors of the domestic economy, controls that were untouched by the wave of reforms of the early 1990s.

Some of these ideas have influenced Indian policymakers. Panagariya is now the Vice Chairman of NITI (National Institution for Transforming India), which was set up recently by the Narendra Modi government to replace the Planning Commission. Another important policy appointment is that of Raghuram Rajan as the Governor of the Reserve Bank of India. Rajan, from University of Chicago's Booth School of Business, is influenced by Friedrich Hayek and Milton Friedman. Rajan wants to create more competition in the financial sector by giving licenses to new banks, allowing foreign banks to expand faster, and privatizing state-owned banks; he is skeptical about the rationality of Indian investors, but also about unintended consequences arising from regulation (*Economist* 2013a; 2013b). "I'm a believer in free markets, but I'm not a believer in laissez-faire. There is a distinction," Rajan says (quoted in Einhorn and Krishnan 2013).

Since 1991: The re-emergence of a liberal movement

After 1991 India witnessed a revival of the liberal movement. While liberals within the Indian academy remain scarce, there has been a re-emergence of a broader movement influenced by liberal ideas, especially in the English-language business press and in policy circles.

An important figure in this revival is Parth Shah, an Austrian school economist, and head of the Center for Civil Society (CCS) a liberal think tank in New Delhi. CCS has led the new liberal movement in India mainly through outreach programs for students and advocacy to promote greater individual choice. CCS often attracts hundreds of applicants for its CCS Academy educational programs. The seminars introduce Indian students to the ideas of Adam Smith, Hayek, and Friedman. CCS has also made significant efforts to reignite popular interest in the Indian classical liberal tradition by making works in this tradition publicly available via the website IndianLiberals.in.

Also associated with CCS, but an independent businessman and scholar, is Gurcharan Das, an advocate for a strong liberal state in India. He has authored several books arguing the perverse and unintended consequences of the large Indian regulatory state. Another scholar at CCS, an economist, author, and columnist, was the late Sauvik Chakraverti. In his columns, he was a fierce critic of the Indian state, specifically with respect to regulation affecting livelihood. He won the International Policy Network's Bastiat Prize for Journalism in 2002.

Another liberal institution is the Liberty Institute in New Delhi, founded by Barun Mitra, with the goal of increasing the understanding of principles such as individual rights, rule of law, limited government, and the free enterprise system. Ayn Rand and Julian Simon are important influences on the efforts of Liberty Institute.

Since 2005 there has been an increase in the number of outlets for liberal writers. An important addition came in 2007 when the *Hindustan Times* and the *Wall Street Journal* collaborated to start a new business daily called *Mint*. The newspaper and its editorial team have an explicitly liberal tilt. In the opening editorial for the daily, its current executive editor Niranjan Rajadhyaksha laid out a manifesto, stating that "The editorial pages of this newspaper will have three central themes: free people, free economies and free societies" (Rajadhyaksha 2007).

The Internet is giving a voice to a number of liberals from different corners of the country through blogs and other channels. One of the first blogs to be explicit about its author's libertarian leanings is *India Uncut*, authored by Amit Varma.[18] Abheek Bhattacharya at the *Wall Street Journal Asia* argues that the revival in the liberal movement in India is a consequence of

---

18. Varma, also an author and columnist at newspapers like *Mint* and *Hindu Business Line*, received the 2007 Bastiat Prize for Journalism.

the increase in the size of the market:

> The burgeoning classical liberal movement is feeding off India's economic growth. ... These new-age commentators are riding the wave of another effect of India's liberalization, a boom in technology and communications. More media outlets, eager to outdo competitors, are listening to diverse opinions. The Internet is often the delivery system. (Bhattacharya 2008)

The paucity of liberalism in the Indian academy: Towards an explanation

Economic research on current policy affects perceptions, which affect the persistence of such policies. If most economists seem to think that government planning improves economic performance, a regime of government planning will in all likelihood persist longer than if the economists, instead, consistently criticize state activism.[19] Consequently government officials have an interest in the content of research by economists.

Authoritarian regimes in the world have at times exercised direct and explicit control over the professoriate. The Soviet Union under Stalin purged several academic disciplines in the 1930s. Notoriously, the Soviets established the bogus theories of Trofim Lysenko as official state doctrine in the fields of biology and agronomy. Economics was tightly controlled as well (see, e.g., Katsenelinboigen 1979). Direct control remains in place in some nations today. But India, of course, was never the Soviet Union. Its universities were established on the British model, and they inherited a tradition of academic freedom. Shenoy, whose criticism of planning greatly upset Nehru himself, was not even dismissed from his position, let alone sent to a gulag.

Nevertheless, throughout the era of central planning as well as during the years of economic reform, the liberal philosophy had a very minimal presence in the halls of Indian academia. Almost all the academics who hailed from India and were influenced by liberal ideas have pursued their careers and their research in universities abroad. This section seeks to outline a possible explanation for this dearth of liberal academics in India.

---

19. For evidence of instances where the research of economists appears to have altered the trajectory of policy in the United States, see Derthick and Quirk (1985) and Leighton and Lopez (2013, Chapter 6).

The means by which economists fund their research will significantly affect the content of the research. As Richard E. Wagner (2012) argues, an economics profession composed of self-financing hobbyists will engage in systematically different research than will a body of professionals paid by others. Institutions of higher education jointly produce research and instruction, using revenues derived from instruction (viz., tuition and government appropriations) to pay faculty salaries. Basic research in economics largely originates from the academy.[20] Control over universities can provide a large measure of control over economic research.

The dominance of public universities in India created a channel for government influence, if indirect, on the economic profession. The colonial government established India's first three universities in 1857, modeled on the university system of London, in the cities of Kolkata, Mumbai, and Chennai (Carnoy and Dossani 2011, 5). Through the course of the second half of the nineteenth and early twentieth centuries, other public universities were established in Punjab (1882), Allahabad (1887), Banaras (1915), Patna (1917), Aligarh (1920) and Dacca (1920) (Naik 1963, 4). These universities were largely under the control of the provincial governments, although the central government also had the authority to intervene in their affairs. India has a number of nominally private colleges offering specialized training in fields like economics, business, and law, but all are affiliated with public universities with control over course curricula, examinations, and awarding of degrees.

The extent of government involvement in higher education increased with national independence and the onset of planning. The newly created state governments replaced their provincial counterparts and now exercised control over the public universities. Control was increased via the establishment of many public colleges. Moreover, the state governments "controlled the university's budget and funding, approved senior staff appointments, staff salaries and tuition fees," and they influenced academic policy through their "membership of the university's senate" (Carnoy and Dossani 2011, 11). Meanwhile, the central government also increased its influence over higher education via the establishment of the University Grants Commission (UGC) in 1956 and the proposal and enforcement of national standards for university

---

20. Almost all of the winners of the Nobel Prize in economics held traditional academic positions when they won the prize.

education.

The dominance of public universities in India kept the employment prospects for critics of planning minimal. Moreover, the intellectual fascination with central planning that had gradually gripped the hearts and minds of the political and intellectual elite in India readily provided a "basic unity of purpose" and created a siege-like mentality in the quest to rapidly industrialize the economy (*First Five Year Plan*, ch. 1). There was thus no need to engage in outright coercion since dissenting would make an intellectual exceedingly unpopular and accordingly limit their career prospects. For instance, Peter Bauer once asked a senior officer of the economics section of the British High Commission in India if he or his colleagues were in contact with B. R. Shenoy, and was told that people on the Commission "were too busy to have time for acknowledged madmen" (Bauer 1998, 3).

Other mechanisms of influence in the academy were in operation in India as well. Wagner (2012) emphasizes the lure of a seat at the table of power as another influence on economists and the views they espouse. The lure of power, and the validation of the powerful, affects economists both at an individual and professional level. Economic theories supportive of a role for government management of the economy—counseled by economists, of course—can create a seat at the table for economists, boosting the profession's standing, influence, and well being.

In the case of India, most members of the economics profession at the time of independence strongly supported central planning (Byres 1998). This was true of prominent economists at all the key intellectual centers for economics such as Bombay University, the Indian Statistical Institute, the Gokhale Institute of Politics and Economics, and the Delhi School of Economics, and in the seventies the Jawaharlal Nehru University. Daniel Klein and Charlotta Stern (2009) discuss how groupthink in academia can become locked in and then expand its domain. Academic disciplines are disproportionately influenced by those departments at the top of the disciplinary pyramid, which produce a large number of new Ph.D.-degree holders. The dearth of liberals among India's economics professoriate may be partially explained by the statist bias of graduate training, which then swept through the entire professorate as students from these institutions secured faculty positions. Once established, the planning bias persists through normal decisionmaking in hiring (Klein and Stern 2009). Exclusion of the liberal perspective contributed further to a lack of exposure and awareness of alternatives, leading many to believe in state planning because 'all reasonable people' do.

Conclusion

There are three interesting trends in the liberal movement in India post-independence. First, the socialist movement and planning apparatus was so aggressive and dominant that it became a target that defined the liberal movement, small and marginalized as it was. As socialist fervor was lost post-Emergency, the target of liberal opposition lost focus, and the liberal movement itself declined. Second, there are few liberals in the Indian academy, and in the 1980s and 1990s, much of the academic critique emerged from Indians educated and working outside India. Since around 2005 the liberal movement in India has been nested primarily within politics and civil society. And finally—now that India has liberalized—the technology, communication media, number of outlets, voices, and opinions have created a new liberal wave within civil society. In the future, the Indian liberal movement will likely have many voices.

References

Arnot, Sandford. 1833. Ram Mohun Roy. *Asiatic Journal* 12 (n.s.): 195–213.

Austin, Granville. 1999. *Working a Democratic Constitution: The Indian Experience*. New Delhi: Oxford University Press.

Balakrishnan, Chandrasekaran. 2011. India's Great Free-Market Economist. *Mises Daily* (Ludwig von Mises Institute, Auburn, Ala.), July 5.

Bauer, P. T. 1971. *Dissent on Development*. London: Weidenfeld and Nicholson.

Bauer, P. T. 1998. B. R. Shenoy: Stature and Impact. *Cato Journal* 18(1): 1–10.

Bayly, C. A. 2007. Rammohan Roy and the Advent of Constitutional Liberalism in India, 1800–30. *Modern Intellectual History* 4(1): 25–41.

Bhagwati, Jagdish. 1966. *The Economics of Underdeveloped Countries*. New York: McGraw-Hill.

Bhagwati, Jagdish. 1969. Joint review of *Indian Economic Policy* (by B. R. Shenoy) and *The Crisis of Indian Planning: Economic Policy in the 1960s* (eds. P. Streeten and M. Lipton). *Economic Journal* 79(Sept.): 634–639.

Bhagwati, Jagdish. 1993. *India in Transition: Freeing the Economy*. New Delhi: Oxford University Press.

Bhagwati, Jagdish. 2001. Interview by V. N. Balasubramanyam. In *Conversations with Indian Economists* by V. N. Balasubramanyam. New York: Palgrave.

Bhagwati, Jagdish, and Padma Desai. 1970. *India, Planning for Industrialization: Industrializa-*

tion and Trade Policies Since 1951. London: Oxford University Press for the OECD.

Bhagwati, Jagdish, and V. K. Ramaswami. 1963. Domestic Distortions, Tariffs and the Theory of Optimum Subsidy. *Journal of Political Economy* 71(1): 44–50.

Bhagwati, Jagdish, and T. N. Srinivasan. 1975. *Foreign Trade Regimes and Economic Development: India*. New York: Columbia University Press.

Bhagwati, Jadish, and T. N. Srinivasan. 1993. *India's Economic Reforms*. New Delhi: Ministry of Finance, Government of India.

Bhattacharya, Abheek. 2008. Liberals of India, Unite! *Wall Street Journal Asia*, September 25.

Briggeman, Jason. 2013. Amartya Sen [Ideological Profiles of the Economics Laureates]. *Econ Journal Watch* 10(3): 604–616.

Byres, Terence J. 1998. *The Indian Economy: Major Debates Since Independence*. Oxford: Oxford University Press.

Byres, Terence J. 2014. Development Planning and the Interventionist State versus Liberalization and the Neoliberal State: India, 1989–1996. In *Two Decades of Market Reform in India: Some Dissenting Views*, ed. Sudipta Bhattacharyya, 27–53. London and New York: Anthem Press.

Carnoy, Martin, and Rafiq Dossani. 2011. The Changing Governance of Higher Education in India. Freeman Spogli Institute for International Studies, Stanford University (Stanford, Calif.).

Chaudhuri, K. N. 1983. Foreign Trade and Balance of Payments (1757–1947). In *The Cambridge Economic History of India*, vol. 2, eds. Dharma Kumar and Meghnad Desai, 804–877. Cambridge, UK: Cambridge University Press.

Das, Gurcharan. 2000. *India Unbound*. New York: Anchor Books.

Datar, Arvind P., Jamshedji Kanga, Nani A. Palkhivala, and Dinesh Vyas. 2013. *The Law and Practice of Income Tax*, 10th ed. Gurgaon: LexisNexis.

Derthick, Martha, and Paul J. Quirk. 1985. *The Politics of Deregulation*. Washington, D.C.: Brookings Institution.

Doctor, Adi H. 1997. *Political Thinkers on Modern India*. New Delhi: Mittal Publications.

Economist. 2013a. Into the Pressure Cooker. *The Economist*, September 5.

Economist. 2013b. Bridging the Gulf. *The Economist*, November 30.

Einhorn, Bruce, and Unni Krishnan. 2013. Mr. Free Market, Raghuram Rajan, Goes to India. *Bloomberg Businessweek*, March 21.

Frankel, Francine R. 1978. *India's Political Economy 1947–1977: The Gradual Revolution*. Princeton, N.J.: Princeton University Press.

Guha, Ramachandra. 2007. *India After Gandhi*. London: Macmillan.

Guha, Ramachandra, ed. 2010. *Makers of Modern India*. New Delhi: Penguin Viking.

Hanson, A. H. 1966. *The Process of Planning: A Study of India's Five Year Plans 1950–1964*. London: Oxford University Press.

Hayek, Friedrich A. 1931. *Prices and Production*. London: Routledge.

Heilperin, Michael. 2010 [1949]. *Studies in Economic Nationalism*. Auburn, Ala.: Ludwig von Mises Institute.

India. Planning Commission. 1953. *First Five Year Plan*. Delhi: Government of India Planning Commission.

Katsenelinboigen, Aron. 1979. L. V. Kantorovich: The Political Dilemma in Scientific Creativity. *Journal of Post Keynesian Economics* 1(2): 129–147.

Khatkhate, Deena. 1994. Intellectual Origins of Indian Economic Reform: A Review of Jagdish Bhagwati's *India in Transition: Freeing the Economy. World Development* 22(7): 1097–1102.

Klein, Daniel B., and Charlotta Stern. 2009. Groupthink in Academia: Majoritarian Department Politics and the Professional Pyramid. *Independent Review* 13(4): 585–600.

Lal, Deepak. 2008. India, Economics in. In *The New Palgrave Dictionary of Economics*, 2nd ed, eds. Steven N. Durlauf and Lawrence E. Blume. London: Macmillan Palgrave.

Leighton, Wayne, and Edward Lopez. 2013. *Madmen, Intellectuals, and Academic Scribblers: The Economic Engine of Political Change.* Palo Alto, Calif.: Stanford University Press.

Mahalanobis, P. C. 1961. *Talks on Planning.* Mumbai: Asia Publishing House.

Manish, G. P. 2011. Central Economic Planning and India's Economic Performance, 1951–65. *Independent Review* 16(2): 199–219.

Manish, G. P. 2013. Market Reforms in India and the Quality of Economic Growth. *Independent Review* 18(2): 241–262.

Manish, G. P. 2014. Qualitative Aspects of the Indian Growth Spurt of the 1980s. *Review of Austrian Economics* 27(3): 325–340.

Masani, M. R. 1936. *Soviet Sidelights.* Mumbai: Congress Socialist Publishing.

Masani, M. R. 1944. *Socialism Reconsidered.* Mumbai: Padma Publications.

Masani, M. R. 1956. The Asian Writer. In *Why I Oppose Communism: A Symposium.* London: Phoenix House.

Morris, Morris D. 1983. The Growth of Large Scale Industry to 1947. In *The Cambridge Economic History of India*, vol. 2, eds. Dharma Kumar and Meghnad Desai, 553–676. Cambridge, UK: Cambridge University Press.

Naik, J. P. 1963. *The Role of Government of India in Education.* Delhi: Government of India Ministry of Education.

Nehru, Jawaharlal. 2004 [1936]. *An Autobiography.* New Delhi: Penguin Books.

Palkhivala, Nani A. 1974. *Our Constitution Defaced and Defiled.* New Delhi: Macmillan Co. India.

Palkhivala, Nani A. 1984a [1965]. The Ideology of Taxation. In *We, the People: India—The Largest Democracy*, 89–100. Mumbai: Strand Book Stall.

Palkhivala, Nani A. 1984b [1972]. Socialism—Its Kernel and Its Shell. In *We, the People: India—The Largest Democracy*, 59ff. Mumbai: Strand Book Stall.

Panagariya, Arvind. 2008. *India: The Emerging Giant.* New York: Oxford University Press.

Prakash, Sandeep. 2013. An Appreciation of B. R. Shenoy, Economist. *Quarterly Journal of Austrian Economics* 16(3): 353–362.

Rajadhyaksha, Niranjan. 2007. In Defence of Freedom. *Mint* (New Delhi), February 1.

Rajagopalachari, C. 1961. *Satyam Eva Jayate.* Madras: Bharathan Publications (Kalki).

Rajagopalan, Shruti. 2015. Incompatible Institutions: Socialism Versus Constitutionalism in India. *Constitutional Political Economy* 26: 328–355.

Ranganathan, A. 1961. Khasa Subba Rau: An Appreciation. *Indian Libertarian* (Mumbai), August 15: 8–9.

Rao, P. Vaman. 2001. Khasa Subba Rau: Pen in Defence of Freedom. In *Profiles in Courage: Dissent on Indian Socialism*, ed. Parth J. Shah, 135–157. New Delhi: Center for Civil Society.

Roy, Tirthankar. 2006. *The Economic History of India 1857–1947*. New Delhi: Oxford University Press.

Sen, Amartya. 1959. Why Planning? *Seminar* (Mumbai), November: 15–17.

Shenoy, B. R. 1955. A Note of Dissent on the Memorandum of the Panel of Economists. In *Papers Relating to the Formulation of the Second Five Year Plan*, 15–26. Delhi: Government of India Planning Commission.

Shenoy, B. R. 1958. *Problems of Indian Economic Development*. Madras: University of Madras.

Shenoy, B. R. 1963. *Indian Planning and Economic Development*. Mumbai: Asia Publishing House.

Shenoy, B. R. 1966. *Fifteen Years of Indian Planning*. Mumbai: Forum of Free Enterprise.

Shenoy, B. R. 1968. *Indian Economic Policy*. Mumbai: Popular Prakashan.

Shenoy, B. R. 1974. *P.L. 480 and India's Food Problem*. New Delhi: Affiliated East West Press.

Shenoy, Sudha. 1971. *India: Progress or Poverty?* London: Institute of Economic Affairs.

Shenoy, Sudha. 2003. The Global Perspective: An Interview with Sudha Shenoy. *Austrian Economics Newsletter* (Ludwig von Mises Institute, Auburn, Ala.), Winter: 1–8.

Shroff, A. D. 1956. *Free Enterprise and Democracy*. Mumbai: Forum of Free Enterprise.

Srinivasan, T. N. 1991a. Indian Development Strategy: An Exchange of Views. *Economic and Political Weekly* 26(31–32): 1850–1852.

Srinivasan, T. N. 1991b. Reform of Industrial and Trade Policies. *Economic and Political Weekly* 26(37): 2143–2145.

Srinivasan, T. N. 1993. Indian Economic Reforms: Background, Rationale, and Next Steps. Economic Growth Center, Yale University (New Haven, Conn.).

Thakurdas, Purushottamdas. 1945. *A Brief Memorandum Outlining a Plan of Economic Development for India*, 2 vols. London: Penguin.

Tomlinson, B. R. 1979. *The Political Economy of the Raj 1914–1947: The Economics of Decolonization in India*. London: Palgrave Macmillan.

Varma, Amit. 2008. Profit's No Longer a Dirty Word: The Transformation of India. *Library of Economics and Liberty* (Liberty Fund, Inc.), February 4.

Wagner, Richard E. 2012. The Social Construction of Theoretical Landscapes: Some Economics of Economic Theories. In *Different but Equal: Documenting the Contribution of Dissident Scholars*, ed. Daniel Sutter, 43–62. West Sussex, UK: Wiley-Blackwell.

Webb, Sidney, and Beatrice Webb. 1920. *A Constitution for the Socialist Commonwealth of Great Britain*. London: Longmans, Green and Co.

White, Lawrence H. 2012. *The Clash of Economic Ideas: The Great Policy Debates and Experiments of the Last Hundred Years*. New York: Cambridge University Press.

Cases Cited

Kesavananda Bharati v. State of Kerala, AIR 1973 SC 1461.
Minerva Mills Ltd. v. Union of India, AIR 1980 SC 1789.

This chapter first appeared as an Econ Journal Watch article in September 2019.
It has not been revised except for the addition of an "Epilogue" at the end.

The Liberal Tradition in South Africa, 1910–2019

Martin van Staden[1]

> *There is nothing 'neo' about my liberalism.*
> —Leon Louw

Part I: Liberalism in South African history

Liberalism in South Africa developed most in the Cape Colony, which later became the Cape Province. British influence was always greatest at the Cape, which was home to most English-speaking South Africans, who have always been somewhat cosmopolitan compared to the other section of South Africa's white population, the Afrikaners.

The story of the Union of South Africa started when South African liberalism—then embodied in the Cape liberal tradition—suffered a great defeat in 1910. The Cape Colony had had a non-racial, but qualified, franchise, which allowed all men who complied with certain literacy and property qualifications to vote and stand for elections.[2] The liberal Cape Colony's delegates at the 1908–09 National Convention that led to the establishment of the Union of South Africa had hoped to negotiate an extension of those rules to the northern territories, where non-whites[3] were excluded from the

---

1. The author is indebted to Eustace Davie, a director of the Free Market Foundation, who read through the initial drafts of this paper and provided valuable historical information and context throughout the duration of preparing this work.
2. Even though any man could stand for an election, by the time of the unification only whites had been elected.
3. Conscious of many of the objections made to the use of the term 'non-white,' it is used here in good faith and for lack of a better (and equally concise) descriptor. When 'non-white'

franchise. They failed, however (Rich 1987, 271). The failure did not mean the end of liberalism in South Africa but represented a setback. The setback culminated in the constitutional crisis of the 1950s—arguably liberals' finest fight for civil rights, but a fight they lost as well. It is therefore correct to say that the history of liberalism in South Africa has been a history of failure, but nonetheless a proud history that climaxed in the adoption of many liberal values in South Africa's current constitution between 1993 and 1996.

The descriptor 'liberal' was almost always regarded as derogatory among Afrikaners, most of whom were conservative and in favor of racist policies in the years before 1994 (McGregor 1990, xi).[4] In 1941, for instance, the Nazi-sympathizing *Ossewabrandwag* ('Ox Wagon Sentinel') had a falling-out with the National Party, their political allies, and referred to them as "liberal" (Malan 1964, 207). The falling-out deeply upset the Nationalist establishment, leading to what was perceived as a *skeuring*, or break, within conservative Afrikanerdom. Another break happened when the Conservative Party split away from the National Party in 1982, with the former accusing the latter of liberalism.

Liberals were seen as foes to Afrikaner national aspirations and enablers of communism; liberals would destroy the Western way of life in Africa, specifically by undermining the Protestant ethic (Swart 1991, 9). Liberals almost exclusively came in the form of English-speaking white South Africans, further adding to the contempt with which the ideology was treated by Afrikaners.[5] During the same era, black nationalists, too, came to regard liberalism as being contrary to their aspirations, with the anti-Apartheid activist and thinker Steve Biko famously criticizing white liberals in essays such as "Black Souls in White Skins?" (Biko 1987/1970, 19–26). Liberals were seen as sanctimonious do-gooders who, to the Afrikaner nationalists,

---

is used, it refers to those people classified by the government as black (or native), coloured (mixed race), and Indian (or Asian).

4. 'Afrikaners' are the descendants of Dutch immigrants who settled South Africa from 1652 onwards. German and French settlers who settled later were also subsumed into the Afrikaner *volk*. Afrikaners constitute the majority of the white population in South Africa.

5. The two white sections of South Africa's population, the English and the Afrikaners, had fought two major wars. The First Boer War between 1880 and 1881 was won by the Afrikaners, and the Second Boer War (or the South African War) between 1899 and 1902 was won by the English. Tensions between these two groups certainly ran high in 1910. Some may say there still exists a tension between them today.

were disloyal to South Africa and, often, were said to be crypto-communists; and, to the black nationalists, were viewed as ultimately comfortable with the status quo, enjoying their privileges as white persons and also indulging a "feeling that [they are] not like the rest of the others" (ibid., 22); they were later criticized for their preference for free markets and non-violent change (Dubow 2014, 7–8). Such were the seeds of the criticism of liberalism that persists today. The Afrikaner criticism of liberalism, while it does still exist, has subsided along with the disappearance of Afrikaners from political dominance. In recent decades, the prevailing attitude toward liberalism—mostly among intellectuals who support the new government's policies of social transformation—is that it is cold and unresponsive to the lived realities of the black poor, that its claim to colorblindness only serves to further entrench white privilege, and that a limited government is incompatible with the requirement for extensive poverty-alleviation programs. When finance minister Tito Mboweni, for instance, proposed some measure of deregulation in an August 2019 policy statement, the South African Federation of Trade Unions and the third-largest party in Parliament, the Economic Freedom Fighters, which subscribes to Marxism-Leninism, decried the proposal as "neoliberal" (Vavi 2019; Nkanjeni 2019). They, like many on the left in South Africa, regard neoliberalism—which is used synonymously with classical liberalism, as opposed to the technical meaning of neoliberalism—as anti-poor (ibid.). The liberal parliamentarian of the Democratic Alliance, Michael Cardo, notes that "those writing about South African history have vilified liberalism as a mere adjunct of imperial conquest, racial segregation and capitalist exploitation." It is thus claimed that liberal economics, if adopted, would retain the economic relationships and structures entrenched during the Apartheid era (Cardo 2012, 17–18).

'Liberalism' in the context of South Africa

Liberalism has had a long tradition with its own unique character in South Africa. Timothy Hughes writes:

> Like those of its classical forebears, the parameters of South African liberalism do not lend themselves to definition with theodolite precision. The South African variant embraces the manifold dimensions of both

> utilitarian and rights-based theory and discourse, but also overlaid within it
> the dynamics of a colonial and post-colonial legacy with which it continues
> to struggle and come to grips to the present. South African liberalism
> exhibits the complexities and nuances of traditional, classical and new
> liberalism, but does so within the context of an ethnically and racially
> divided society. (Hughes 1994, 15)

Generally speaking, liberalism in South Africa is not understood to be quite as far to the left in the field of economics as it is usually understood to be in America, but it is also not the undiluted free-market liberalism of Ludwig von Mises or Albert Venn Dicey. There has been a constant tug of war between classical liberals and left-liberals (Sunter 1993, 41; Dubow 2014, 9). Phyllis Lewsen wrote of the liberals of the interwar period as scoring "fairly well on the factious-minority scale" (Lewsen 1987, 110). But through much of South Africa's history it has been common to refer to *all* liberals as being on the "left," for until very recently "left" almost exclusively connoted a support for non-racialism over Apartheid (Swart 1991, 160). And today both left-liberals and classical liberals claim the word 'liberal' (Johnson 2011; Shandler 1991, 21–22).

In the interwar years, two white parliamentary representatives set aside for blacks (known as 'native representatives'), Margaret Ballinger and Donald Barkley Molteno, certainly liberal in outlook on cultural and interpersonal affairs, regarded themselves as economic socialists, whereas two of their colleagues, also native representatives, Edgar Harry Brookes and John David Rheinallt Jones, believed in the free-market system (Lewsen 1987, 115). At the end of Apartheid, one would have found personalities like David Welsh and Terence Beard in the left-liberal camp, and Leon Louw and Ken Owen in the classical liberal camp (O'Malley 1988, 5).

While recognizing this diversity of thought within the liberal tradition, this paper is concerned mainly with the history and current state of *classical liberalism*. Moreover, it is concerned with classical liberalism after the formation of the independent nation-state of South Africa in 1910 (from 1910 to 1961 the country was known as the Union of South Africa, and thereafter it became the Republic of South Africa).

Today, the electoral system is one of party-list proportional representation. As of 2019, the African National Congress holds 230 of the 400 seats in the National Assembly, with the other 170 seats divided among 13 other parties.

As we shall see, liberalism is largely missing in today's parliamentary politics.

In South African academic economics, there has been little discernible classical-liberal thought, except for a select few figures like William Harold Hutt, Ludwig Lachmann, and Karl Mittermaier. The contemporary South African undergraduate economics curriculum, according to Stephen Graham Saunders (2008), is almost entirely mainstream material, viz., "the synthesis of Neoclassical Economics and Keynesian Macroeconomics." The economic discipline is rarely placed "into its philosophical context," and the "philosophical underpinnings of economic theory…are often not taught or ignored," at least in first-year classes, Saunders writes. The "conceptual, methodological and ethical issues" of the discipline are left unaddressed. Discussion of schools of economic thought like the Austrian school is left to advanced or postgraduate levels of education (Saunders 2008, 740–741).

Up to 1994, when Apartheid ended, liberalism, like most other ideologies and political groupings in South Africa, was preoccupied with matters of race, and economics was often ignored. The two camps of South African liberalism, the classical and left-liberals, also obviously could not agree on what economic direction South African policy should pursue (O'Malley 1988, 6). Yet liberals throughout South African history have been opposed to Apartheid, which was in large part an economic system, that is, a system of restrictions on human activity, notably economic activity.

In many respects, therefore, 'liberal' usually meant little more than 'not racist' or 'anti-Apartheid' before 1994, and more often than not was presumed to refer to an ideology of whites exclusively. It comes as no surprise then that the *de facto* leader of South African liberals before his death in 1948, Jan Hendrik Hofmeyr, would have declared in 1935: "When I speak of Liberalism I think especially of the Native people of this land" (Robertson 1971, 4). Both the Progressive and Liberal parties—each having a strong commitment to free enterprise in their statements of principles—were widely referred to as 'left-wing' before the end of Apartheid.[6] The question of race was foremost in giving content to where one stood on the political spectrum in South Africa.

Still there is a substantive liberal tradition in South Africa that, apart from race, goes into aspects of politics, economics, and philosophy. Much

---

6. As readers will learn, 'progressive' too is different in South Africa than in the United States.

has changed since 1994. The 'liberal' identity today is known to embrace all races but continues to have some unfortunate baggage, such as the idea that its 'neoliberal' policies benefit only the elite and particularly whites, and the perception that its colorblind approach to public affairs amounts to a refusal to acknowledge and redress the suffering black South Africans endured under Apartheid. Liberals of all races today have the difficult task of convincing a very skeptical population of why individual freedom should be the apex political goal in South Africa.

My focus lies in the years up to 1994—the year Apartheid is said to have formally ended and was replaced by a democratic dispensation. Works on liberalism in South Africa peaked in the political transition between 1990 and 1994. After 1994, there was a significant decline in liberal works, for reasons that may become apparent. Also, since 1994 the use of the word 'liberal' has declined. As a result, many liberals today call themselves all sorts of names, from 'libertarians' to 'democrats' to 'pragmatists,' so it is considerably more difficult to craft a historical narrative about the liberal movement after 1994. It is also the case that the attention paid by historians and commentators to liberals and the liberal movement has declined considerably, given that during the period before 1994 liberalism was the main political opponent of the dominant nationalist ideology. Since 1994, when South Africa's political paradigm changed completely, liberalism's relevance appears to have taken a knock. Nonetheless, the few liberal individuals, and liberal organizations and political groupings that have persisted into the democratic era and their views on public policy, will be considered.

The character of South African liberalism

The principles of South African liberalism were largely transplanted in the nineteenth century from Britain into the then-Cape Colony. Liberalism there traces its roots to the Scottish missionary John Philip in the 1820s (Cardo 2012, 16). Most liberals in South African history have been white and their primary language English. Among non-whites, liberalism was largely discredited during Apartheid because they felt its "promises have been endlessly deferred and its assurances betrayed by discrimination and a white monopoly of Africa's favors" (De Kiewiet 1955, 36). There were some Afrikaner liberals, such as Jan Hofmeyr as well as, in the 1950s and 1960s,

Philip Pistorius, a professor at the University of Pretoria, and Nic Olivier, a professor at the University of Stellenbosch (Swart 1991, 118). Those two universities were then and are still today considered to be more conservative and Afrikaans than the traditionally English universities. That is because their embrace of the government's post-Apartheid social-transformation policies was slow and gradual, and the bulk of the student body are still white Afrikaans speakers. It should not, however, be assumed that Apartheid was an exclusively Afrikaner enterprise. Many, perhaps most, English-speaking South Africans were conservative on the question of race relations despite their opposition to Afrikaner nationalism (ibid., 104). By the time of Hendrik Verwoerd's premiership in 1958, the National Party, led by the Afrikaners, was actively courting white English South Africans to support Apartheid (ibid., 90).

Along lines set by Hughes (1994, 22–31), I would put forward the following as generally uniting principles of, or dimensions to, South African liberalism:

- *The individualist dimension*: Racial discrimination in state policy is rejected. The individual must be the object of emphasis in social and political institutions, and the principle of equal liberty must be respected.
- *The Millian[7] dimension*: The conditions conducive to individual freedom are freedom of thought, conscience, expression, movement, and association.
- *The Diceyan[8] dimension*: The rule of law is necessary to protect individuals and minority groups.
- *The pragmatic dimension*: History and context are allowed to adjust the practice and outlook of liberalism. On the other hand, Kierin O'Malley of the Liberal Forum and a lecturer in political science at the University of South Africa provided a brief description of what South African liberalism constituted in 1994. He argues that there is a core of liberalism that does *not* shift over time. He pointed out why it is important to appreciate the fixed nature of this core by referring

---

7. That is after John Stuart Mill.
8. That is after Albert Venn Dicey.

to the *liberal slideaway*—where liberals abandoned their principles for expediency—that has occurred in South Africa from the 1980s. The liberal core that was slid away from is said to be "individual self-determination and self-realisation (which can only be achieved within a noncoercive framework)" (O'Malley 1994, 29–30). Ken Owen, a popular anti-Apartheid classical liberal journalist, too described the core of liberalism in 1988 as a belief in "individual liberty, the rule of law, the democratic method and the free market" (O'Malley 1988, 36).

- *The institutional dimension*: Liberty must be safeguarded by institutions specifically aimed at checking and balancing government power.
- *The economic dimension*: An economy unhindered by unnecessary and artificial government intervention will tend to produce more wealth and prosperity.
- *The gradualist dimension*: Political change should be brought about not through revolutionary violence but through gradual or incremental steps. Perhaps the one constant and unifying feature of South African liberalism has been its opposition to revolution, and its insistence on evolutionary change from the Apartheid order to a liberal-democratic order (O'Malley 1988, 31).

John Kane-Berman (2002, 2–5) has given a useful account of South African classical liberalism. Kane-Berman served as chief executive officer of the Institute of Race Relations (IRR). Founded in 1929, IRR is South Africa's oldest think tank and is one of the oldest classical-liberal think tanks in the world. In the following paragraphs I summarize Kane-Berman's account.

Kane-Berman finds that within liberal theory the role of the government should be to protect individuals' rights so that they may forge their own paths and destinies in society. These rights "are in the nature of man as a sentient being with free will and the ability to imagine, reason, and create."

Kane-Berman criticizes the left and the right for both assuming that the government, instead, has a duty to engage in social engineering: in essence, to reshape man. Liberals are skeptical of granting government this kind of power, for fear of the abuses and potentially tyrannical consequences. Indeed, governments in practice tend to promote only the interests of specific lobbies or interest groups, rather than the so-called common good. Thus, liberals prefer man to be free even though highly imperfect.

It is sufficient, writes Kane-Berman, for people to be protected from harming one another in their own divergent pursuits. Individuals are better judges of their own interests. Freedom promotes the taking of responsibility rather than the outsourcing of that responsibility to others. This, argues Kane-Berman, was partly how the Apart-

John Kane-Berman, former CEO of the Institute of Race Relations, speaking at a Free Market Foundation event.

heid system was defeated: with ordinary South Africans of all races pursuing their economic interests, many Apartheid laws were undermined to the extent that the system collapsed.

The dignity of the individual, freedom of expression, freedom of association, equality before the law, an independent judiciary, supreme constitutions and the rule of law, the right to participate in governance, and a free press are considered by Kane-Berman to be "vital components of the package of rights and freedoms characteristic of the liberal state." He hastens to add that it is arbitrary to distinguish between these aforementioned rights and freedoms, and rights of an economic nature:

> the liberal view is that…freedom of contract, freedom to trade, and freedom to engage in economic activity are logical extensions of individual liberty, as are property rights.

Kane-Berman says the market system is what logically follows from freedom of choice. Markets are where producers meet consumers. A free market is more democratic than the political 'market' because in politics the voting age is restricted and participation in governance, like voting, happens only occasionally, whereas in a market one votes continuously with one's resources.

But to Kane-Berman liberalism is not akin to anarchism. The government has a role to play in protecting the vulnerable from abuse: keeping inflation stable and low and ensuring big businesses do not succeed in "manipulating markets to the detriment of consumers." Unlike socialists and interventionists who see intervention as a desirable foregone conclusion, liberals regard intervention as justified only where it is absolutely necessary and where a thorough cost-benefit analysis has been conducted. Taxes within a liberal regime should be low, and used only to allow government to perform its limited role. Tax monies are "held in trust on behalf of the nation."

Liberalism before 1994

Cape liberalism in early South Africa (1910–1948)

The Union of South Africa was established, at least in part, on considerations that might be described as classically liberal. The historian Leonard Monteath Thompson, in his comprehensive account of the events surrounding the South African National Convention of 1908–09, writes that the last prime minister of the Cape Colony, John Xavier Merriman, who would also go on to play a leading role in the convention, was a Whig in the British tradition. According to Thompson, Merriman believed that:

> The functions of a Government should be limited; taxation and public expenditure should be kept to a minimum; an unbalanced budget was a major evil; and Parliament should be the sovereign element in a Constitution—the real forum of a nation, where decisions should be made by free votes after full public debates. (Thompson 1961, 95)

Merriman, along with Jan Christiaan Smuts, later multiple-time prime minister of South Africa, insisted that the new country's constitution be unitary instead of federal, and that Parliament must be sovereign and not subject to substantive constitutional safeguards (ibid., 97–98). This was because Merriman was concerned that a federal dispensation and/or a dispensation with constitutional rights would be too costly to the taxpayer (ibid., 102–104).

Despite this economic liberalism, the Whig ideology was intensely conservative in some respects. It opposed equal representation of constituencies in the legislature, preferring that rural areas be given weighted preference, and it opposed women's suffrage. But Merriman was also opposed "to the increase in the range of government action" (Thompson 1961, 95). In the end, however, Merriman and the other unitarists convinced the convention of the downsides of federalism and strict constitutionalism (ibid., 105), and from 1910 to 1993 South Africa had a centralized political system that, in part, enabled later governments to relatively easily extend their racially discriminatory policies across the whole country.

The Cape liberal tradition, of which Merriman was said to be a part (Bickford-Smith 1995, 70), represented four principles of classical liberalism: free expression, economic freedom, political rights (in the form of a non-racial but qualified franchise), and access to justice (Hughes 1994, 16). The Cape liberal tradition is associated with the slogan "equal rights for all civilized men" (Johnson 2011).

The delegates of the Cape Colony at the National Convention represented the only liberal tradition existing in the region at the time. As the South Africa Act (i.e., the 1910 Constitution) was being drawn up, however, the delegates abandoned these liberal principles (Hughes 1994, 20). They were faced down by the uncompromising Afrikaner conservative nationalists from the northern colonies, the Orange River Colony and the Transvaal Colony. Even their fellow English-speaking colonists from the Natal Colony, which had a more restricted form of qualified franchise, resisted the Cape liberals' attempts to extend the franchise throughout the whole Union (Robertson 1971, 3–4).

The liberals had believed that from the time of the unification of the South African colonies, whites would gradually grow more liberal in their outlook on race and race relations, a hope maintained as late as the 1950s (Robertson 1971, 7). The first notable liberals[9] within the Union of South Africa who were concerned about the freedom of non-whites under the political dominance of the whites were the chief justices John Henry de Villiers and James Rose Innes, the journalist F. D. Malan, and the politicians Jacobus Wilhelmus Sauer, Walter Ernest Mortimer Stanford, John Xavier Merriman, William Philip Schreiner, and Jan Hofmeyr (Robertson 1971, 2–3).

Liberals initially focused on establishing forums, known as joint councils, to facilitate contact and cooperation between the politically dominant whites and the other racial groups, outside of politics (Hughes 1994, 20). The joint councils were based on the American model spearheaded by W. W. Alexander in the southern United States to promote good relations between blacks and whites toward the end of World War One. J. D. R. Jones was behind the joint council idea in the South African context, where they would afford "an

---

9. It must be emphasized that some of these individuals were not necessarily as liberal as one would today desire.

opportunity for whites and blacks to get to know each other personally, and they did a good job in furthering black adult education, child welfare and other social services" (Byrne 1990, 21).

The councils steered away from politics partly because it was expected that the United Party, formed in 1934, would provide the progress needed on the political front to end racial prejudice (Hughes 1994, 21). Until the 1950s, the United Party was the only political home of liberals. It enabled certain liberals, like Jan Hofmeyr, to serve in government and to work toward a gradual loosening of authoritarian racial policy. But early liberal trust in the United Party would be progressively disappointed—by the United Party abolishing the limited black franchise in the Cape in 1936, for example—until the eventual formation of the breakaway Liberal and Progressive parties in the 1950s (Hughes 1994, 34; Robertson 1971, 12).

The liberal doctrine of trusteeship—the notion that oppressed peoples in what are today the developing countries should be protected and their status and rights elevated to that which was enjoyed in the West—was ironically used as a basis for both the Cape liberal tradition *and* what would later be known as Apartheid. The white regimes of the Union of South Africa accepted the powers that came with trusteeship but employed them to the benefit of whites, paying only lip service to the elevation of blacks. The National Party, the party that created and implemented the Apartheid system— acknowledging that the South African Party and United Party, too, contributed their share to entrenching racial discrimination in public policy—was primarily concerned with the protection of white political supremacy, which it considered to be compatible with trusteeship (Malan 1964, 282). As a result, Apartheid reinterpreted trusteeship as paternalism rather than as a system of empowerment. Trusteeship, which by its nature was intended to be temporary, was made into a permanent institution by the time of Apartheid (Ntsane 1994, 22).

The Cape liberal tradition did not die out with the formal establishment of Apartheid in 1948. In October 1952, for instance, the Liberal Party was founded. Indeed, some of the founders declared in an article that non-whites should be offered "a reasonable status in our common society," something only possible by reviving "the liberal tradition which prevailed for so many years with such successful results in the Cape Colony." This liberal tradition, they wrote, was based on the principle of "equal rights for all civilized people and equal opportunities for all men and women to become civilized" (Robertson 1971, 86).

Economics and the state before 1948

The National Party was founded in 1914 by James Barry Munnik Hertzog and governed South Africa as the senior partner in the Pact Government with the Labour Party between 1924 and 1934. In 1934, the National Party split, with the larger section following Hertzog, then prime minister, into a merger with the South African Party to form the United South African National Party (the United Party), and the smaller section—one of Afrikaner nationalists—following Daniel François Malan.

The National Party secretary and historian M. P. A. Malan wrote with pride that the National Party recognized and was faithful to the "political and traditional policy of whites from generation to generation to keep power in the hands of whites" (Malan 1964, 267).[10] M. P. A. Malan was chronicling the political successes of the Afrikaner nationalist faction of the National Party, which would be reunited with the Hertzog faction in 1940. He wrote in 1964 that the National Party had always been "a good friend of the workers." The Labour Party died, as its traditional working-class members went to the Nationalists. Malan noted that the party had been advocating for an industrial color bar since 1922 in gold mining and other industries. The Nationalists, through legislative intervention, put an end to racially "mixed trade unions" and ensured that "white workers are legally protected in selected professions, so that they cannot be pushed out of their jobs by non-white competition" (Malan 1964, 269).[11]

By 1922, the National Party's Federal Council demanded that the government take measures to ensure the continued viability of certain "essential" industries, by means of protectionist measures or otherwise (Malan 1964, 79). According to Malan, the direction in which the NP was moving by then was clear: jobs for locals, support and protection of local industry, and economic self-sufficiency for South Africa. This direction culminated in 1923, when the NP and the small Labour Party formed a coalition known as the Pact Government. A 1922 NP Federal Council report confirmed that the Labour and National parties would stand together to "reduce or stamp out the evil

---

10. My translation from the original Afrikaans.
11. My translation from the original Afrikaans.

that is the dominance of mining magnates and their financial power" (ibid., 80).[12] The Pact Government coalition continued until 1933, a year before the United Party was formed.

The Labour Party's involvement in government came with its insistence on the "Civilised Labour Policy" as a response to the "rapid dissolution of racial barriers" in employment. Racial discrimination in matters of employment became even more conspicuous after 1948 (Hutt 1975, 57–58). The Pact Government wanted to set a color bar against non-whites in competition with whites for jobs, mostly in industrial areas. The free-market liberal Edgar Brookes (1956, 190) wrote that nationalism "is fundamentally an emotional rebellion against harsh facts rather than a readiness to face the facts and to see what can be done with them," alluding to the small number of whites in South Africa. Most available white foreigners were not allowed to immigrate to South Africa at the time of his writing because the National Party was afraid of importing Roman Catholics or liberals. Needs for unskilled labor were being met by the blacks, coloureds, and Indians of South Africa. Herein Brookes identified a fatal flaw in the Apartheid ideology, which rendered the success of the "ideal" of total segregation impossible (ibid.). As the numbers of skilled black, coloured, and Indian workers increased, they would not be content with being kept out of the professions by the so-called Civilized Labor Policy, which was later a cause of the unrest that erupted throughout the country against racial discrimination.

There was also an education color bar. Prior to Apartheid in 1948, university councils had the right to reject or admit students. English universities allowed a small number of non-whites to attend, but the Afrikaans-language institutions did not. Some universities, like the University of Fort Hare, were reserved for blacks (Davies 1996, 321). Brookes wrote of an instance pre-1930 in which a black person who qualified academically tried to enroll in the Transvaal University College (today the University of Pretoria), in the veterinary science program, which was the only program of its kind in Africa. The Senate of the college voted by 20 votes to 12 to refuse admitting him (Brookes 1956, 197). After 1959, special permits were required for blacks to be admitted to white universities (Davies 1996, 322).

The Pact Government also established state control over South Africa's

---

12. My translation from the original Afrikaans.

steel industry in 1928—creating the Iron and Steel Corporation (ISCOR)—to the widespread, if somewhat hypocritical, condemnation of the South African Party (SAP), the official opposition and main precursor to the United Party. The former and future prime minister and leader of the SAP, Jan Smuts, supported the government's intention to establish a steel factory outside Pretoria but did not want to see the industry falling under state protection or receiving state support. As reported by Malan, Smuts said that the "dead hand of the State will rest upon [the industry]"[13] and that the enterprise would thus not succeed. Smuts went as far as to say that state control would act as an adhesive for a socialist "blemish" on the industry. Sir Ernest Oppenheimer, another member of the SAP, condemned the initiative as follows:

> A failed industry will be a disadvantage [to South Africa] especially if it is to be State property, because the pressure that will be exerted in the direction of protected rights will be much greater than if it were a private enterprise.[14]

The South African Party was also concerned that a state-subsidized and controlled enterprise would undermine, if not totally destroy, the existing private steel companies in South Africa. The opposition's attempts to stop the creation of ISCOR, however, failed, and the bill that established this state-owned enterprise was passed in 1928, with 78 votes in favor and 50 against (Malan 1964, 104–105).

Before the National Party was elected to power, it intended to nationalize the mining industry, a powerhouse of white English-speaking capitalists (Giliomee 2008, 774; Laissez-Fair 1987, 174), but did not follow through when it became apparent that economic ruin would follow. Interestingly, the liberal Harry Oppenheimer, son of Ernest Oppenheimer, assisted Afrikaners in the 1960s to take over the General Mining company to overcome their exclusion from the industry, and to create an English/Afrikaner alliance against state intervention in the mining industry.

Apartheid and liberty

There was a hope among black South Africans generally and liberals in particular that whatever party governed, the Second World War and its

---

13. My translation from the original Afrikaans.
14. My translation from the original Afrikaans as found at Malan (1964, 104).

elevation of the notion of human rights regardless of race, would lead to a loosening of domestic legislated racial discrimination. But the hope was to be bitterly disappointed. The National Party, which returned to power in 1948, went about implementing Apartheid. It took existing racial discrimination in the statute books and systematized it into a comprehensive policy program (Swart 1991, 40–41).

Apartheid was often presented as an ideology. "Apartheid is sometimes described as the 'philosophical basis' of the Afrikaner's racial philosophy meaning the approach to life which has developed around the colour question and, after three centuries, crystallised into a unique formula for the regulation of race relations" (Rhoodie and Venter 1959, 19). In that conception, government was described as "the Afrikaner's political instrument" to release "the ideal they had set themselves," that is, "the comparatively permanent and concrete separation of White and Black in South Africa" (ibid., 22–24).

Janet Robertson argues that the decision of Smuts's United Party government to enter South Africa into the Second World War in 1939 is what led to the breakdown of the "fusion" between white Afrikaners and white English South Africans that had come about when the South African Party and the National Party combined in 1934 to form the United Party. Entering the war enabled D. F. Malan's faction, the Reunited National Party, to surge in support and replace the United Party in government in 1948 (Robertson 1971, 12). With their vanquishing in 1948 and the entrenchment of National Party rule

Jan Hofmeyr (left) and Jan Smuts (right). *Source*: Wikimedia Commons.

until 1994, liberals were henceforth excluded from positions of formal power.

Edgar Brookes and J. B. MacAulay wrote that 1948 can be described as the year of the "great divide," when statutes encroaching on liberty became more striking (Brookes and MacAulay 1958, 8). South Africa prior to 1948 was no bastion of freedom, of course, as before that year the country "experienced that trend towards bureaucracy caused by the development of the Welfare State" as well as laws infringing on individual rights along racial lines. But the restrictions on civil liberty during the Apartheid era were systematic, and more brazenly restricted the freedom of black, coloured, and Indian South Africans as well as that of whites (ibid., 5).

The bedrock policy instrument of Apartheid, as a system of political, social, and economic racial discrimination, was the Population Registration Act of 1950. It provided for the classification of the South African population into four racial categories: white, black, Indian, and coloured. Each race would have its own areas, institutions, and amenities. Black, Indian, and coloured persons were thus blocked from many advantageous situations. The manner for classification into these racial categories was dependent upon the discretion of census officials. The discretion placed the totality of persons' destinies in those officials' hands. If, say, a white person was 'reclassified' to any other race, at once he or she would be politically disenfranchised and no longer enjoy the multitudes of advantages accruing to or set aside for whites. Reclassified people would need to move to an area designated for the new racial category into which they had been placed. Their children would be forced into inferior educational circumstances. Anyone from whatever race who had the misfortune of being classified as black would have their whole world upended, as they would then have to endure the worst possible treatment at the hands of the state and participate in the worst possible education. Many coloureds were reclassified as black, meaning they, being a mostly Afrikaans-speaking community, were put among mostly Xhosa-speaking blacks in the Cape Province (Brookes and MacAulay 1958, 15–17).

Under the various Group Areas Acts,[15] all South Africans were restricted from residential or commercial property ownership in areas not assigned to their race. Applied to corporate persons, government would look at the race of those with a controlling interest in the company. The determination of where one lived and worked became highly governmentalized. The government enjoyed a statist presumption; if the minister of the interior or someone working in the deeds office maintained that someone or a company belonged a particular racial group, they would be presumed to be part of that group unless they could prove otherwise. Prime commercial real estate— urban centers—were almost invariably 'white' group areas. In the town of Lydenburg, for instance, all the Indian traders were already self-segregated into one part of the shopping district. The whites who had shops in the same area were willing to sell. The bureaucracy, however, moved the Indians out of

---

15. Most prominently the Group Areas Act of 1950.

the district across the river (Brookes and MacAulay 1958, 18–21).

Liberals and the constitutional crisis (1951–1957)[16]

One factor behind the desire to disenfranchise blacks (which took place in 1936) and the Cape coloureds (in the 1950s) is to be found in the early history of the Cape Colony, where the non-racial franchise originated in South Africa. By the 1880s, Cape politicians became concerned that increasing numbers of blacks and coloureds were qualifying to vote in terms of property and literacy qualifications, and as a result were playing a larger and larger role in political battles. The qualifications for franchise were thus raised at various junctures, long before the Union of South Africa came into existence (Robertson 1971, 4). After the Union was formed, the Cape liberals drew a line in the sand over the existing rights of coloured and black voters in the Cape Province, saying that those rights should persist and should not be modifiable unless in terms of the strict procedure set out in the 1910 Constitution drawn up at the National Convention (May 1955, 11).

In 1936, the Representation of Natives Act removed blacks from the Cape common voters roll. They were placed on a separate roll entitled to elect three white "native representatives" to represent them in the House of Assembly and four in the Senate. They also received the ineffectual Native Representative Council (Robertson 1971, 9).

The native representatives tended to side with the liberal-spirited United Party, as when they assisted Prime Minister Smuts in gaining a majority in Parliament to enter South Africa into the Second World War (Lewsen 1987, 102). According to Brookes, he and the other liberal white native representatives regarded their mission as bringing about an end to the existing native representative system and replacing it with one where South Africans of any race, directly elected by enfranchised blacks, could sit as parliamentarians (Lewsen 1987, 110).

Early 1950s politics was defined by what became known as the constitutional crisis, which represented one of the biggest clashes between the new National Party government and the opposition United Party. In what may be its most liberal moment, the United Party stood for the supremacy of the 1910 Constitution in the face of attempts by the National Party to amend it in

---

16. The legal aspects of this event as set out below are based on the work of Geoffrey Marshall (1957, 139–248) and Henry John May (1955, 22–78).

order to remove coloured voters from the common electoral roll in the Cape Province, by way of the Separate Representation of Voters Act in 1951. The Constitution—the South Africa Act of 1910—entrenched two provisions: that providing for equality of English and Afrikaans, and that which protected the existing non-racial, qualified franchise in the Cape Province. The only way to amend the entrenched provisions was by obtaining a two-thirds majority of both houses of Parliament in a joint sitting. The United Party's English constituency particularly feared that allowing the government to do away with the provision protecting the non-racial franchise would open the door to the Afrikaner-dominated National Party also doing away with the provision protecting their language rights. Thus, Jan Smuts, the former prime minister, declared that, "To break away from the Constitution is to break away from the very foundation of Union" (Robertson 1971, 48).

The Separate Representation of Voters Act was passed only with bare majorities (not two-thirds), and in separate sittings as opposed to a joint sitting of both Assembly and Senate, thus contravening the constitutional procedure on two counts. In future attempts to force the bill through it also failed to obtain the requisite two-thirds majority in a joint sitting. Its supporters, as a result, relying on the doctrine of parliamentary sovereignty, attempted to bring the Act into operation despite failing the procedure. Their argument, simply, was that Parliament was sovereign: because the 1910 Constitution was an ordinary piece of legislation, and because Parliament cannot bind its successors, the current Parliament must be allowed to amend any law by a simple majority.

The United Party responded, via Smuts's successor, Koos Strauss:

> The United Party...will fight this Bill inch by inch and all the way. It will fight it not only in this Parliament by every legitimate means at its disposal, but should the fight of the United Party not prevail in this House, that fight will be carried on in the law courts of this country. And if it should happen that the United Party does not prevail in its fight in the law courts, if it should be held by the highest court in this land that the entrenched clauses are no longer in full force and effect, then the United Party will make it its business to see to it that a new entrenchment will take place of these fundamental provisions in our Constitution. (quoted in Marshall 1957, 163)[17]

---

17. Marshall cites the parliamentary Hansard: 75 *House of Assembly Debates* col. 4483.

On 20 March 1952, the Appellate Division of the Supreme Court, consisting of Chief Justice Centlivres and justices Greenberg, Schreiner, Van den Heever and Hoexter, unanimously held that the Separate Representation of Voters Act was invalid, as its passing did not comply with the procedures set out in the 1910 Constitution. According to the court, legislation affecting the entrenched provisions had to be passed by two-thirds of the members of a joint sitting, and not by a bare majority of each house (Marshall 1957, 171).

The prime minister, D. F. Malan, announced on the same day that:

> Neither Parliament nor the people of South Africa will be prepared to acquiesce in a position where the legal sovereignty of the lawfully and democratically elected representatives of the people is denied, and where an appointed judicial authority assumes the testing right... (Marshall 1957, 185)

After this announcement that government would not abide by the decision of the Appellate Division and would take action to circumvent it, Sailor Malan (no relation to D. F. Malan) of the liberal Torch Commando reportedly said:

> The mask of respectability is there for all but the blind to see. The sheepskin has fallen off and the fascist wolf is snarling at the courts. We accuse the government of preferring jungle law to the rule of law. We accuse them of preferring unfettered dictatorship to a constitution which binds them to certain standards of procedure. (quoted in Kane-Berman 2018)

In light of these developments, the Torch Commando, the United and Labour parties, and the Defenders of the Constitution formed themselves into the United Democratic Front to agitate against the National government in the 1953 general election (Robertson 1971, 60).[18] In 1956, the Women's Defence of the Constitution League—later and today known as the Black Sash—committed itself to "the restoration and encouragement of political morality and the preservation of Constitutional Government." They argued that the National Party government was besmirching South Africa's honor by so brazenly refusing to comply with the 1910 Constitution's prescripts (Black Sash 1956, 1–2).

The National Party was so outraged by the audacity of a court defying the

---

18. This United Democratic Front should not be confused with the United Democratic Front that composed a substantial segment of the anti-Apartheid movement in the 1980s.

will of the sovereign Parliament that it attempted to create something known as the High Court of Parliament. This 'court' would, in fact, be Parliament sitting as if it were a court, and would have the authority to review decisions of the Appellate Division that related to the constitutionality of legislation. Margaret Ballinger said in the House of Assembly that this legal absurdity amounted to "Parliament establishing Parliament in a new form to say that a majority of the Government was itself right by a verdict of its members." Abe Bloomberg, the United Party MP for the Castle constituency in Cape Town, whose electorate was mostly coloured (Green 2004, 163), said that the High Court of Parliament was a "phoney," "fake court," that amounted "to nothing more than a Select Committee of this Parliament that gives effect to the decisions of the Nationalist Party Caucus" (Marshall 1957, 192).[19]

When the legislation creating this 'court' was challenged, the Appellate Division found on 29 October 1952 that it was unlawful, because in substance no court was being created. The legal reality was that if Parliament fails to secure a two-thirds majority in a joint sitting, it could not legislate repugnantly to the entrenched provisions (Marshall 1957, 222). This decision by the Appellate Division further angered the National Party, which again vowed to ensure a return to what it considered constitutional normalcy.

It proved relatively easy for the National Party to get around the Appellate Division's findings of unconstitutionality. The size of the Senate, the upper house of Parliament, and the size of the Appellate Division bench were not entrenched provisions, meaning no special procedure had to be followed if government wished to modify them. As a result, government introduced legislation that expanded the size of the Appellate Division bench in constitutional matters from five to eleven. Thereafter, the government introduced the Senate Act, which enlarged the Senate, allowing the National Party to secure a two-thirds majority in a joint

The Appellate Division of the Supreme Court of South Africa found Parliament's Separate Representation of Voters Act unconstitutional in 1952. Today the Appellate Division is known as the Supreme Court of Appeal and is housed in the same building in Bloemfontein. *Source*: Wikimedia Commons.

---

19. Marshall cites the parliamentary Hansard: 78 *House of Assembly Debates* col. 4209.

sitting of Parliament after itself nominating new senators. Parliament consequently passed the Separate Representation of Voters Act, which became law on 2 March 1956 (Marshall 1957, 236).

The Senate Act was also challenged for its constitutionality, with the applicants arguing that government was using underhanded means to circumvent the entrenched provisions of the 1910 Constitution, as it did with the High Court of Parliament. The Appellate Division, however, now composed of eleven judges and no longer five, found against this argument and confirmed the validity of the Senate Act on 9 November 1956, thus ending the constitutional crisis in favor of the National Party government (Marshall 1957, 240–242). Only one judge, the liberal Oliver Deneys Schreiner, agreed with the applicants in his dissent:

> I hold accordingly that on the proper construction of the [1910 Constitution,] a Senate constituted *ad hoc* for the purpose of securing, by nomination or its equivalent, a two-thirds majority in a contemplated joint sitting is not a House of Parliament within the meaning of the proviso. The application of this conclusion to the facts creates no difficulty. It is clear that the Senate set up under the Senate Act was as certain to provide the requisite two-thirds majority as if the names of its members had been scheduled to the Act or the Government had been empowered to nominate all of them. It is not seriously disputed by the respondents, and the history of the legislation proclaims, that the Senate Act was part of a legislative plan to create a Senate that would in that way provide the two-thirds majority required to remove the appellant from the common roll, and that it was enacted only for that purpose. (*Collins v. Minister of the Interior and Another* 1957)

The disappointing end of the constitutional crisis made it evident that the flexible 1910 Constitution itself would be no asset in the cause of liberalism (Brookes 1956, 194). As Ballinger noted in the House of Assembly during the debate on the Separate Representation of Voters Bill:

> The people of South Africa...believed that they had a Constitution. ... If we have not got a Constitution, if we are assuming, as we all seem to be assuming in a broad general fashion, that Parliament is sovereign, we are also assuming...that our Constitution is completely elastic, and that [we, Parliament] can do what we like. (Marshall 1957, 159)[20]

---

20. Marshall cites the parliamentary Hansard: 75 *House of Assembly Debates* col. 4638.

Subsequently, legal-constitutional challenges to Apartheid legislation were of negligible significance. The constitutional crisis was, however, the United Party's and the judiciary's finest hour from a liberal perspective (Swart 1991, 15).

Liberalism during Apartheid (1948–1994)

The 1950–1961 Assembly speaker for the National Party, Johannes Hendrik Conradie, usefully summarized the National Party's apparent intentions with its Apartheid policy:

> If we yield in every sphere, in the political sphere and in the economic sphere, we shall be forced later on to yield in the social sphere. We would like to see the native develop in his own sphere and there attain a high standard of civilisation. We are not opposed to that but he must be separated from us. (quoted in Robertson 1971, 44)[21]

With Hendrik Verwoerd's tenure as minister of native affairs (1950–1958) before becoming prime minister in 1958, the lives of black people in South Africa became rigidly centrally planned. They were expected to live in rural reserves, or 'homelands,' and could come into so-called 'white' areas, which constituted about 80 percent of the surface area of the country, only if they had a pass. Yet for those non-whites who lived in 'white' areas—and in their own houses—their stay in such areas was by government considered to be temporary. Therefore, within the Apartheid logic, they could never truly call the houses they lived in, sometimes for generations, their homes. Their home, according to government, was always to be in the rural homelands set aside for them (Swart 1991, 39–40).

Blacks were promised eventual sovereign independence from South Africa in these homelands, where they could then fully exercise political rights and have their own political and economic institutions. But by this time South Africa already had a high degree of integration, especially economically—an egg that could not be unscrambled, said Ray Swart. The plan also ignored the fact that many millions of blacks were urbanized with no real ties, as individuals, to the rural areas to which they were assigned (Swart 1991, 47–48). Even by 1956, less than a decade after Apartheid began, Brookes noted that

---

21. Robertson cites the parliamentary Hansard: 64 *House of Assembly Debates* col. 1602.

the quickly integrating economy undermined the Apartheid vision (Brookes 1956, 195).

The lack of economic opportunities in the rural areas spurred black people to move into urban 'white' areas in defiance of laws, threats, arrests, and demolition of their makeshift houses (Wentzel 1995, 20). The phenomenon was later known as the Defiance Campaign. The laws that reserved specific kinds of jobs for members of specific racial groups had the same consequence. By the 1970s there were not enough white South Africans to fill the jobs that had been reserved for them, leading to employers hiring blacks in contravention of the law. The government was powerless to stop them. Also, private schools and universities, in defiance of law, admitted black pupils (ibid., 18–19).

Brookes and MacAulay (1958, 1) wrote that civil liberty amounts to the rule of law "in the sense of basic principles of right, not merely of any and every statute or regulation that has force, but not the right, of the State behind it." The government moved away from its British heritage, gradually destroying the principles of individual freedom and the rule of law (ibid., 5). For example, under the Suppression of Communism Act of 1950, the government issued a banning order against Albert Luthuli, a moderate from the African National Congress preaching non-racialism. For five years he could not legally leave the magisterial district in which his black reserve was located. For this ban the government gave no reasons, despite its severity. Luthuli noted to United Party MP Ray Swart that the United Party equivocated on the race issue over the years, and that black South Africans had come to not expect any solution to their lot to come from that party (Swart 1991, 42–43). According to R. W. Johnson (2011), "Luthuli was a liberal through and through who always lived a modest life."

The Suppression of Communism Act was a particularly illiberal piece of legislation. The Act said, in essence, that a communist was one who was 'deemed' by government to be a communist. The result of being deemed a communist was that the government could prohibit that person from being in certain areas, attending meetings, or being a member of certain organizations (Brookes and MacAulay 1958, 23–24).

Helen Suzman of the Progressive Party was the only representative of the liberal cause in the South African Parliament between 1961 and 1974. Since communist and liberation movements were banned by law in the 1950s and

1960s, the National Party government faced insignificant political opposition (Wentzel 1995, 9). The core of the liberal movement at that time consisted of the Liberal Party, the Progressive Party, the Institute of Race Relations, Black Sash, the National Union of South African Students, and the Civil Rights League (Hughes 1994, 26). Other organizations that could be considered allies, at least partially, were the Torch Commando and the Defenders of the Constitution, as well as the English press and universities.

The English universities, also referred to as 'open universities' because they did not discriminate along color lines, were often considered by Nationalists as "provocatively liberalistic" and posing an existential threat to the continued existence of whites in South Africa (Lavin 1965, 436). Despite this apparent liberal threat, Brookes and MacAulay wrote that liberty as an ideal had by 1948 already been defeated "in the schools and universities of the Union before [it was defeated] at the polling-booths and in Parliament" (1958, 6).

By the 1950s, the Cape Province was still the heartland of South African liberalism. There coloured, but perhaps not necessarily black, South Africans could sit on municipal councils and engage with whites in various jobs where they would come into regular contact, even in hierarchically superior positions such as a traffic police officer. The National Party government however started applying Apartheid more strictly in the Cape in the early 1960s, which put an end to much of this (Robertson 1971, 22).

A major test for South African liberals came on 24 July 1964. The Institute of Race Relations' Michael Morris writes of how Frederick John Harris, a senior Liberal Party member, planted a bomb at the whites-only platform of Johannesburg Park Station, the main railway station in South Africa's largest city. Immediately after setting the bomb, Harris, who did not want to harm any innocents, contacted both the press and the police, urging them to evacuate the platform before the bomb went off. No action was taken, leading to an explosion that injured 23 and killed one. Harris was the only white anti-Apartheid activist to be hanged by the South African government on murder charges. Today, perhaps ironically, the liberal Harris is regarded as a hero by many, but not necessarily by many liberals (Morris 2019b).

By the 1960s, Apartheid was seen as inexcusable by the international community. The South African government was losing sympathy and was forcing its own international isolation (Swart 1991, 107). When the members of the Progressive Party met with foreign statesmen, they urged them to soften their approach to South Africa so as to not push white South Africans further into the arms of the National Party, which had been capitalizing on international condemnations of Apartheid. The Nationalists spun these condemnations as being from foreigners who did not appreciate the complexities of South African life, and, should foreign powers succeed in bringing about change in South Africa, black majority rule would mean the end of the Afrikaner and Western civilization in this part of the world. The Progressives, as a result, wanted to abate the foreign element in the narrative of the National Party, an element which they felt was making the project of non-racialism more difficult (Swart 1991, 105).

As late as the 1980s, liberals, it now seems, did not realize that the Apartheid system was already collapsing (Wentzel 1995, 17; Kane-Berman 2017, xi). Starting in the 1970s, Apartheid laws were being flouted not only by the black, Indian, and coloured victims of the system, but also by white businessmen and educational administrators. In many cases, government simply acquiesced to the civil disobedience (Wentzel 1995, 18–19). The crumbling of the system had the effect of bringing about a *de facto* freer market. Although the welfare state was rather minimal, between 1970 and 1991 "the white share of total income dropped by 24% while the [black] share rose by 67%." Real wages among blacks in the manufacturing industries also rose by 29 percent in the 1980s, with that of the whites only going up by one percent. Ordinary white South Africans adapted to these changing circumstances, with Jill Wentzel noting that by the time Nelson Mandela was released from prison in 1990, post-Apartheid South Africa was already being created (1995, 20–21). Liberals, however, were largely conditioned by the authoritarian Apartheid from the era of prime minister Verwoerd (1958–1966); they seem to have largely not noticed how the system they so vehemently opposed was crumbling around them. Thus, while the liberals correctly noted that the reforms to the Apartheid system were structurally insignificant and aimed mostly at whitewashing Apartheid or trying to dress it in more politically correct terms, the fact is that these reforms gave people on the ground room to maneuver in ways government never intended (Wentzel 1995, 23).

Michael O'Dowd, a polymath liberal who served as chairman of the Free Market Foundation from 1978 to 2005, head of the Anglo American mining corporation's Chairman's Fund between 1974 to 1997, and former president of the liberal National Union of South African Students, famously (Keniston

2010, 28) predicted in 1966 that economic growth and capitalism would lead to the crumbling of Apartheid by 1980 (O'Dowd 1996, 13). O'Dowd's timeline was off by 14 years, which he later freely admitted (ibid., 33), but the essence of his predictions turned out to be true. Because liberals were largely unconvinced that Apartheid was already collapsing, they reacted adversely to his prediction (Wentzel 1995, 24).

Private enterprise before 1994

Now let us look at private enterprise in South Africa and its relation to liberalism. The story is turbulent and quite confused.

The arrival of British private industry in the eighteenth century in South Africa contrasted with the largely subsistence existence of Afrikaner farmers. The English, as well as Eastern European Jews, established commercial wool farming, import-export businesses, etc. Many Afrikaners regarded private commerce and industry as the driving force behind the South African War (the Second Boer War) and the conquest of independent Afrikaner states (Giliomee 2008, 767–768), especially considering the fact that it was the influx of non-Afrikaner whites to the Johannesburg gold fields in the 1890s and the apparent displacement of local Afrikaner interests that provided impetus to the outbreak of hostilities.

According to Hermann Giliomee, it was said at a conference dedicated to the economic emancipation of poor Afrikaners in 1939 that Afrikaners must "conquer the capitalist system and [transform] it so that it fits our ethnic nature." Giliomee writes that there was a north-south divide between Afrikaners, with southerners tending to favor private enterprise and coopera-tion with English businesses, and northerners being wary of "the excesses of the capitalist system," and preferring cooperative enterprises where profit was not necessarily the main driver. William Harold Hutt, the acclaimed classical liberal economist who was teaching in South Africa at the time, in 1941 likened the Afrikaner organizing along ethnic lines to preparation for war (Giliomee 2008, 772–773).

Despite this general Afrikaner opposition to 'capitalism,' the National Party, which represented Afrikaners politically, repeatedly claimed its commit-ment to the private enterprise economy throughout the twentieth century. As Ian J. Hetherington notes, the South African government, as well as many intellectuals at South African universities, sincerely believed the economic system of the country to be one of free enterprise (Hetherington 1985, 190–191). But as Peter Berger and Bobby Godsell noted:

> The vocabulary of the present government would suggest that South Africa is currently organised along capitalist, or even libertarian lines. In a country where state regulation is central to most aspects of the lives of black South Africans in particular, this is clearly not the case. (Berger and Godsell 1988, 296)

From the left, too, Apartheid has been described as essentially capitalist (Lazar 1988, 105). Racial oppression, the argument goes, was intended to benefit wealthy capitalists (Vorhies 1990, 19). Liberals were criticized for being "beneficiaries of the very racist system that they claimed to oppose" (Dubow 2014, 10). But the classical liberal economist Clem Sunter notes that despite the presence of crony businesspeople during the era, Apartheid amounted to putting ideology above the natural principles of economics, and as such had nothing in common with capitalism (Sunter 1993, 55). The system "placed major restrictions on entrepreneurship, on free enterprise and on the movement of people, capital and goods to where the markets demanded they should go." Apartheid was "completely incompatible with capitalism," which means "free enterprise, entrepreneurship, laissez-faire and voluntary exchange" (Vorhies 1990, 19).

Economists Brian Kantor and H. F. Kenny of the University of Cape Town criticized the Marxist analysis of Apartheid. They write that the labor theory of value was convenient to Marxists because of the difference in income between whites and blacks. Examples throughout Africa, argued Kantor and Kenny, showed that capitalists rejected Apartheidesque labor controls, to the benefit of the workers (Kantor and Kenny 1976, 27–28). To Kantor and Kenny, it was peculiar that Marxists argued that the South African government knew what was good for capitalists when capitalists themselves, in neighboring states with similar circumstances, were rejecting the kinds of policies the South African government was implementing (ibid., 31).

Kantor, an economic liberal, was appointed professor of economics at the University of Cape Town in 1981. Shortly thereafter, at a meeting of the Free Market Foundation, he argued that ordinary businesspeople need not understand the theory of economics. This is because in the market, information that is communicated through mediums like prices, wages, rents, interest, and competition, is sufficient for ordinary people to read the economy. Government, on the other hand, certainly had to understand the theory and principles of economics. In particular, to Kantor, they had to appreciate from the discipline of economics "why planners were not needed" (*Witness* 1981).

The Apartheid regime, then, was heavily interventionist. The Price Control Act of 1964 authorized the government to control the prices of goods and services. These goods included "electrical and non-electrical household appliances and parts therefor," which included hairdryers, sewing and knitting machines, vacuum cleaners, toasters, etc.; movie tickets; bricks; cameras and their parts; films, flashlights and their parts; margarine; lawnmowers and their parts; tobacco; cigarettes and cigars; sugar; coal; milk; firearms and ammunition; whisky; television receivers; mineral water and fruit juice; bread; butter; and cheese (Swanepoel 1976a). The classical liberal Don Caldwell also writes of subsidized exports, rent paid to the state, Sunday trading restrictions, control boards, state financing of politically favored projects, job reservation, unemployment insurance, monopolization and protection of favored industries, occupational licensing, tariffs, exchange controls, agricultural subsidies, and a complex tax collection system, among other things (Caldwell 1989, 39–41).

In 1976, Milton Friedman, who had just been awarded a Nobel prize, was in Johannesburg hosted by the Graduate School of Business of the University of Cape Town. He said he opposed the idea of egalitarianism for South Africa. By this Friedman meant state policy directed at addressing wealth inequality. For him, the pressing issue of income discrepancies between whites and blacks had to be resolved by removing barriers and "artificial impediments to the advancement of the individual in accordance with his capacity and ability," and not by government programs (Feldberg et al. 1976, 48–49).

In 1981, ZSA Gurzynski, professor and head of the School of Economics at the University of Cape Town, wrote in defense of the free-market system in the Free Market Foundation journal *Free Market*. After problematizing the fact that the notions of "private enterprise" and "free markets" have been misrepresented and mischaracterized in South African discourse, especially by socialists, Gurzynski wrote:

It is essential, therefore, to place the terms Private Enterprise and Free Mar-

kets in their proper perspective and to show that far from being conditions
under which people are enslaved and exploited, they are the very conditions
which are essential to the maintenance of the freedom and dignity of the
individual. (Gurzynski 1981, 24)

Gurzynski criticized the government for having "taken upon itself the task
of promoting and co-ordinating the development of the country's various
ethnic groups." The reasoning advanced by government was that black South
Africans required "special protection, since their backward economies could
not possibly compete with the highly productive and aggressive white
economy." This and the concomitant control exercised over the so-called
white economy made "the government the key economic agent for the whole
country." While it was, according to Gurzynski, indeed a legitimate role for
government to create the conditions necessary for enterprising individuals
to operate freely, it would be better to rely "on individual freedom, private
property, free enterprise and free markets," as these are "the most conducive
to development and economic growth." "The more control the government
exercises, the greater is the regimentation of society and the smaller is the
freedom of the ordinary, individual citizen" (Gurzynski 1981, 24).

Piet Meyer, former chairman of the Afrikaner Broederbond—a semi-
secret society to which most of the holders of power in politics, culture, and
business belonged during the Apartheid era—said in 1981 that Afrikaners had
to resist the free-enterprise economy because it intended to integrate racial
groups:

> An integrated economic system tends inevitably towards an integrated
> society at all levels—political, educational, church and eventually also in
> cultural and social spheres. May the Afrikaners never allow themselves to
> adapt passively to the tendencies and demands of the free enterprise system
> especially where it involves well-being for its own sake. (Meyer, quoted in
> Zille 1981)

The article in which Meyer was quoted, written by Helen Zille—who is today
one of South Africa's most prominent and controversial liberals—illustrated
the tension between the *verligte* ('enlightened') and the *verkrampte* ('close-
minded') factions of Afrikanerdom and particularly the National Party (Zille
1981). That tension reflected what Caldwell noted—that there is no such thing

as "Apartheid capitalism," and that the architects of Apartheid knew that they had to make great onslaughts on property and freedom to implement their policies (Caldwell 1989, 24).

After 1985, large-scale disinvestment took place as foreign companies withdrew from South Africa. The companies tended to sell their interests in the country to local buyers, which, wrote the classical liberal University of the Witwatersrand economist Duncan Reekie, had the result of increasing concentration in particular industries and "at an aggregate, cross-economy level." Complaints were subsequently heard about having a 'free market' like this in South Africa, but the increased concentration was essentially induced by government. Reekie points, for example, to the tax advantages that long-term insurance companies enjoyed that enabled them to tailor more beneficial outcomes than can a saver who invests directly. He also notes the strict exchange controls that inhibited domestic companies from expanding their operations abroad, thereby causing them to focus on local expansion (Reekie 1990, 115–116).

The liberal slideaway (1980s–1990s)

In the 1980s, there occurred what Wentzel (1995, vii) referred to as a "liberal slideaway," the consequences of which South Africa still experiences today. Liberals had warned that the indignity of Apartheid policy would eventually lead to a violent reaction. In 1906 John Xavier Merriman said that the "inferior race" would sooner or later rebel if they were excluded completely from the regime of political rights. Merriman was advancing the cause of a qualified franchise to be applied universally to all men, regardless of race, but which he felt would continue to secure "European political supremacy" for several generations to come. The argument did not catch on, and for most intents and purposes non-whites were denied political rights. The non-racial, qualified approach was still being advocated by the Progressive Party as late as the 1970s (Robertson 1971, 6).

The warnings of violence came true in earnest in the 1980s after the so-called Tricameral Parliament was established, and violence would continue until the dawn of democracy in 1994. This violence in response to the indignity of Apartheid was perpetrated by both black and white South Africans, largely to enforce rent and school boycotts. It was during this period that the influence of liberals was at its highest, especially with the international community. That influence flowed in part from the liberals' credibility with facts and the avoidance of unnecessary ideological pontification (Wentzel 1995, 1).

A large contingent of people who considered themselves liberals at this stage, however, started supporting the violence or responding with silence. Wentzel said these liberals would not dare to be seen as "'criticising blacks' and failing to 'understand why' black people were compelled to resort to violence" (1995, 45). It had become "anathema publicly to criticise one's own side (defined as any individual or group opposed to apartheid)" (ibid., 4–5). Apartheid itself tended to be blamed for the violent means enacted by revolutionary organizations (52). White liberals especially believed "that to show goodwill to black people it was necessary not to criticise the strategies of some of their leaders" (6). There were some liberals who regarded criticizing revolutionaries as taboo, if not treasonous (Kane-Berman 2017, xii). Illiberal leftists used the struggle against Apartheid as a useful tool to attack traditional liberalism (Douglas 1994, 12) because of its preference for peaceful and gradual change.

Wentzel attributes this change in the "liberal" attitude to the "tyranny of 'political correctness'" which was developing in the United States around the same time the liberal slideaway in South Africa was developing. Many liberals had "lost their pragmatism, their critical faculties and their willingness to court unpopularity in the pursuit of truth, and succumbed instead to the kind of romanticism they had always despised" (Wentzel 1995, 1–2). Jack Bloom criticized the liberal slideaway as "an unwillingness everywhere to firmly challenge the myths of the 'underdog' liberation movements," saying instead that liberals' humaneness and open-mindedness "must not make us the 'useful idiots' of the new tyrannous forces in our society" (Bloom 1994, 8). Peter Coleman later noted that political correctness is what happens when liberalism and leftism come together (Coleman 2000, 6).

A factor and manifestation of the liberal slideaway was that from the 1980s the English universities increasingly lurched leftward, particularly in the social sciences. By 1994, the library at the University of the Western Cape, for example, did not include works by notable liberals like Friedrich A. Hayek. The history faculties, too, opted to not teach their students about liberal revolutions throughout history, but instead focused on avowedly socialist revolutions. And the National Union of South African Students, formerly an unashamedly liberal student association, once it fell in with the left-nationalist South African Students Congress, started marginalizing liberals from student governance and channeling funds to socialistic causes (Hughes 1994, 26). The silence of classical liberals on campus during the 1980s was, according to Wentzel, not because classical liberals stopped believing in their ideas "but because they were too timid, guilt-ridden and lacking in confidence to expound them." The Democratic Party, which Wentzel identified as a holdout against the liberal slideaway in the 1990s (Wentzel 1995, 292), however, won some battles on behalf of liberalism on campuses (Douglas 1994, 15). Meanwhile the National Union of South African Students was at the forefront of fighting against liberalism, despite its own historically liberal character, because they now considered liberalism to be "capitalist" (Welsh 1998, 5).

The early 1990s represented a time when (classical) liberalism enjoyed a slight uptick from the slideaway of the 1980s, with academic leftists fazed by the fall of the Berlin Wall and Afrikaner nationalists losing their powerbase during the democratic transition (Douglas 1994, 16). In the mid to late 1990s South Africa's democratic transition was completed, and many, perhaps most, liberals believed their mission to be over. As Keirin O'Malley noted during the transition: "Belief in a liberal victory prompts the inappropriate view that all that is now needed is a little more of what was done in the past" (O'Malley 1994, 31).

Where white liberals did propound classical liberal principles, to both the Apartheid regime and to the illiberal forces fighting it, they were often labelled as 'right-wing.' Black liberals were labelled 'sell-outs' of the revolutionary cause. Such labels carried with them the implication that one was racist or an apologist for the regime. As Wentzel writes: "For liberals [the 'right-wing' label] became the psychological equivalent of necklacing, and the fear of it kept many people very quiet at meetings of liberal institutions" (Wentzel 1995, 271–272).[22]

O'Malley wrote that the so-called "right wing economic liberals"—by which he meant classical liberals—have been better able to withstand the liberal slideaway than the left-liberals, or "left wing economic liberals" (O'Malley

---

22. Revolutionary movements in South Africa, particularly the African National Congress, engaged in the "necklacing" of black people who were deemed to be traitors to their cause or informers to the police. This meant a vehicle tire was hung around the alleged traitor's neck, doused in fuel, and then set afire.

1988, 5). Wentzel lists some liberal groups that did not fall victim to the liberal slideaway: the Free Market Foundation, Groundswell, the Institute of Race Relations, and the Democratic Party (Wentzel 1995, 288–297). In the latter half of the 1980s the Liberal Democratic Association was formed as a non-slideaway organization. It was to oppose government's tyrannical policies but also oppose violent overthrow of the state, a tendency of many revolutionary organizations. It would cooperate with government reforms away from authoritarianism and also provide its own innovative solutions to the problems facing South Africa (ibid., 288).

Kane-Berman (2019c) summarizes the pronounced schism caused by the slideaway in the following words:

> Classical liberals versus social democrats, liberals who rejected violence versus apologists for revolutionary violence, liberals who believed that apartheid was being peacefully overwhelmed by economic forces versus liberals who refused to believe that that system could be overcome by anything other than revolution (which some of them romanticised), and liberals who opposed economic sanctions on the grounds that they would damage the economy versus liberals who said that that was just too bad and that most blacks supported sanctions anyway.

The liberal slideaway continues to this day, in modified form, and is often spoken of as relating to 'political correctness.' In October 1999, the Institute of Race Relations and the Friedrich Naumann Stiftung (FNS) hosted a conference about the problem of political correctness in South Africa. Temba A. Nolutshungu, a director at the Free Market Foundation, noted that the "moral ugliness of apartheid and the very real atrocities that accompanied it are such that a timorous critic of [politically correct] positions can be cowed into silence by the mere suggestion that his or her views represent a disguised defence of the old order and show an insensitivity to the plight of black people." Nolutshungu mentioned that critics of the Employment Equity Act, a mainstay of post-Apartheid racially discriminatory legislation, are the target of attacks alleging that they are defending Apartheid's legacy. Whites who embrace politically incorrect positions are considered racist and blacks are considered heretical traitors to the black cause (Nolutshungu 2000, 23–24). As Rainer Erkens of the FNS said, political correctness does not translate into social justice or a prosperous society, but simply stifles freedom of expression which is a precondition for progress (Erkens 2000, 2).

Economics during the transition years (1990–1996)

Apartheid caused a very peculiar thing: there existed, and some argue today still exist, parallel economies. One is a developed economy of immense wealth, development, and prosperity, and the other is a developing economy of great poverty, dilapidation, and destitution. The existence of the latter economy has provided impetus to the post-Apartheid regime and civil society to call for further and expansive governmentalization of social affairs.

Pierre van den Berghe wrote in 1979 that after Apartheid was abolished, and a free market system was implemented in South Africa, there would be "a drastic reduction of the standard of living of most whites" and that the living standards of blacks, coloureds, and Indians would "improve only marginally." He was arguing that Apartheid propped up whites economically (Van den Berghe 1979, 15). In reality, while Apartheid intended to prop up whites, almost immediately after Apartheid ended in 1994, and South Africa attained the highest level of economic freedom it had ever experienced, white incomes skyrocketed (*Economist* 2013).

Van den Berghe was thus wrong on most counts. For whites and Indians particularly, a freer market has meant a considerable rise in welfare. Coloureds and blacks benefited as well, albeit to a far lesser extent. The average incomes of blacks seem to have plateaued in the year 2000, shortly after the post-Apartheid government's new labor laws came into operation. Van den Berghe was, however, correct in noting that Apartheid was "grossly at variance with a free market" (Van den Berghe 1979, 62).

It is today widely assumed "that extensive state intervention is required to undo the legacy of apartheid and that traditional liberalism is irrelevant" (Kane-Berman 2002, 2). This assumption is based on the idea that because the Apartheid government caused the poverty South Africa is burdened by today, the democratic government should be the entity to undo it. A cruder basis for this reasoning is the idea that because the Apartheid government succeeded in uplifting whites from poverty and providing whites with benefits, the democratic government must do the same on behalf of blacks. Such reasoning, to liberals, exalts collectivist endeavor.

It is more difficult for liberals to criticize the post-Apartheid government than the Apartheid regime (Kane-Berman 2017, x), especially from an economic standpoint. Jack Bloom of the Democratic Party related in the year of transition, 1994, that campaigning for liberal values in areas considered by the African National Congress to be their turf was incredibly difficult, and that the Democratic Party encountered intimidation when working in those areas (Bloom 1994, 3–4). Kane-Berman (2019a) relates that many liberal organizations joined the ANC-affiliated United Democratic Front during the transition, and the "Mandela years after 1994 helped to ensure that almost everyone continued to see the ANC through rose-tinted spectacles."

Kierin O'Malley (1994, 39) specified the dangers:

> It is not impossible that the market consensus alluded to above is simply a subterfuge and that once Nkrumah's adage about seeking first the political kingdom has been achieved, the domestic left will be forced by populist pressures from below to embark on a more radical socialist economic project.

Clem Sunter, too, warned in 1992 that the end of Apartheid would cause domestic and foreign "effendis" to regard South Africa as a prime location to, once again, try a new model of socialism. They would argue that socialism failed elsewhere for reasons other than its inherent impossibility, and as such it would be worth a try in South Africa (Sunter 1992, 162).

To guard against those dangers, O'Malley argued, liberals had to ensure that there were adequate constitutional protections for the market economy, such as the right to private property. These protections were taken up in the 1996 Constitution; for instance, in the Section 25 right to private property and the Section 22 right to freely choose one's trade and occupation. Some of these guarantees, as O'Malley and Sunter predicted, are today in the crosshairs of an increasingly left-populist regime.

Liberals warn that intervention exacerbated the poverty that contemporary intervention is meant to remedy. State-owned companies represented substantial interference in the economy during the Apartheid era, with the largest of such companies having been among the largest enterprises in the whole economy: the Post Office, Transnet, and the power utility Eskom, with the latter having been the single largest company by 1990 (Leach 1990, 95). By 1990, too, television-producing firms in South Africa were statutory monopolies that received tariff and import quota protection from foreign competition (ibid., 100). Duncan Reekie wrote then that wealth distribution would be better through deregulation and privatization. Privatization could be pursued not only by sale but also by simply giving state companies, freely, to South Africans (Reekie 1990, 111). Kane-Berman too notes the truism that under regimes of economic freedom there is more prosperity and less poverty (Kane-Berman 2002, 3).

Since the late 1980s, the South African government has declared itself to be pursuing privatization. Some steps were taken, like the privatization of ISCOR in 1989 and the passage of the Minerals Act of 1991, but little else was achieved by 1990 according to Reekie (1990, 120), and certainly little else was achieved thereafter. Regardless, by the end of Apartheid, private enterprise had proven to be competitive when contrasted with the statutory monopolies. The Cooperative Wine Growers Association was an unnatural state monopoly over the wine production industry of some 6,000 farmers. It had the ability to fix prices and set production quotas. South African Breweries, on the other hand, was a private enterprise that controlled 99.9 percent of the malt beer market, but with no protection from competition. Economist Daniel F. Leach argued that SA Breweries dominated the beer market "because the economics of beer production dictates that it is efficient for one firm to serve the market," and was, as such a natural monopoly (Leach 1990, 97) but with no "monopoly power" (ibid., 105).

Sunter wrote that the notion that "the State will provide" has led to big government, itself a phenomenon of the 20th century. Ordinary people have outsourced their responsibility to care for themselves and their families and communities to government. Hitherto the government had provided extensively for the welfare of the white minority. Going forward the majority would expect a similar arrangement. Sunter wrote that this would never come to be. The promises would not be fulfilled (Sunter 1993, 69–70).

Liberalism after 1994

When Apartheid ended, the political paradigm in South Africa changed completely, especially as it related to liberals. Liberals participated in the negotiations for a post-Apartheid constitution during a time that seemed like a moment of liberal victory, but soon thereafter and to this day liberals have had to respond to renewed government attacks on liberal institutions.

Constitutional negotiations

Bloom (1994, 5) set out the liberal position during the constitutional negotiations that brought South Africa out of Apartheid:

> One of the key issues in the interim Bill of Rights that has been tabled is the appropriate balance between the principles of liberty and equality. The true liberal understanding is that liberty is the more important of these principles and is consistent only with equality before the law and equality of opportunity. This is a battle that dare not be lost. Equality of result, of outcome, of condition, is a tyranny that must be ardently fought not only in the interests of a free society but also for a dynamic, prosperous economy.

Bloom notes that the institutions of "property, family, local community, religion and voluntary association" necessarily involve hierarchy and kinds of inequality but are imperative in a free society because they "are the social and cultural walls that provide checks and limits" against the overthrow of the liberal-democratic political order.

Bloom said that affirmative action is "a woolly term" that eventually develops "into group-based schemes inimical to individual merit." Institutions then "become hostage to spurious claims as to whether they are fully 'representative'" (1994, 5). Paul Pereira, commenting on Bloom's speech, said that discussions about affirmative action, whether a program is justified or not, often ignore the fact that the economic-wealth pie is not fixed but can grow (1994, 63).

Today, indeed, it is constantly questioned whether the private sector, judiciary, the press, etc., have been adequately 'transformed.' Even the Democratic Alliance itself, the successor to the non-slideaway Democratic Party, today makes much ado over its own racial makeup, with spokesperson Phumzile van Damme recently proudly proclaiming on Twitter that fewer than half of the Alliance's parliamentary candidates are white (Leng 2019; Cele and Khumalo 2019). The Democratic Party, the final embodiment of the Progressive Party founded in 1959, in contrast, opposed the very principle of racial discrimination, especially in politics and representative institutions.

Bloom said that liberals were concerned about "protecting the realm of the social from being swallowed up by the political" by way of centralized power. Some social or private institutions require reform, but liberals must nevertheless protect them "against all forms of unwarranted state intrusions."

Bloom spoke of a kind of judicial activism that South Africans may come to regret, if the law were allowed "to intrude into the delicacy of private social arrangements" (1994, 6).

Liberals and the new Constitution

Despite the fact that liberals had seemed not to make any significant political gains over the course of the Apartheid era, especially nearer Apartheid's end, liberal values ended up being adopted as constitutional content in the interim (1993) and current (1996) Constitutions (Hughes 1994, vii). Bloom however argued that liberalism was "accepted in form but not wholly in content in the current negotiations" (1994, 4). The constitutional content included the rule of law over arbitrary discretion, the recognition of legal equality, the protection of civil liberties and property rights, and a government with clear lines of separation between the executive, legislature, and judiciary.

In 1993, the Tricameral Parliament, with its dominant white chamber, enacted the interim Constitution, which would apply after the first broad-based democratic election in April 1994. The interim Constitution put an end to parliamentary sovereignty and, for the first time, gave South Africa a justiciable Bill of Rights. In 1994, the first democratic Parliament was elected, with the African National Congress scoring an overwhelming victory and ending 46 years of continuous white National Party rule. This Parliament, sitting as the Constitutional Assembly, would be responsible for formulating the current Constitution, which came into operation in February 1997. The current Constitution remains the Constitution of South Africa today, and includes a Bill of Rights in its chapter 2.

Liberals were not completely satisfied with the Constitution, however. Both the Institute of Race Relations and the Free Market Foundation made submissions on two crucial shortcomings in the Bill of Rights. Firstly, both organizations regarded it as a mistake to make the Bill of Rights apply horizontally and vertically rather than simply vertically. Horizontal application means the rights—including socio-economic rights—were not only enforceable against government but also enforceable between private persons *inter se*. For instance, this might mean that farmers would be constitutionally required to provide education (which is a constitutional right) to the children of farmworkers, or at least allow the government to construct a school on their farm. Secondly, the FMF and IRR challenged the inclusion of socio-economic rights—i.e., not only first-generational, or liberty, rights—in the Bill of Rights. To the IRR, including socio-economic rights and horizontal application in the Bill of Rights could result in government using the Constitution to justify illiberal interventions in the economy (Kane-Berman 2019c). The FMF, in particular, argued that the State did not have adequate resources to give effect to these rights, and that the courts would be required to adjudicate matters properly within the purview of the legislature. The FMF also pointed out that the rights as worded were vague, and that socio-economic rights were unprecedented in South African law, meaning the courts would have to develop a new jurisprudence to accommodate them (Free Market Foundation 1996, 2–3).

The years immediately after Apartheid ended can be described as South Africa's brief experiment with classical liberalism. Privatization, deregulation, and respect for property rights were briefly considered by the new government to be key policy objectives. Tshepo Madlingozi (2006) writes:

> [The Growth, Employment, and Redistribution (GEAR) policy] is essentially a conservative policy that affirms the virtues of a neo-liberal free-market economic system. This programme promises the following: cutting down on government spending; keeping inflation in the single digits; encouraging 'wage restraint'; speeding up privatisation of government assets; tax breaks for corporate capital; and the creation of a flexible labour market. Although criticised severely by ANC alliance partners, GEAR was meant to be the vehicle with which to transform the legacy of inequality, poverty and stagnant growth. (Madlingozi 2006, 9–10)

With the end of the Apartheid era, then, many liberals believed their work to have been completed, at least until a new status quo came into focus (Kane-Berman 2017, x). The J. H. Hofmeyr Memorial Trust, an organization tasked with keeping alive the spirit and values of Jan Hofmeyr, decided to close down shortly after the current Constitution was adopted. It was thought that the Constitution adequately enshrined the liberal values Hofmeyr stood for (Deane 2001, 63).

O'Malley writes that the movement toward economic liberalism had been successful in the years leading up to 1994, and for two reasons: many communist governments had recently fallen, discrediting socialism; second, there was a "vociferous free-marketeer and radical capitalism grouping in South Africa." This group included the Free Market Foundation and Ground-swell (O'Malley 1994, 39), a grassroots movement spawned by Leon Louw and Frances Kendall's book *South Africa: The Solution* to promote direct democracy and the Swiss canton system as an alternative for South Africa (*Sun* 1987).

Radical economic transformation

Ace Magashule, the Secretary General of the African National Congress, said in the aftermath of the 2019 general election that the ANC is determined to

> foster a new momentum for the fundamental radical economic transforma-tion (RET) of our socio-economic landscape. Our mandate is to expropriate land without compensation…to nationalise the Reserve Bank…to trans-form the financial institutions and banks in order to serve the needs of our people…to stop privatisation of state-own[ed] enterprises…the transfer of the political and socio-economic power into the hands of the overwhelming majority of our people, Africans in particular, and the black people in general. (African News Agency 2019)

This is a useful summary of the agenda the ANC has been pursuing to greater and lesser extents since the GEAR years ended. Labor policy and land reform are key aspects of this agenda to which liberals have had to respond over the last two decades.

Labor policy

Unemployment has in general been the most pressing issue to most South Africans according to Institute of Race Relations surveys (Kane-Berman 2002, 5; Institute of Race Relations 2018, 3). In 2019 the unemployment rate in South Africa was around 27 percent. The answer to this problem, writes Kane-Berman (2002), is not for government itself to create work by merely using taxes to hire people into the public service. But that is what government has, unfortunately, done with the public sector, employing more than 1.6 million people across all levels and spheres of government. In 2014, the public service wage bill amounted to 11.5 percent of South Africa's GDP, according to research done for the Helen Suzman Foundation (Franks 2014, 55).

Kane-Berman describes a liberal solution to the joblessness crisis. The government must cease strangling the labor market with restrictions, collective bargaining mandates, and minimum wages, and should free small businesses from overregulation. These interventions by the state have served only to protect the employed at the direct expense of the unemployed, who have been priced out of the market. "They must be empowered to sell their labour to the highest bidder." A liberal solution would include having government fulfill its core mandate of protecting rights by keeping people and their property safe, enabling market competition, and privatizing state functions. Government must also voucherize education as far as possible to encourage private schooling. This would help poor children gain access to good schools. The government must also play a role in healthcare, while making maximum use of the private sector (Kane-Berman 2002, 6–7).

The IRR opposed the ANC's new labor regime from the beginning. Notably, the Labour Relations Act of 1995, the Employment Equity Act of 1998, and the Broad-Based Black Economic Empowerment Act of 2003 were all resisted (Kane-Berman 2019a). The purpose of the Black Economic Empowerment policy is "to increase the number of black people that own, manage, control and gain employment in South Africa's economy" (Investment House 2016). It does this, for instance, in the mining industry by requiring that the shareholders of a company be 30 percent black (Ritchie 2018). The IRR notes that Black Economic Empowerment, affirmative action, and employment equity policies have failed, as they have only assisted "those who are already fairly advanced on the social ladder" instead of poor blacks (Roodt 2018, 1).

As historian Hermann Giliomee writes, the "policy of ethnic preferment provides new opportunities to the politically dominant group for generating wealth, income and employment. It bolsters the support of ethnic leaders, even from those who are not benefiting from the policies" (Giliomee 2008, 767).[23] The IRR has proposed a liberal alternative to the government's Black Economic Empowerment model. Rather than using race as a proxy for disadvantage, disadvantage itself should be considered. The result would be that the majority of beneficiaries of state assistance would continue to be

---

23. Here Giliomee was referring to Malaysia's New Economic Policy, which in part inspired South Africa's policy of Black Economic Empowerment.

black, but the stain of racial discrimination will no longer taint South African law (Kane-Berman 2002, 7). Policy should "shift away from a focus on numerical targets, [and] rather look to provide the inputs which would improve the lives of poorer people." It should prioritize "rapid economic growth, excellent education, more employment, and the promotion of vibrant and successful entrepreneurship" (Roodt 2018, 11).

On 1 January 2019, South Africa's National Minimum Wage Act came into operation, creating one single standardized minimum wage across all sectors in the South African economy.[24] Sunter had warned 25 years earlier that social engineers should not interfere in how wages are arrived at in the market, because it would lead to unemployment (Sunter 1993, 59). As of 14 May 2019, South Africa's unemployed plus discouraged workers made up 38 percent of the potential labor force (*BusinessTech* 2019). The generally free-market Centre for Development and Enterprise (CDE), led by Ann Bernstein, argued in an October 2018 report that South Africa must undergo labor policy reforms, chiefly in the form of exemptions from the national minimum wage, to arrest the crisis of slow growth and unemployment. The authors, economist Nicoli Nattrass and political sociologist Jeremy Seekings, concluded that there must be an "expansion of lower-wage, labour-intensive sectors" to make room for the unemployed (2018, 5). In an earlier spotlight notice, the CDE concluded that upon "sober examination," government's national minimum wage policy "reveals unacceptably high levels of risk and a very high chance of exacerbating poverty, inequality, and unemployment, while also slowing economic growth" (CDE 2017).

Land reform and expropriation without compensation

The post-Apartheid regime's determination to carry out land reform came to a head in 2018, when Parliament adopted a resolution that committed the institution to amending the Constitution to allow for the expropriation of private property, mostly rural land, without compensation.[25] In the words of president Cyril Ramaphosa, the measure would address the "original sin" of land dispossession (quoted in Herman 2018). Others too, like Julius Malema, leader of the Economic Freedom Fighters (EFF), a radical Marxist-Leninist

---

24. Subject to limited exceptions.
25. For a broad discussion about the question of land and property in post-Apartheid South Africa, see Van Staden (2019, 272).

party, believe that the answer to poverty in South Africa is land redistribution, and that South Africans are poor because they do not own land (Cronje 2014).

Sunter, however, noted that peasant or subsistence farming will not provide the answer to South Africa's poverty woes. Indeed, the Apartheid homeland policy—requiring blacks to live in rural areas—was particularly directed toward "depositing masses of people on semi-arable land in rural areas remote from markets." Instead, it is principally in urban areas that people learn trades and entrepreneurship (Sunter 1993, 73–74).

When the government expropriates property for public purposes or land reform, the Constitution requires government to pay just and equitable compensation based, among other things, on market value. Expropriation without compensation would remove that provision. A similar process was followed in Zimbabwe in the early 2000s, when farms owned by whites were violently expropriated without compensation, crashing the banking sector and consequently the economy. The EFF, which has been the greatest champion of expropriation without compensation, has lauded the Zimbabwean situation as one to emulate (Head 2019).

According to the CEO of the Institute of Race Relations, Frans Cronje, prospects for blocking expropriation without compensation in the May 2019 general election hinged on keeping the ANC and the EFF, collectively, under 66 percent of the seats in the National Assembly. In terms of the 1996 Constitution, that coalition would need a two-thirds majority in the lower house of Parliament to amend the Constitution to implement its program (Cronje 2019a). The ANC and EFF collectively attained 68 percent of the vote, however, and now do possess a two-thirds majority of the seats in the National Assembly.

Recent discourse about 'liberalism'

Criticism of liberals and liberalism has continued after the end of Apartheid. For example, Ismail Lagardien (2019) has accused the liberal former premier of the Western Cape, Helen Zille, of "stepping into the alt-right, and hiding behind the fig leaf of 'classical liberalism.'" He lambastes Zille for fondly citing Thomas Sowell, "the right-wing economist" who is associated with "the most notorious paleo-conservatives" in America. Above all, Lagardien criticizes classical liberalism for its emphasis on "individual liberty, meritocracy, [and] rational thought" and the notion that people "are responsible for their own misery and poverty." He concludes that liberalism thus glosses over the unearned privileges white South Africans gained from colonialism and Apartheid. Liberalism is therefore a dog whistle to racists. To Lagardien, "atomistic individualism is one of liberalism's worst aspects."

The former minister and Communist Party central committee member Jeremy Cronin (2019) lauds the "progressive liberalism" of "the founders of the ANC," but has criticized the liberalism that "is also invoked by the likes of the Free Market Foundation, calling for the unleashing of untrammelled market appetites with all their ecocidal implications."

Etienne Mureinik, like many liberals at the end of Apartheid, warned of this kind of sentiment:

> Liberal has again become the stigma label. Under [former Apartheid prime ministers] Verwoerd and Vorster liberal was the stigma-label of choice. It meant so far left as to be almost Communist. But now it [means] so far Right as to be almost racist. It is a new psycho-trick, calculated to taint the democrats on one's Right with the authoritarianism of those much further to the Right. (quoted in Leon 2019)

Part II. Classical liberal personalities and institutions

In Part II, I turn to particular persons and organizations, and specifically liberals in politics. What follows is episodic, sometimes doubling back chronologically.

Liberal organizations and liberals in civil society

Historically, the liberal movement was supported by the South African English-language press, the English-language universities, some English-language churches, some businesses, lawyers, and literary and other artists (Hughes 1994, 25). But in the twenty-first century the liberal movement received support from foreign quarters. A German political foundation, the Friedrich Naumann Stiftung, has been described as the most helpful foreign institution to South African liberals (Johnson 2011). Also, the Atlas Network, a United States-based global network of classically liberal think tanks and organizations, assists partners in South Africa (Sayyid 2019).

There are several civil society organizations in South Africa today that can broadly be described as "liberal." Arguably, however, only two can be described as classical liberal, the Institute of Race Relations, founded in 1929, and the Free Market Foundation, founded in 1975.[26] This part of the essay will cover these and other organizations and individuals important to liberalism.

Institute of Race Relations

The South African Institute of Race Relations (IRR) was established on 9 May 1929 by John David Rheinallt Jones, Charles Loram, Howard Pim, Edgar Harry Brookes, J. du Plessis, D. D. T. Jabavu, J. H. Nicholson, and J. G. van der Horst.[27] The IRR is perhaps one of Africa's oldest think tanks, and certainly its oldest classically liberal think tank (Shandler 1991, 21). It was located in the basement of the University of the Witwatersrand until February 1947 (Byrne 1990, 27).

By 1936, the IRR was engaged in welfare activism, which contributed to stimulating an emerging liberalism in South Africa. Phyllis Lewsen writes that although the IRR was not politically partisan, it "was broadly liberal in its quest for individual freedoms and social advancement." Socialists at the time attacked the IRR for being capitalist. Lewsen writes that the IRR had a "belief that accurate information can change attitudes" (Lewsen 1987, 101). Its annual *South African Survey of Race Relations* began in 1936 and continues today.

J. D. R. Jones, the "Forgotten Man of liberal politics," has been described as "South Africa's first full-time professional liberal," given that he was the first director of the Institute of Race Relations, serving between 1930 and 1947 (Byrne 1990, vii). His successors were Quintin Whyte (1947–1970), Frederick Johannes van Wyk (1970–1980), John Rees (1980–1983), John Kane-Berman (1983–2014), and currently Frans Cronje (Byrne 1990, 30; University of the Witwatersrand 2011; Spector 2013). The IRR relied mainly on American funding since its founding at least up to 1990, at which time the Kellogg Foundation and the American Aid Programme were the main financial supporters of the IRR. Other large funders over the IRR's history were the Carnegie Corporation, the Phelps-Stokes Fund, and the Ford Foundation (Byrne 1990, 28–30). The IRR's reliance on American organiza-

---

26. The Free Market Foundation is the author's employer.
27. C. de B. Webb, however, includes as founders Rheinold Frederick Alfred Hoernlé and Leo Marquard, and excludes Pim, Du Plessis, Nicholson and Van der Horst (Webb 1979, 40).

tions declined beginning around 1983. USAID and the Kellogg Foundation provided funding mainly for bursaries, but others refused to fund the think tank due to their criticism of international economic sanctions and the violence employed by the ANC to further its cause. The IRR survived financially mainly as a result of local fundraising efforts. Michael O'Dowd of the mining corporation Anglo American is noted as having been instrumental in sourcing funds from that company for the IRR's most contentious work (Kane-Berman 2019c). The government was so threatened by the IRR's research and stature in civil society that in 1948 it established its own, pro-Apartheid counterpart, the South African Bureau of Racial Affairs at the University of Stellenbosch (see Overy 2002, 66 n.9).

Widely respected by those who opposed the idea of Apartheid before 1994, the IRR is today regularly labelled as reactionary, conservative, and right-wing, despite the fact that the IRR has simply continued to advocate personal and economic liberty (*News24* 2011; Cloete 2011; Bond 2015). Compare, for instance, the 1958 IRR-sponsored publication *Civil Liberty in South Africa* by Brookes and MacAulay and its 2018 publication *Race Relations in South Africa: Reasons for Hope 2018*. In both there is a clear overtone favoring the dignity and worth of the individual and an unashamed advocacy of private property rights regardless of race. Indeed, Kane-Berman describes the IRR as "unashamedly liberal" (Kane-Berman 2017, ix).

The IRR claims that it has described itself as liberal since 1929, and by that it means to take the view that society is "made up of various interest groups, political and otherwise, but as essentially comprising a collection of individuals, each with inalienable rights" (Kane-Berman 1994, 1). In April 2019, the IRR's Sihle Ngobese described the IRR as "an advocacy organization that fights for your right to make decisions about your life, your family, and your business, free from unnecessary government, political and bureaucratic interference. We are an actual, classically liberal organization" (Ngobese 2019).

In the same month, April 2019, President Ramaphosa conferred the Order of the Boabab in Silver posthumously on Ray and Dora Phillips, Americans who were involved with the IRR at its founding (Morris 2019a), for their social work among poor black South Africans in the early twentieth century (Lubisi 2019).

In May 2019, Frans Cronje summarized how the IRR believes South Africa should "rebuild" after ideological mismanagement and corruption in recent years:

> Rebuilding will mean, among other things, jettisoning over-zealous labour regulation that prices poor people out of jobs, repealing all race-based policy, reducing the state's role in the economy, and allowing parents control over the education of their children. Do these things, and South Africa might achieve the growth rates sufficient to substantively erode levels of poverty and inequality to take the wind out of the racial nationalist sails. (Cronje 2019b)

Free Market Foundation

The Free Market Foundation (FMF) was founded in August 1975, and its inaugural congress took place in March 1977 (Swanepoel 1976b). The FMF's goal was and remains "to encourage a free market economy in South Africa" and stop the trend of "increased government participation in and control of the economy" (Swanepoel 1975). In 1976 the FMF complained of a "paradox" where South Africa had a "declared pro-capitalist position" and "anti-communist laws," but "against a background reality of extending, creeping state tentacles which envelop, constrict and eventually stifle" (*Daily News* 1976). The FMF said of itself: "The Free Market Foundation is the only organization in the Republic with the singular goal of advancing capitalism" (FMF 1976, 7).[28]

Leon Louw described the work of the FMF as follows in 1987: "We mobilise public opinion, we lobby, we fight government, any government, and make representations and submissions. Our objective is to create a climate of public opinion among politicians, radical groups and unions in favour of free markets" (quoted in Kennedy 1987). The American classical liberal James U. Blanchard III wrote that the "growing group of intellectuals who understand individual liberty and the free market" in South Africa were "centered around the Free Market Foundation" (Blanchard 1979, vii).

The FMF was born out of the South African Association of Chambers of Commerce (Assocom), of which Louw was the legal manager (*To the Point* 1977). Louw has been executive director of the FMF from 1978 to the time of writing. Assocom gave the FMF direct assistance for the first ten months

---

28. My translation from the original Afrikaans.

of its existence before the FMF became independent (Louw 1978, 5). Lou Sher, the former president of Assocom, was the FMF's first chairman (Segal 1977). Louw was the chairman of the steering committee constituted to form the FMF (Robertson 1975) and was joined by Ed Emary, Mike Lillard, Fred Macaskill, Andre Spies, and Mark Swanepoel (*Daily News* 1976). After its establishment, the FMF's interim executive committee was chaired by Dirk Hertzog, a relative of the former prime minister J. B. M. Hertzog, and was formally supported by Assocom, the South African Society of Marketers, the South African Federated Chamber of Industries, the National African Federation Chamber of Commerce, and the Afrikaanse Handelsinstituut (*Clarion* 1976). In March and April 1978, the FMF and the University of South Africa co-hosted Friedrich A. Hayek in Johannesburg.

Stephan du Toit Viljoen, the first president of the FMF and chairman of the Bantu Investment Corporation, argued at the FMF's inaugural congress that the unrest in South Africa was due to the inability of blacks to identify with the system in which they lived. For conflict to be abated, all races had to be included in the administration of the country. A free market in South Africa could not be successful if this was not done (Segal 1977). Louw echoed this in 1978, saying in a response to a survey showing that most blacks self-identify as communist or socialist that this was because the *status quo* in South Africa—Apartheid—was described as capitalist by both its promotors and detractors, which was not in fact the case (Norton 1978). At a 1987 symposium in honor of Martin Luther King Jr. in Atlanta, Louw said that peace in South Africa could only be achieved if the white electorate gave blacks citizenship and equality before the law and abolished Apartheid (*Citizen* 1987).

Michael Conway O'Dowd (1930–2006) has been described alongside William Harold Hutt (1899–1988) as a "doyen of the free market school" in South Africa (O'Malley 1988, 6). In addition to being an executive of the mining corporation Anglo American, O'Dowd was chairman of the Free Market Foundation from 1978 until 2005 and known for his "O'Dowd Thesis." The O'Dowd Thesis, initially circulated privately in 1966, held that industrialization would lead to the end of Apartheid, just as it had led to greater democracy in

O'Dowd in 1996.
Source: FMF.

Britain (Keniston 2010, 28). The thesis was inspired heavily by Walt Whitman Rostow's *The Stages of Economic Growth* (O'Dowd 1996, 1). In 1987, O'Dowd wrote that the privatization of South Africa's state-owned enterprises would make it easier for disempowered blacks to enter the market. The reform had to be combined with the liberalization of regulations that were causing small enterprises to be priced out of the market (*Sowetan* 1987).

Fred Macaskill, then a director of the FMF, wrote that the problem in South Africa was "not a question of violating the rights of blacks or whites." Instead, the issue was "the state's violation of individual rights," implying that the racial element of oppression in South Africa drew attention away from the machinery of oppression. He criticized certain constitutional proposals—those which would ultimately culminate in the 1983 Tricameral Constitution—for not contemplating a limited government but instead further entrenching the absolute power of government. The only way to solve the problem of oppression according to Macaskill was to limit the government's powers, especially the power to discriminate (Macaskill 1979, 215–216).

In November 1980, Terry Markman, a council member of the FMF and well-known transportation consultant, called for the deregulation of South Africa's state-run airline monopoly, South African Airways (SAA). He advocated that the domestic market be deregulated immediately, that SAA be required to make a profit and eventually be privatized, that airports finance themselves, that the country enter into generous bilateral agreements with other countries, and that private airlines be allowed to compete on international routes (*Cape Times* 1980).

1991: The FMF's Terry Markman was a member of the South African government's International Aviation Policy Steering Committee, which culminated in the demonopolization and deregulation of the aviation industry. Markman is standing fourth from the left. *Source*: FMF.

In 1981, Markman called on the then-Monopolies Commission to investigate SAA, then effectively a monopoly that had the right to license other operators, for refusing a "right to operate" to another airline, Sky Couriers. Sky Couriers had been taking a large amount of cargo business from SAA, angering the freight agents' union. Markman condemned SAA for its "coercive monopoly" and lambasted the fact that a market player could deny, by force of law, the right to participate in the market to its competitors (Duncan and Paris 1981). In 1991, the domestic aviation market in South Africa was deregulated and SAA demonopolized, allowing private airlines to compete against the state's carrier (Mhlanga 2017, 3–5).

The FMF continues to argue for the privatization or liquidation of SAA itself, as the government persists in propping up the thoroughly uncompetitive and unprofitable airline. Since deregulation, SAA's market share went from 95 percent in 1994 to 17 percent in 2018. By June 2018 the airline needed R9.2 billion ($6.3 million) to pay off its debts and R15 billion ($1.03 million) for operating costs (eNCA 2018). In June 2018, Louw made a R100,000 ($6,916) wager with the CEO of SAA, Vuyani Jarana, that the airline would not be profitable within Jarana's three-year timeline. Jarana accepted the wager (Smith 2018) but resigned from SAA on 29 May 2019 (Gernetzky 2019), less than a year after taking office, citing red tape and an unwillingness of the government to help SAA succeed (*TimesLive* 2019).

Louw has been considered the face of the free-market movement in South Africa since the 1970s. In a December 1987 biographical article by journalist Stan Kennedy in the Johannesburg paper *The Star*, Louw was described as "the driving force for a free-market society" in South Africa. Louw came from an Afrikaner family, initially flirted with fascism, then at university became a Marxist and acted as a courier for the then-banned African National Congress (Lawson 2013). He was weaned away from Marxism when he discovered that there was "no sign of any great struggle between the working classes and capitalists," instead seeing cooperation between consumers and sellers (Kennedy 1987).

Louw wrote in 1981 in the FMF journal *Free Market* that adopting a free-market paradigm would solve South Africa's most important social, political, and especially racial problems. His major points were three:

- There needed to be rapid wealth creation, without which any political solution to South Africa's problems would be stillborn. Even if all the wealth white people owned at the time were redistributed, this ultimately would do little to help the impoverished black majority. Only a free market would be conducive to such rapid wealth creation.

- South Africa's woes would not come to an end unless racial intergroup domination is eliminated. By embracing the free market, life would be less politicized, with the important decisions that affect people's daily lives being made by them individually or as communities.
- Such a depoliticization, furthermore, is not possible except under a constitution that provides for a limited government, especially insofar as government's economic powers are concerned. Such a constitution would defuse the intense racial and ethnic tensions.

Louw concluded, "the promotion of a free market, or stated conversely, the reduction of statism, whether it be left or right, is the most urgent and important priority in South Africa" (Louw 1981, 2).

Louw was the principal author of the Ciskei's Small Business Deregulation Act (Blundell 1985), and chairman of the Commission of Inquiry into Ciskei Economic Policy (*Financial Mail* 1980). The Ciskei was an Apartheid homeland considered by the Apartheid regime to be "independent" from South Africa but rightly seen by the international community as a puppet meant to legitimize the Apartheid system. Louw and the FMF pressed to take advantage of the South African government's self-declared non-involvement in domestic Ciskeian affairs. The Small Business Deregulation Act, among other things, exempted small businesses from a host of interventionist legislation still imposed upon the homeland by the central South African government, and it established the office of the Small Business Commissioner, who could exempt small businesses from other bur-

1986: Frances Kendall and Leon Louw in a promotional photo for their book *South Africa: The Solution. Source*: FMF.

densome laws or regulations unless Parliament overruled it. The Act also legalized child labor when there is consent from parents or guardians. And the Act certainly did not create a free-for-all of economic anarchy; for one, it explicitly provided that all the rules of employment and public health that exist

under common law shall persist (Hetherington 1985, 192).

The FMF-advanced reforms in the Ciskei included the abolition of various taxes, and they led to the development of new industries and greatly increased foreign investment. The FMF's slogan for taxes in the Ciskei was "Simple, Flat, and Low," as the personal income tax return was simple and one page long, and those who earned more than R8,000 had to pay a flat 15 percent rate. There was no company tax. The reform led to 90 percent of those who used to be liable for personal tax being liable no longer. In the wake of these reforms, over about three years, the Ciskei had an annual economic growth rate of 6 to 8 percent, whereas South Africa's growth was near nil (*Business Day* 1987).

By the mid-1980s, the FMF's funding largely came from big companies, augmented by membership contributions from individuals and smaller companies and paid consultancy work for firms and government institutions. In the late 1980s, FMF's training program Justice For All taught politics and economics to millions of South Africans employed by participating companies, and it contributed 60 percent of the FMF's total income (Kennedy 1987).

In 1986, Louw and his wife Frances Kendall co-wrote the best seller *South Africa: The Solution* (Louw and Kendall 1986). Widely acknowledged as a potential path forward for South Africa, the book recommended a direct democracy system patterned on the Swiss canton system: "Democracy is a complicated array of checks and balances, intended to protect individuals and minorities and limit the power of central governments" (*Sun* 1987). The book was widely promoted by the FMF and Groundswell at forums like the 1987 Dakar Conference and the first national congress of the Institute for a Democratic Alternative for South Africa (*Pretoria News* 1987). Groundswell was formed specifically to promote the Swiss-style direct democracy and federal canton system ideas offered in the book. The book opened the way for FMF's participation in the constitutional negotiations that brought South Africa out of Apartheid. Louw and Temba A. Nolutshungu "played a role in negotiations to democracy, and successfully included property rights in the Constitution" (Bloor 2019).

In line with its support of entrenching property rights protection in the 1996 Constitution, FMF opposes the government's policy of expropriation without compensation. In November 2018, the FMF hosted a conference in

Johannesburg that drew participants from Venezuela, India, Nigeria, Kenya, Ghana, and the United States, who related their own countries' experiences with similar anti-property rights laws (Van Staden 2018).

The FMF is known for its Khaya Lam (Xhosa for "My Home") land reform project. The goal is to facilitate the transfer of title deeds from municipalities to indigent tenants. Under Apartheid tenure law, black South Africans could not own property in 'white' cities and had to rent houses from the municipalities in 'black' townships on the periphery of the cities. By 2019, many of these tenants had lived on these properties for more than a generation. As a pro-property rights method of realizing the constitutional commitment to land reform, the FMF believes these tenants must become full freehold owners of those properties (eProperty News 2018). By May 2019, Khaya Lam had successfully facilitated the processing of 3,610 title deeds, with another 3,525 titles in process.[29]

William Harold Hutt (1899–1988)

William Hutt was a renowned economist from Britain who came to work in South Africa at the University of Cape Town in 1928. He became dean of the Faculty of Commerce in 1931. His best-known contribution to South African liberal economics was his book *The Economics of the Colour Bar* in 1964, which addressed the economics of Apartheid (see also Hutt 1975).

Hutt had always been an opponent of racial discrimination by the state in South Africa, even before the National Party won the 1948 election and implemented its Apartheid policy. In 1937, Hutt warned of the coming threat to the entrenched clauses of the 1910 Constitution, a threat that was realized in the 1950s during the constitutional crisis discussed above. The entrenched clauses had protected the equality of the English and Afrikaans languages, as well as the non-racial but qualified franchise in the Cape Province. In 1961, when South Africa was to become an independent republic outside the British Commonwealth, Hutt argued that all South Africans should be offered British citizenship (Hutt 1964, 6–7).

William Harold Hutt. *Source*: Mises Institute.

---

29. Numbers obtained from Perry Feldman, Khaya Lam project manager, via email.

Hutt described Apartheid as an economic injustice, that is, "any policy or action which is intended to perpetuate the inferiority of material standards or status of any racial group" (Hutt 1964, 9). According to Hutt, Apartheid South Africa was characterized by two opposing forces. The first force—the free market—tended to liberate non-whites from coercion and subservience, and the second force—interventionism—tended to subjugate them (ibid., 173). Unchecked state power, wrote Hutt, "deliberately or unintendedly, patently or deviously" represses politically vulnerable groups (174). In South Africa, Apartheid was not a "truly free enterprise" system, but instead a state-directed economy, where the spontaneous order of the market was "replaced by planning with political objectives" (177).

Hutt argued that the elimination of racial discrimination in state policy was not going to solve South Africa's problem with authoritarianism. In the context of South Africa having had parliamentary sovereignty as opposed to constitutional supremacy, Hutt wrote: "Universal suffrage would merely mean the transfer of power to a new political majority, with no constitutional limitations to prevent retaliatory abuse" (1964, 178). Instead, South Africa needed to adopt the political philosophy of liberalism. "The rule of law," wrote Hutt, "must be a rule of non-discrimination and a rule, therefore, of limited state intervention in the sphere of markets and free contract" (ibid., 179).

Ludwig Maurits Lachmann (1906–1990)

The economist Ludwig Lachmann, well-known for *Capital and Its Structure* (1956) and *The Market as an Economic Process* (1986), taught at the University of the Witwatersrand in Johannesburg, South Africa, between 1948 and 1972, and was president of the South African Economic Society between 1961 and 1963.

In September 1976 Lachmann addressed a meeting of the Free Market Foundation, alongside Dirk Hertzog and Leon Louw, on the topic of economic freedom. He explained how politicians trade promises for votes, arguing that the more they promise, the more votes they attain. This was the basis for his argument that democracy, as it was then widely practiced, threatens economic freedom (Swanepoel

Ludwig Maurits Lachmann. *Source*: Mises Institute.

1976c). In an interview with the FMF in August of the same year, Lachmann (1976) argued that inflation, too, threatens economic freedom. Governments, which are invariably unwilling to stop increasing the supply of money, will use methods like price, wage, and rent controls, among other restrictions on the market, to restrain inflation.

Torch Commando

The Torch Commando was a group of former South African soldiers who had served during the Second World War (Robertson 1971, 51). Founded in 1951, the Torch Commando was organized specifically to oppose the introduction of the Separate Representation of Voters Act, which gave rise to the constitutional crisis in the early 1950s. Having recently fought fascism in Europe, Torch Commando members felt that the National Party government was exhibiting signs characteristic of their former enemy: the prioritization of race, extreme nationalism, and dictatorial government.

The national chairman of the Torch Comman-do was Louis Kane-Berman, father of John Kane-Berman, the latter of whom became and remains today one of South Africa's most prominent classical liberals. The Torch Commando was one of the largest resistance movements in the country's history, once boasting 250,000 regis-tered members (including civilians who were not veterans), including five judges and ten generals, amounting to about 10 percent of South Africa's white population. Other prominent members of the Torch Commando were its national president, Adolph "Sailor" Malan (1910–1963), and Alan Paton (1903–1988), who would later be a founder and leader of the Liberal Party (Kane-Berman 2018). Sailor Malan referred to the National Party government as "fascist in spirit," while the Torch was founded on principles of constitutionalism, democracy, individual liberty, and the rule of law (Robertson 1971, 52–53).

Adolph "Sailor" Malan was the president of the Torch Commando. *Source*: Wikimedia Commons.

Black Sash

The Black Sash was founded in 1955 during the constitutional crisis as the Women's Defence of the Constitution League, "an organization of white women to promote respect for the constitution and protest the loss of voting rights for Coloureds" (Michigan State University 2005). Jean Sinclair, Ruth Foley, Elizabeth McLaren, Tertia Pybus, Jean Bosazza, and Helen Newton-Thompson were among the League's liberal founders. The League employed marches, convoys, protests, and vigils to oppose government policy (South African History Online 2011).

At the League's protests against what it considered unconstitutional government action, the women wore black sashes fastened to white cards reading *"Eerbiedig ons Grondwet,"* Afrikaans for "Respect our Constitution." The protesters became associated with these black sashes. They gave rise to the name (Black Sash 1956, 2), which was formally adopted at the organization's April 1956 National Conference (Black Sash 2017).

Circa 1955–1960: Black Sash members protesting with a placard reading "Justice demands a National Convention of all races." *Source*: Wikimedia Commons.

Their role expanded after the unsatisfactory resolution of the constitutional crisis. Wentzel argues that after the dissolution of the Liberal Party in 1968 the Black Sash was the most effective human rights organization in South Africa, working directly in communities that were threatened with forced removals and trying to ensure the injustices were exposed (Wentzel 1995, 10).

In the 1970s, increasing numbers of Marxists joined the Black Sash, leading to the sidelining of liberals; Wentzel writes that Marxists were "in many ways the traditional foe of liberals" (Wentzel 1995, 12). Today, the Black Sash makes submissions and advises government on legislation and welfare (South African History Online 2011).

Anton Rupert and Johann Rupert

Anton Rupert (1916–2006), the business magnate who established the international Rembrandt Group, was another Afrikaans liberal. In 1985, for example, Rupert pointed to building codes, health regulations, restricted operating hours, licensing requirements, transportation regulations, labor regulations, and minimum wages as reasons for poverty in South Africa.

In part as a result of Rupert's activism in favor of a free-enterprise economy, in the late 1980s South Africa went about a process of regulatory reform designed to benefit small businesses and the informal economy (Esterhuyse 1986, 66–67). Rupert opposed influx controls, i.e., controls on black movement into 'white' urban areas. For Rupert, without freedom "private initiative and creative ingenuity cannot develop fully" (ibid., 102–103). Rupert's was one of various voices pointing out that Apartheid measures did not work in light of the economic realities in South Africa. Rupert assisted with the initial funding of the Free Market Foundation (Louw 2011).

Anton Rupert.
Source: Wikimedia Commons.

Rupert's son Johann Rupert, who inherited his father's empire, continues Anton's liberal legacy. Recently, Johann partnered with the Free Market Foundation's Khaya Lam land reform project, sponsoring the title deeds of 70 Aberdeen residents (Free Market Foundation 2018).

Liberals in politics

A number of South African liberals and liberal organizations had an important role in politics throughout the twentieth century. This participation has continued, but to a lesser extent, into the twenty-first century.

Jan Hendrik Hofmeyr (1894–1948)

Jan Hofmeyr was seen as the leader of South Africa's fledgling liberal political movement in the 1930s and 1940s. He had been a veteran politician, but was also "convinced that prevailing South African racial attitudes and policies could not be reconciled with either his Christian principles or his understanding of liberal democracy" (Deane 2001, 58–59). As a minister in the United Party government in 1936, he opposed his own party's legislation that disenfranchised blacks and cordoned them off in the homelands (Robertson 1971, 15). He was vice president of the Institute of Race Relations from 1944 until his death in 1948 (ibid., 27).

Hofmeyr, a political polymath, held five Cabinet positions between 1933 and 1938. After he threatened to resign in 1937 when his party made threats against coloured rights, the prime minister, Jan Smuts, wrote that his resignation would "be a great loss," and that Hofmeyr was "a good liberal with a fine human outlook." Hofmeyr did resign from Cabinet later because of a different issue—the appointment by prime minister J. B. M. Hertzog of an unqualified person to a vacant 'native representative' Senate seat. The 1910 Constitution required such senators to be "thoroughly acquainted" with black affairs, which Hertzog's appointee was not (Lewsen 1987, 109).

Hofmeyr had been the deputy prime minister under Smuts since 1938 and was expected to be Smuts's replacement as leader of the United Party and prime minister of South Africa when Smuts

Circa 1940s: Jan Hendrik Hofmeyr was considered to be the political leader of South African liberalism until his untimely death at the age of 54.

retired. Hofmeyr's untimely death in 1948—the same year as the National Party's electoral victory over the United Party—represented a significant setback for liberalism in South Africa, and with him probably died any possibility of the United Party becoming more dependably liberal (Hughes 1994, 32–33; Robertson 1971, 27).

African National Congress prior to the 1940s

Despite its inherent appeal to nationalism, the African National Congress (ANC), which rules South Africa today, was a largely liberal organization from the time of its founding in 1912 to roughly the end of the 1940s. It advocated the removal of discriminatory government policy but tolerated a qualified franchise. Above all, it sought equal rights, including property rights, across racial lines (Robertson 1971, 28–29).

The ANC Youth League was founded in 1944. One of the founders, Jordan Kush Ngubane (1917–1985), said in a 1964 interview that he split with more militant elements within the League partly for "ideological reasons." He was from a family that owned land, with a traditionalist mother and a realist father. These influences made him become, in his own words, "a non-racialist and a liberal." His father, for instance, "rejected race as criterion by which to fix the position of the individual in society" (Ngubane 1964). Ngubane wrote that, "True liberalism recognises every man's right to a life of his own; to a culture of his own, so long as these do not constitute a threat to his fellowmen," and that liberalism was "the only philosophy on which we can build a lasting Union of South Africa" (Ngubane 1954).

Ngubane wrote that he "rejected Communism," "a foreign ideology." His own "liberal background," however, led him to stop short of expelling communists from the Youth League. He thought they, the liberals in the League, should instead come up with an idea more powerful than communism. A fellow Youth Leaguer, Anton Lembede, opted for Africanism, "a racially exclusive attitude among the Africans which would be similar to that of the Afrikaner nationalists," an idea that did not sit well with Ngubane. Some, like Ngubane, "wanted a liberal democratic republic," while others "preferred a socialist community." The differences between these groups would be set aside until the common enemy—the white government—was vanquished. Lembede "dis-

Circa 1940s–50s: Jordan Kush Ngubane was one of the liberals in the African National Congress in the 1940s. *Source*: Ntongela Masilela.

liked [Ngubane's] friendship with white men and women of liberal persuasion." But Ngubane was not prepared to consider all whites as "sinners"—he "did not wish to judge any human being as a member of a racial group." He thought that "the element of liberalism on the race question had always been an important ingredient in the makeup of African nationalism." Ngubane's thinking on what the liberation movement should have done is handily summarized in his own words: "Our task was to move events in the direction of our choice; to establish a new social order where liberty would mean the freedom to make the best possible use of our lives as human beings and not just as members of a particular racial group" (Ngubane 1963–64).

In 1961 Ngubane went into exile in Swaziland, before going on to lecture about Apartheid in the United States. By 1980, Ngubane had allied with Inkatha, the main black group opposing the African National Congress in South Africa (Ngubane 1980). His 1963 book, *An African Explains Apartheid*, contains a chapter titled "Communists versus Liberals," wherein he wrote about the impotence of the Liberal Party, which had been formed in 1952 to oppose Apartheid and promote full rights for all South Africans. It would dissolve five years later (Trewhela 2017).

Jan Smuts, while prime minister, was instrumental in drafting the World War II Atlantic Charter, a fact that gave liberals and the ANC hope that the United Party regime would soon adopt a policy resembling respect for equal rights. This was especially true after Smuts declared economic segregation impossible (Robertson 1971, 30). Smuts also composed the preamble to the United Nations Charter (Lewsen 1987, 108). Smuts was later evicted from power by the National Party, which turned "his international standing against him" and attacked him "for being under the sway of liberalism and for prioritizing his personal international reputation over white national interests" (Dubow 2019). But in reality, as Saul Dubow writes: "Smuts was nowhere as hard line as some of his white compatriots, but neither was he in favor of black political rights. Like many paternalistic and 'moderate' whites, he was inclined to defer problems of race equality to the future" (ibid.).

The ANC's proposed bills of rights in 1943 (Nthai 1998, 142) and 1945 (Robertson 1971, 31)[30] were inspired by the Atlantic Charter, thereby seeking, according to Janet Robertson, "freedoms which democrats outside South Africa regarded as inalienable rights" (ibid.). Importantly, the ANC wanted protection for the right to land ownership. Both the ANC's 1923 and 1943/ 1945 bills of rights sought the entrenchment of property rights as an individual right founded in the British common law tradition (Nthai 1998, 142–143).

Despite the ANC's early liberal and moderate character, white South Africans, including many white liberals, did not believe that fully extending political rights to blacks would end well for the rights of whites (Robertson 1971, 31). This attitude was largely in response to the views of the younger, more radical Africanist members of the anti-Apartheid movement, chiefly those in the ANC Youth League (ibid., 34). Immediately after the end of World War II, and the failure of the government to grant rights to the blacks who served in the armed forces, the ANC's character started to move away from moderate liberalism (Robertson 1971, 32) and toward cooperation with communists. That relationship persists to this day, and it has led to the effec-

---

30. Robertson quotes Carter (1958, 484–485).

tive end of liberalism within the ANC and to a break in the relationship between white liberals and the ANC.

Robertson usefully outlines the three reasons why the ANC warmed up to communism. First, the leadership of the Indian Congress in Natal was already communist, and Apartheid forced the ANC and the Indian Congress into a close relationship to resist racial discrimination. Second, the communists in South Africa did not act condescendingly toward black aspirations for equal—as opposed to "qualified"—rights. On this second reason, Robertson quotes Nelson Mandela at his terrorism trial in 1964:

> [F]or many decades communists were the only political group in South Africa who were prepared to treat Africans as human beings and their equals; who were prepared to eat with us; talk with us, live with us, and work with us. They were the only political group which was prepared to work with the Africans for the attainment of political rights and a stake in society. (Mandela 1964; quoted in Robertson 1971, 75)

Third, the government's clampdown on communism from 1950 onward with the Suppression of Communism Act was interpreted by the ANC as a thinly veiled attack on activism for equal rights between blacks and whites, rather than as only the suppression of communist ideology (Robertson 1971, 69–78). Thus, by 1965, liberals found themselves caught between the twin extremes of Afrikaner nationalism and black nationalism fused with communism, both of which were hostile to the values underlying a liberal democratic order (Spence 1965, 56).

Edgar Harry Brookes and the native representatives

Edgar Brookes (1897–1979) was a Liberal Party senator in Parliament for 15 years, representing the blacks of Zululand (Brookes 1956, 190) between 1937 and 1952. He was national chairman of the Liberal Party between 1963 and 1968 (Webb 1979, 40). In the Senate, he edified the chamber with Institute of Race Relations reports, himself having been a co-founder of that organization and its president in 1933. Brookes likened "himself to a second-rate J. H. Hofmeyr," referring to the historical leader of South African liberals whom he greatly admired (Webb 1979, 39). Although less critical of government policy than were Margaret Ballinger and Donald Molteno, his counterpart native representatives in the House of Assembly, by 1947

Brookes had demanded qualified common roll franchise for black South Africans at every level of government (Lewsen 1987, 102). That is, black South Africans would be part of the general electoral list rather than be limited to electoral rolls defined by race.

Ballinger (1894–1980) had represented blacks in the lower house of Parliament from 1938 until 1960, the entire period during which the native representative system was in operation (Robertson 1971, 26). Ballinger was an economic historian at the University of the Witwatersrand who had a track record of work in the black community (Lewsen 1987, 101). She was a founding member and early leader of the Liberal Party. Another liberal associated with the IRR, J. D. R. Jones, represented the blacks of the Transvaal and Orange Free State provinces in the Senate between 1938 and 1943 (Robertson 1971, 26).

Liberalism in the United Party (1934–1959)

The United Party (UP) had traditionally been the political home of English-speaking South Africans, and, as a result that of liberal South Africans, as the bulk of liberals had been English. While it did falter substantively and often on the question of race relations—which perhaps did not have a simple solution, since immediate and unqualified universal suffrage might have entailed its own dangers to liberal democracy—the UP did have notable liberal characteristics. It sought a limited government that did not infringe too wantonly on individual liberty and maintained the rule of law and constitutionalism (Robertson 1971, 15–16). Chiefly, it sought the protection of *existing* rights, and did so admirably during the 1950s constitutional crisis (Robertson 1971, 42). The rule of law "is fundamental to freedom, and freedom is fundamental to the good life," wrote Brookes and MacAulay. It was undermined during the Apartheid era because the destinies of millions of South Africans were placed in the hands of a "thousand petty tyrants"—ordinary officials with virtually unlimited discretion—without effective control by the courts (Brookes and MacAulay 1958, 26).

In the late 1930s, the UP increased state benefits for many blacks: a housing and pension scheme, grants for education and welfare, an agreement by Jan Smuts to recognize black trade unions, and higher wages for blacks working on the railways. In 1942, the minister of native affairs, Deneys Reitz, attacked the pass law system, hinting at its potential future abolition (Lewsen

1987, 104–105).

The tumultuous history of the United Party and the Progressive Party's attempt to advocate liberalism in white politics is well chronicled by Ray Swart in his 1991 book *Progressive Odyssey*, which is an important source for the pages ahead. Swart was a rebel member of the United Party, and his book reflects close familiarity with its past. As we will see, the Progressive Party broke away from the United Party in 1959, became the Progressive Reform Party in 1975, then the Progressive Federal Party in 1977, and, finally, in 1989, the Democratic Party. The modern Democratic Alliance, established in 2000, was based on the Democratic Party plus two other parties.

The United Party was for many years, before 1948, the governing party of South Africa, and for many years thereafter the official opposition. It would be incorrect, however, to consider the UP as the liberal alternative to the racist National Party. The UP, instead, was a big-tent organization (Swart 1991, 23), with a run-of-the-mill, generally Afrikaner wing that agreed, in principle, with legalized and systematic racial discrimination. Indeed, Swart, a new young parliamentarian in the UP in the late 1950s, relates how a senior UP official admonished him for waving a greeting to black children (ibid., 13).

Lewsen (1987, 110) writes that conservative segregationists made up the majority of the rank-and-file of the United Party, even though it had notable liberal-spirited leaders and representatives. The UP also broadly supported the intentions of various pieces of Apartheid legislation, but opposed the means they sought to employ. On the Prohibition of Mixed Marriages Act, for instance, Robertson relates how many in the UP were opposed to mixed marriages but felt that legislation was not needed. Robertson attributes this to the UP's support for the rule of law—i.e., the notion that government officials must not have broadly defined discretions stated in vague legislation. The UP opposed the Suppression of Communism Act not because the UP welcomed communists, but because the law assigned sweeping powers of political suppression to the minister of the interior (Robertson 1971, 45–47).

The UP also had a centrist faction that consisted primarily of English South Africans who simply feared living under a system of Afrikaner nationalism outside the British Commonwealth, and a small wing that was liberal on questions of race (Spence 1965, 61). Because of the performances of both the conservatives and the liberals of the UP in parliamentary debates, the party was often accused of speaking with two voices (Swart 1991, 28). Because of its lack of a coherent, direction-giving philosophy, the UP would during the 1960s and 1970s lose its right wing to the National Party. And earlier, in 1959, Swart and others in the centrist and left factions broke away from the UP to form the Progressive Party, which had as a core policy pillar the rejection of racial discrimination and an insistence on equal opportunities and a common franchise (ibid., 9). What had united the United Party was opposition, for different reasons, to the National Party (ibid., 14).

So the UP was not entirely illiberal. In fact, Jan Smuts, as prime minister, addressed the staunchly liberal IRR in February 1942 and acknowledged that segregation had failed because of economic reasons. Many liberals believed that gradually the UP would adopt a more racially inclusive policy, especially in light of the fact that its racial policy at the time was already far more inclusive than that of the National Party (Robertson 1971, 24).

The liberal backbench of the UP right after the watershed 1953 general election[31] was composed of Jan Steytler, Helen Suzman, Owen Townley Williams, Sakkies Fourie, John Cope, Zach de Beer, and Ray Swart (Swart 1991, 14, 21–22). Another MP, Bernard Friedman, had sympathies with this clique, as did the business mogul and MP Harry Oppenheimer (ibid., 35).[32] After the 1958 general election they were joined by Clive van Ryneveld, Boris Wilson, and Colin Eglin. It was only in the 1958 general election that the National Party secured a majority of votes from the white electorate. In the two previous elections the UP was the largest party, but the majority of votes were split among the opposition parties (ibid., 44).

In the late 1950s these younger, more liberal backbenchers tended to be shunned by the UP's old guard, even though the party required their energy and talents to be blended with the experience of the senior members if it hoped to be successful (Swart 1991, 32–33). The UP was known in the 1950s for "the equivocation inherent in the party's approach to matters of principle," which ultimately led to the formation of the Progressive Party

---

31. This was the election immediately following the National Party's victory over the United Party in 1948 (the year described as the beginning of Apartheid). The United Party had strong hopes that it would oust the Nationalists in 1953, but this was not to be. UP leaders, after this election was lost, seemed to resign themselves to the fact that the NP would remain in power for some time to come.

32. Oppenheimer also contributed funds to the founding of the Free Market Foundation (Louw 2011).

(ibid., 36). Perhaps ironically, the Progressive Party's big-tent successor in recent times, the Democratic Alliance, is also known among liberals for often being equivocal and having a turbulent relationship with principle (Gon 2019; Berger 2018).

Harry Lawrence, a UP frontbencher from the days of the old South African Party, also counted himself among the liberals' ranks, and along with Steytler was the most senior liberal in the party. In a June 1959 letter to the UP leader, Sir De Villiers Graaff, for instance, Lawrence said that time was running out for white South Africans to find a peaceful and equitable way of living with non-whites:

> If my premises are accepted, then Verwoerd's aims [viz., Apartheid] require the posing of a clear alternative—an alternative, moreover, which must rest on sound moral and ethical grounds, which must not involve permanent discrimination for all time. (Lawrence, quoted in Barnard and Marais 1982, 110–113)

At the August 1959 UP Union Congress[33] in Bloemfontein, the liberals were openly treated as pariahs and hissed as they went to the podium to speak. The leader of the liberal wing, Jan Steytler, was to be the chair of the congress because that office rotated among the provincial leaders of the party. Steytler was the head of the party in the Cape Province. A delegate at the congress objected to this by way of a point of order, asking whether it was appropriate for a liberal to chair the occasion. A large number of delegates applauded the objection, showing the level of contempt in which the liberals were held, but eventually Steytler was allowed to take the chair. While the party formally wished to keep its liberal wing to ensure it sustained its dominance of urban centers, the liberals' attempts to reform the party from within along more tolerant lines was treated with contempt. Such occurrences at the congress made the liberals believe their future in the UP to be precarious (Swart 1991, 53). The decisions taken at the Union Congress and the UP's lack of coherent race policy finally sparked the resignation of the liberals from the party, and soon thereafter they resolved to establish a new political party (ibid., 53, 64).

Swart was the first rebel from the UP to address a public meeting, in Eshowe, Natal. Similar meetings were held by the other dissidents in their

---

33. The annual Union Congress was the UP's highest decision-making body.

own locales to explain why they had resigned from the UP but intended to keep their parliamentary seats (Swart 1991, 66–67). At Eshowe and elsewhere motions of confidence in such individual liberal dissidents were passed. Motions of no confidence, on the other hand, were routinely defeated, except when the UP succeeded in packing a meeting in Empangeni and narrowly passed a vote of no confidence in Swart. The UP, however, knew that the liberals had significant support in those constituencies. The English newspaper media, which have historically associated with the UP as opposed to the Afrikaans newspapers, which supported the National Party, proved sympathetic to the liberals, with the popular *Rand Daily Mail* going as far as outright support (ibid., 67–69, 71).

Liberal Party (1953–1968)

The Liberal Party was founded in 1953 on the tenet that "non-racialism is the only sure foundation for a multi-racial society of such complexity" as South Africa. It sought the non-racial extension of "full political, social, and individual rights to all adult South Africans." The Liberals rejected the qualified franchise, color bars, and authoritarian government (Paton 2011).

Initially, the Liberals sought to participate in white electoral politics, but due to the party's failure to make any inroads, it adopted electoral boycott as a legitimate means of pursuing political change (O'Malley 1988, 32). Only its white

The Liberal Party was a non-racial party from its founding in 1953 to its disbandment in 1968. *Source*: Wikimedia Commons.

"native representatives" in Parliament, who were either appointed by the government or elected by blacks, could act as the party's bridge into government. But the party lost these seats when black South Africans were deprived of their white representatives in 1959, and it was robbed of the majority of its grassroots members—blacks—when mixed racial membership of parties was outlawed in 1968 (Hughes 1994, 38–40). The Liberal Party voted to disband itself after mixed racial membership in political parties was outlawed, as it did not wish to comply with legislation that offended its core principles (South African History Online 2012a).

Cardo says of the Liberal and the Progressive parties that the Liberal

Party was largely progressive, in that it pushed for state-provided welfare, and the Progressive Party on the other hand was largely liberal, in that it focused on civil rights (Cardo 2012, 19–20). Hughes, on the other hand, describes the early Liberal Party as focusing public attention on "the core classical liberal values," including "strict adherence to the rule of law and Parliamentary democracy as the primary institutional guarantees of the liberty of the individual." He goes so far as to write that in the face of South Africa's realities, the party "never transcended its preoccupation with classical liberal principle." By 1963, however, the party appointed a commission to reconsider the party's identity as the organization shifted focus to "social and distributive justice" (Hughes 1994, 35, 37).

Progressive Party (1959–1975)

While the Liberal Party was multi-racial, with most members black (Hughes 1994, 38), the Progressive Party consciously decided to direct its attention at the white electorate where political power legally resided, in order to convince that electorate to shun prejudice and embrace individual freedom (Swart 1991, 11). The Progressive Party was formally launched on 13–14 November 1959 at the Cranbrook Hotel in Hillbrow, Johannesburg. The inaugural congress attracted 300 delegates. Jan Steytler was elected unanimously as the party leader, and former UP stalwart Harry Lawrence became the national chairman (ibid., 75–76, 79–80). The party's basic principles were:

- The maintenance and extension of the values of Western Civilisation, the protection of fundamental human rights and the safeguard of the dignity and worth of the human person, irrespective of race, colour or creed.
- The assurance that no citizen of the Union of South Africa shall be debarred on grounds of race, religion, language or sex, from making the contribution to our national life of which he or she may be capable.
- The recognition that in the Union of South Africa there is one nation which embraces various groups differing in race, religions, language and traditions; that each such group is entitled to the protection of these things and to participate in the government of

the nation; and that understanding, tolerance and goodwill between the different groups must be fostered.

- The maintenance inviolate of the Rule of Law.
- The promotion of social progress and the improvement of living standards through the energetic development of a modern economy based on free enterprise, whereby the national resources of men and materials can be fully utilised.
- The promotion of friendly relations with other nations, more particularly the members of the Commonwealth and those who share with us the heritage of Western Civilisation. (Kruger 1960, 105)

It was also decided at the inaugural congress that a commission would be established that would draw up proposals for a new constitution for South Africa. This constitution would bring about non-racialism in governance and entrench individual rights, which were absent from the 1910 Constitution (Swart 1991, 77–78). Donald Molteno was a constitutional lawyer and civil rights champion at the time of the founding of the Progressive Party and joined the party to chair its constitutional policy commission.[34] He was previously a native representative in the House of Assembly.

1960: The parliamentary caucus of the Progressive Party. Left to right: Walter Stanford, Ray Swart, Harry Lawrence, Clive van Ryneveld, Boris Wilson, John Cope, Jan Steytler, Zach de Beer, Helen Suzman, Ronald Butcher, Colin Eglin, and Owen Williams. *Source*: Wikimedia Commons.

Molteno grew up in Cape Town with a tradition of liberalism in his family (Lewsen 1987, 101).

Douglas Mitchell, a conservative United Party frontbencher considered to

---

34. Other commissioners on the party's constitutional commission included the former chief justice of South Africa, Albert Centlivres, native representative Edgar Brookes, judge Leslie Blackwell, businessman Harry Oppenheimer, Selby Ngcobo, Richard van der Ross, Eugene Marais, former UP leader Koos Strauss, and Kenneth Heard (Swart 1991, 80).

have been a leading cause for the breakaway of the Progressives, had this to say about the split in the UP:

> No, I don't take the blame for kicking out the Progressives. I take the credit. We must always have a political rubbish bin on our left in South Africa into which all the curious people with their curious political ideas can be safely packed together. Indeed, I go further and say that if there was no such a thing called the Progressive Party it would have paid us in the United Party to have manufactured such a political creature to have on our left otherwise we would become the party of the left. (quoted in Barnard and Marais 1982, 135)

Despite Mitchell's elation, S. L. Barnard and A. H. Marais opine that the liberal rebellion was one of the worst setbacks the UP experienced during its existence. There were liberals who remained in the UP, however, who did not want to give the conservatives the pleasure of thinking they had scored a victory over the progressive cause. This group of liberals—known as the "Young Turks"—would be relevant again in the 1970s, when they joined the Progressives after a brief period as the independent Reform Party (Barnard and Marais 1982, 136).

Disaster for South Africa and the Progressives in the 1960s

On 21 March 1960, there was protest throughout the country against the so-called pass and influx control laws, which excluded blacks from so-called white areas unless they possessed a pass book with the necessary stamps and permits from employers and government officials. Thousands were arrested across the country, but the black township of Sharpeville was where the unrest came to a head: the South African Police shot and killed 68 people in Sharpeville.

The government imposed press censorship around these events, but it could not censor Parliament, where freedom of expression was absolute. The Progressives thus used their parliamentary podium to keep the public informed about what was going on, while calling for restraint on the part of the police. The Progressives had opposed the pass law system as "an unjustifiable invasion of personal liberty" (Swart 1991, 84–85).

Days after the Sharpeville massacre, the government introduced the Unlawful Organisations Act, which banned the African National Congress and the Pan-Africanist Congress, which were behind the demonstrations. The Progressives opposed this legislation as well. Steytler said in Parliament that the law would simply drive the ANC and PAC underground and lead to violent fanaticism—something that proved to be true as the years went on (Swart 1991, 86).

After South Africa became a republic in 1961, independent of the British Commonwealth,[35] it became "more important than ever" for the Progressives to mobilize white liberals in opposition to the Nationalists' racial Apartheid platform (Swart 1991, 90). It was around this time—the 1960s—that the UP finally abandoned any pretense of liberalism, joining the National Party in condemning those foreign countries that criticized domestic South African political arrangements (Robertson 1971, 42). But while the Progressives did operate exclusively within formal white electoral politics, the party engaged in cross-racial dialogues from its overriding commitment to creating a non-racial society (Swart 1991, 73–74).

The general election of 1961, however, spelled disaster for the Progressives, who retained only one seat in Parliament, down from ten (Swart 1991, 97). This seat was held by Helen Suzman, who would be the lone Progressive member of Parliament for the next thirteen years. Swart (ibid., 102) provides highlights of what Suzman stood for as the sole representative of South African liberalism in Parliament:

- Abolition of detention without trial
- Abolition of pass laws and influx control
- Abolition of job reservations on the basis of race
- Recognition of trade unions with mixed racial profiles
- Abolition of separate amenities and the Group Areas laws
- Abolition of the forced removals system
- Better wages and working conditions for the poor

Suzman's performance in Parliament won her admiration from the coloured community, which was entitled to political representation in the Provincial

---

35. The National Party resolved in 1941 that only the approval of the white population should be necessary for South Africa to become a republic without a British connection. Prior to 1941, the party's platform said it would only take South Africa to republican status under a Nationalist government if it was the "people's will" (Malan 1964, 292).

Council of the Cape Province and to four seats—represented by whites—in Parliament. Coloureds were placed on a separate voters' roll from whites after being disenfranchised during the constitutional crisis of the 1950s, and as such had to be politically represented by whites.

In the 1964 provincial elections, two Progressives were elected to the Cape Provincial Council representing the coloureds, and it was likely that the Progressives would also receive the four seats contested on the coloureds' voters' roll in Parliament in the 1966 election. The Progressives had not contested those seats because of their opposition to the separate representation system, but it appeared that the coloured community desired representation. With the potential of having to deal with a renewed Progressive caucus in Parliament joining Suzman, however, the National Party introduced legislation that prohibited political parties from having mixed racial constituencies, and also abolished the coloureds' representation in Parliament in favor of a separate Coloured Representative Council (Swart 1991, 109–110).

In 1970, Swart became chairman of the National Executive of the Progressive Party, and Colin Eglin became the party leader (Swart 1991, 112). In 1973, the Progressive Party hosted the Bulugha Conference in the Ciskei homeland with leaders of all the major non-banned black, Indian, and coloured groups, with liberal whites. The result of the conference was a declaration in favor of a non-racial federal system with a bill of rights that protects individual rights and outlaws discrimination (ibid., 117).

Shortly thereafter, the government set up a commission to investigate various liberal civil society organizations, specifically the National Union of South African Students, the Christian Institute, the IRR, and the University Christian Movement. The United Party, to the condemnation of the English press, liberals around the country, and those few liberals among their own ranks, participated in this commission's proceedings (Barnard and Marais 1982, 220). Swart considered the work of this commission to be a witch hunt against those who opposed Apartheid, and the press at the time likened it to McCarthyism. The UP's participation in the commission further evidenced its abandonment of liberalism, and this close cooperation with the National Party likely contributed to the UP's demise (Swart 1991, 120).

The Young Turks and the 1974 election

At the same time, a liberal coup was staged in the UP's Transvaal Province branch by the so-called "Young Turks" of the party, led by Harry Schwarz. The individualist Young Turks ousted the conservative Transvaal leader of the UP, Marais Steyn, at the party's 1973 provincial congress. Schwarz was not on good terms with the Progressive Party, but they did share common views on matters of racial policy. A year later, for instance, Schwarz and Mangosuthu Buthelezi, then chief minister of the KwaZulu homeland and today leader of the Inkatha Freedom Party, co-signed the Mahlabatini Declaration of Faith, in which they resolved that South Africa should adopt a federal constitution that guaranteed equal rights and limited government (Swart 1991, 120–121; Dhlamini 2017).

Harry Schwarz, once leader of the UP in the Transvaal, prominent member of the future Progressive Federal Party, and ambassador to the United States between 1991 and 1995. *Source*: Wikimedia Commons.

While the Schwarz faction and the Progressive Party were in talks, the 1974 general election was announced. The Progressives' financial and human resources situation had greatly improved from 1970, and the electoral climate was also more favorable. Against even the most optimistic expectations, the Progressive Party attained six seats in total. A seventh Progressive was added to Parliament in a by-election shortly after the general election (Swart 1991, 123, 127).

Schwarz and the Young Turks founded the Reform Party in February 1975 after breaking away from the United Party. Because they already controlled the Transvaal branch of the UP, the Reform Party became the official opposition in the Transvaal Provincial Council as all ten UP members became Reformists. The Reform Party was always intended to be a mechanism through which the Young Turks could enter into talks with the Progressive Party with a view toward amalgamation. In the lead-up to such talks, Swart notes one attitude within the Progressive Party at the time:

> There was a deep concern within our ranks that in our attempts to broaden
> our base by forging links with others who had opposed us through the years,

in hope of winning more support from amongst the white electorate, our political thrust as a tough-principled anti-racist group might become diluted and that we would fall to temptations of political expediency. (Swart 1991, 129)[36]

Progressive Reform Party (1975–1977)

Although the Progressive Party endorsed the qualified franchise, many members acknowledged that the principle of universal franchise would need to be adopted sooner rather than later, within the framework, they hoped, of a constitution that protected individual rights and barred racial discrimination. The Reform Party also supported universal franchise, and the two parties looked to merge. There was also some quibbling over what the name of the newly merged party would be (Swart 1991, 129–130).

The two parties congressed simultaneously in Johannesburg in 1975. It was agreed that should each party's congress adopt the details of the proposed merger, the congresses would merge into one inaugural congress of the new Progressive Reform Party (PRP), which indeed transpired. Eglin would remain party leader, Swart would remain national chairman, and Schwarz would become chairman of the National Executive (Swart 1991, 130–133).

Shortly after the PRP's establishment, it won its first by-election in Durban North, with Harry Pitman becoming the eighth Progressive to sit in Parliament. This was the Progressives' first victorious incursion into the UP stronghold of the Natal Province. As Swart notes pertinently, however, the liberals' political success was of "symbolic rather than practical" significance to the black majority, who were still locked out of South African politics. The Progressives were only making progress against the weak UP opposition rather than the relatively strong National Party government (Swart 1991, 137–138).

Progressive Federal Party (1977–1989)

In 1977, the UP finally met its end after merging with the small Democratic Party and forming the New Republic Party (NRP). Many sitting United Party

---

36. It is today believed by some that the Democratic Alliance—the Progressive Party's descendant—has in fact been so tempted by political expediency and has largely abandoned its classical liberal roots in its attempts to appeal to the black electorate (Van der Westhuizen 2018).

members, among them Japie Basson, Nic Olivier, Derek de Villiers, and Gavin McIntosh, were unhappy with this decision and instead decided to join the Progressive Reform Party. It rebranded again, becoming the Progressive Federal Party (PFP), with the controversial political chameleon Basson becoming the deputy national chairman.[37] The party's position on the franchise was then subjected to a review commission chaired by Frederik van Zyl Slabbert. In September 1978, the commission made its proposals, and the PFP adopted them. The Progressive policy was now one of non-racial universal franchise within a strong federal system, thereby abandoning the qualified education and property franchise that had characterized the Cape liberal tradition for a century (Swart 1991, 149).

Swart beat the leader of the newly formed New Republic Party, Radclyffe Cadman, in the Durban Musgrave constituency during the 1977 election. The Progressives replaced the NRP as the largest opposition party in Parliament, winning 17 seats to the NRP's ten. The National Party increased its majority (Swart 1991, 143–145).

By 1977, however, Nationalist dedication to the Apartheid idea was falling apart due to the policy's obvious unworkability and the violent protests that had erupted throughout the country against it. The government went about trying to adapt Apartheid while enacting ever more stringent security measures to ensure law and order (Swart 1991, 147). The political establishment's abandonment of Apartheid as an ideology, in favor of a kind of pragmatism, was becoming increasingly apparent (Kane-Berman 2017, x). Kierin O'Malley writes that the Progressives' victories in the 1970s flowed principally from the demise of the UP and the breakdown of "monolithic Afrikanerdom" (O'Malley 1994, 32).[38]

The Progressive Federal Party was the political home of white South African liberalism. *Source*: Wikimedia Commons.

---

37. Basson began his political career in the National Party, then started his own National Union in 1960, then joined the United Party in 1961, then the Progressive Federal Party in 1977, and finally rejoined the National Party in the mid-1980s.

38. Here O'Malley was likely referring to the fact that Afrikaners were no longer only represented by the National Party in national politics, in light of the emergence of the popular

In September 1979, the academic Frederik van Zyl Slabbert became the leader of the Progressive Federal Party, replacing Colin Eglin, who became national chairman in the place of Swart.[39] Slabbert was a well-credentialed Afrikaner schooled in the conservative far north of the country, with a degree from Stellenbosch University. That he was now the face of "liberal values in white parliamentary politics" led to consternation on the part of his Nationalist opponents (Swart 1991, 156–157). Slabbert's leadership proved productive, as the PFP increased its representation in Parliament from 17 to 27 in the 1981 general election. The liberals, despite this victory, still feared that it might have been too late for liberalism to gain support among white South Africans, given that the conflict between whites and blacks was reaching a boiling point (ibid., 160).

To make Apartheid seem more acceptable, the Nationalists proposed what would become the Tricameral Parliament in 1984, a legislature consisting of three houses constituted along racial lines: one for whites, one for coloureds, and one for Indians. Blacks were excluded because the Nationalists argued that their political and constitutional activities were sufficiently accommodated in their homelands. The Progressives opposed the idea of a tricameral legislature, dismissing it as a sham in light of the facts that blacks were excluded and that whites would retain political supremacy even if both other houses voted against a measure. In the following white referendum to approve or reject the new constitution, the National Party government used state resources like public broadcasters to promote the new composition of Parliament, putting the opposition at a disadvantage. Sixty-six percent of the white electorate approved the 1984 Constitution, and the Tricameral Parliament was inaugurated (Swart 1991, 161–164).

The Progressives now faced an old liberal dilemma: should they participate in a fundamentally illegitimate system in order to reform it from within, or boycott the system knowing that the void will be filled by others? The PFP decided to continue serving in this flawed Parliament (Swart 1991, 165). To their credit, the Progressives and the anti-Apartheid movement succeeded in convincing the government to repeal measures that banned political race mixing, to relax strict labor laws and regulations, and to abolish pass laws and

---

Conservative Party of Andries Treurnicht and to a lesser extent the Reconstituted National Party of Albert Hertzog.

39. Swart was chosen as the leader of the party in the Natal Province in 1980.

relax influx control (ibid., 175).

Slabbert's unhappiness with the effectiveness of opposition within white parliamentary politics wore heavily on him, and the Progressives' ambivalence toward the 1984 Constitution led to his and Alex Boraine's resignations in 1986 (O'Malley 1994, 33). They went on to establish the Institute for a Democratic Alternative for South Africa (IDASA), which would play an influential role in the remainder of the struggle against Apartheid (Swart 1991, 181).

The resignation of the popular Slabbert signaled a downturn for liberal politics. In the 1987 election the PFP lost six seats in Parliament, losing its position as official opposition in the process. The New Republic Party, the successor to the once-dominant UP of Jan Smuts, was reduced to having only one seat in Parliament. But these losses for the liberals did not mean the Nationalists gained, for this time the Conservative Party, which thought the National Party itself had become too liberal on the race question, sailed into the slot of official opposition (Swart 1991, 191).

By the end of the 1980s, the situation in South Africa was critical. Large parts of the country had been under an almost continuous state of emergency from July 1985, a state of affairs that only ended in June 1990 (South African History Online 2012b). The tumult combined with international sanctions led many to believe that there would be no return to normalcy (Swart 1991, 197–198).

Democratic Party (1989–2000)

Delegates at the 1988 Federal Congress of the Progressive Federal Party were eager for closer cooperation with two new independent parliamentary groups, the Independent Party of Denis Worrall and the National Democratic Movement of Wynand Malan (Swart 1991, 198). Various *verligte* ("enlightened") Afrikaners, mostly associated with the National Party, were also involved in the negotiations that followed. The PFP's principles were accepted as the basis of the new Democratic Party, founded on 7 April 1989. The co-leaders of the party would be Zach de Beer, Worrall, and Malan (ibid., 199–201).

At the same time, the National Party itself started adopting positions historically advanced by liberals, now realizing that keeping South Africa committed to Apartheid would be disastrous. Such was the agenda of Frederik

Willem de Klerk, the reformist and pragmatist National Party leader (Swart 1991, 200). His predecessor Pieter Willem Botha had declared at the opening of Parliament in 1986:

> We believe in the sovereignty of the law as a basis for the protection of the fundamental rights of individuals as well as groups. We believe in the sanctity and indivisibility of law and the just application thereof. ... We believe that human dignity, life, liberty and property of all must be protected, regardless of colour, race, creed or religion. (quoted in Du Toit 1988, 240–241)[40]

The last general election to take place in Apartheid South Africa was on 6 September 1989. The strife within the National Party between the reformist faction of De Klerk and the conservative faction, combined with the ailing state of the economy as well as the relative principledness of its opponents, led to the Nationalists losing much ground to the Conservative and Democratic parties. The Conservatives, still the official opposition, won 39 seats and the Democrats 33, with the latter up from 21 in the 1987 election. The National Party lost 29 seats, but still emerged victorious with 94 total seats. This was the first time since the 1961 election that the Nationalists received less than 50 percent of the vote—having taken 48.2 percent. Nonetheless De Klerk, now state president, considered his party's victory as an endorsement of his reformist agenda, and he pressed forward (Swart 1991, 202).

On 2 February 1990, what could be described as the death of Apartheid occurred, when De Klerk announced the unbanning of the African National Congress and other anti-Apartheid groups, as well as the releasing of Nelson Mandela from prison. By this time, various Apartheid laws and restrictions had been repealed, with more repealed thereafter. These actions paved the way for the Convention for a Democratic South Africa (CODESA) and the first multi-racial democratic elections on 27 April 1994. The Nationalists had by now adopted practically every substantial proposal made by liberals throughout South Africa's history, at least in principle. In 1994, the Democratic Party itself attracted less than 5 percent of national popular support according to survey data and received only 1.73 percent of the vote in the April elections. But the former chief opponents of liberalism—Afrikaner and

---

40. Du Toit cites the parliamentary Hansard: *House of Assembly Debates* 31/1/1986.

black nationalists—had adopted many liberal values during the transitional period (Hughes 1994, viii). At the time, the Institute of Race Relations considered the Democratic Party as "the oldest party-political vehicle for liberalism in South Africa" (Kane-Berman 1994, 1).

O'Malley makes the point that even though liberals thought their work to be over by the mid-1990s, that was incorrect. During the years approaching the start of the political transition in 1990, liberals suffered political defeat after defeat. It was the left that had forced the situation:

> The [National Party's] sudden adoption in the early 1990s of many of the liberal policies of the [Democratic Party] was thus not a voluntary and considered adoption of liberal policies, but a forced retreat from a defeated ideological position towards the centre. (O'Malley 1994, 33)

Helen Suzman disputed O'Malley's characterization of political liberalism as a failure, given how the Progressives had achieved the status of official opposition within Parliament at one stage and that the party was largely responsible for the acceptance of the notions of a bill of rights, universal suffrage, and freedom of expression (Kane-Berman 1994, 41).

In a June 1995 speech in Parliament, the Democratic parliamentarian Tony Leon said that there was "clear blue water" separating the National and Democratic parties, not simply because the parties had long disagreed about key policy issues, but because they had fundamentally different political philosophies. For the Nationalists after the end of Apartheid, their core philosophy was built around the notion of power-sharing. The Democrats, on the other hand, placed "the liberty of the individual as the highest priority of public policy" (Leon 1998, 34). A year later, Leon became the leader of the Democratic Party, "introducing a more aggressive approach to opposition politics." The DP became the official opposition again in 1999, reclaiming the position they lost in 1987 as a result of this new approach and the NP's growing irrelevance (Brand South Africa 2014). Helen Suzman wrote that Leon stood squarely in the South African liberal tradition, having "a staunch commitment to civil rights and to the rule of law, and a total opposition to racial discrimination" (Suzman 1998, ix).

The Democratic Party's support grew quickly among white South Africans (Kenny 2019). The National Party now all but disintegrated as its historical purpose—Apartheid—was gone. The Democratic Party, under the leadership of Leon, was aggressively liberal and rejected the ANC's new affirmative action policies on that basis. Former white Nationalist supporters now largely became Democratic Party supporters. In 2000, the "New" National Party, the Federal Alliance, and the Democratic Party merged to form the Democratic Alliance.[41]

Democratic Alliance (2000–present)

Leon Louw, executive director of the Free Market Foundation, described the Democratic Alliance (DA) as the "more pro-market, capitalist, classical liberal" political party in South Africa (Louw 2011). Indeed, shortly after the Democratic Alliance was created in 2000, it included in its statement of principles freedom of expression and association, a dedication to the rule of law, federalism, an independent and vibrant civil society, a free enterprise economy, and the right to private property (Democratic Alliance 2000).

In November 2018, the Friedrich Naumann Stiftung awarded the Democratic Alliance its 2018 African Freedom Award. The DA's leader since 2015, Mmusi Maimane said, in accepting the award, that the DA had "been fighting for a free and open society with opportunities for all for the past 60 years." He said that liberals have "to become a lot better at crafting and explaining liberal solutions." He criticized the government's policies of expropriation of property without compensation, free university education, and the proposed nationalizations of healthcare, the information technology sector, and the Reserve Bank, pointing to Venezuela and Zimbabwe as examples where similar ideologies had failed. Maimane (2018a) has written that for the Democratic Alliance a prosperous society can only arise "in a liberal democracy with a market economy, a capable state, a zero tolerance for corruption and a Constitution that guarantees its people their rights, including the right to own property."

The DA has had remarkable electoral successes in a country often thought to be dominated by one party. In the 2006 municipal elections, the DA took control of the city of Cape Town, where the South African Parliament is based. It governs the city to this day. The former journalist, Helen Zille, became the mayor of Cape Town, the first time any liberal party in South

---

41. The NNP and FA later "left" the merger, but many of their members remained, and the new DA name was kept. The NNP merged with the ANC in 2005.

Africa governed a major city. In the same year, Tony Leon declined to run for the position of leader again, with Zille being elected. Zille won the World Mayor prize in 2008, the only time the prize has been bestowed upon a mayor of an African city.[42]

In the 2009 general election, the DA was elected as the government of the Western Cape Province, which it has governed since then with an outright majority in each successive election. The provincial government and municipalities in the Western Cape have received successive clean audits from the Auditor General on financial management, outperforming all other provinces in South Africa (Winde 2019).

In the 2016 municipal elections, the Alliance won pluralities in the cities of Port Elizabeth, Pretoria, and Johannesburg under Maimane's leadership. The coalition government in Port Elizabeth fell apart soon thereafter and was returned to effective ANC rule, but the DA remains in power in Pretoria and Johannesburg today as the result of an informal and precarious arrangement with the Marxist-Leninist party, the Economic Freedom Fighters. Through 2014, the DA had gained in every national general election since 1994: 1.7 percent in 1994, around 10 percent in 1999 when it became the official opposition, 12.4 percent in 2004, 16.6 percent in 2009, and 22.2 percent in 2014. But the DA has been the subject of intense criticism from contemporary classical liberals, especially in recent times. In the 2019 general election the DA attained 20.8 percent of the vote—the first time since 1994 it had lost voter share (Johnson 2019).

At a 2015 meeting of the DA caucus in Johannesburg, Paul Pereira said that "when messages become blurred, when a pursuit of electoral reward trumps common sense and political principles," the DA could destroy itself, which he felt was in progress at the time. The DA, noted Pereira, had already flip-flopped on racial policies in defiance of its colorblind tradition (Pereira 2015). Andrew Kenny (2019) has said that after Tony Leon left the DA as leader in 2003, the party "began to stray from its liberal values," became apologetic, and adopted affirmative action and Black Economic Empowerment into its policies, thereby becoming an "ANC-lite," "in the hope of appealing to ordinary black people." Frans Cronje (2019b) later

---

42. The prize is awarded biennially by the City Mayors Foundation, a London-based think tank.

accused the DA of "jettisoning" its liberal heritage.

Even among the party leadership all has not been well. On 20 March 2017, the popular former leader of the DA, Helen Zille, herself a social democrat (see Zille 2013, xi), warned that the DA might, as it tried to secure more black votes, "start to swallow every tenet, myth and shibboleth of African racial-nationalist propaganda, including the scape-goating of minorities, populist mobilization and political patronage" (Zille 2017). Zille was that same week penalized by the DA for innocuously noting that Singapore, a former colony of Britain, had in part benefited from being a colony. She said it was incorrect to claim that the legacy of colonialism was purely negative. Maimane responded by referring Zille to a disciplinary hearing and said Zille's views were inconsistent with the party's values (Mngadi 2017). The settlement subsequently reached between Zille and the party was that she would, and did, apologize for her remarks, and that she would no longer participate in DA political activities (*News24* 2017).

An historical contrast may be helpful: at the Progressive Party's inaugural congress in 1959, it became clear that liberal South Africans who were involved in the party would not be whipped into line. Leadership and party positions could be criticized, making the party dynamic with a "healthy, enquiring, and individualistic attitude" (Swart 1991, 77). The contemporary DA, however, shows much less tolerance for public disagreements with leadership figures (Cele 2019).

In the days leading up to the 2019 general election, the IRR's Gareth van Onselen accused Maimane of leading the DA down a "vacuous, ambiguous, directionless and anti-intellectual" path. Van Onselen continued that Maimane and the DA had abandoned the battle of ideas and opted to give the "[African National Congress's] ideas a fresh coat of paint, and present them as [their] own." Through all these criticisms, however, the DA's leadership holds fast that the party represents liberal values "that put the individual first" (Van Onselen 2019). Maimane (2018b) says the DA "will never abandon [its] liberal values." In May 2019, after the DA's disappointing showing in the 2019 general elections, Zille (2019), who was DA leader between 2007 and 2015, acknowledged that she had played a role in having the DA join the racial-nationalist narrative, and she apologized for it.

Conclusion

South Africa during Apartheid has often been described as fascistic, undemocratic, and authoritarian. Whilst this is accurate to an extent, it ignores some nuances. South Africa during Apartheid was not a liberal democracy, and not an upholder of freedom and human rights. But as the second post-Apartheid chief justice and prominent anti-Apartheid activist Arthur Chaskalson has observed: "Some unjust societies lack any semblance of [a commitment to legality]. There was, strangely, a commitment to legality in apartheid South Africa, and that is what makes it such an unusual case" (Chaskalson 2003, 598). The word "unusual" to describe the Apartheid regime is apt.

Press freedom, while often undermined, was respected far more than one could expect today in Venezuela, China, the Gambia, Eritrea, or North Korea. The judiciary, too, was well-respected among black South Africans and anti-Apartheid activists for its commitment to the civil libertarian themes underlying South Africa's Roman-Dutch common law (Wacks 1984, 270). It cannot be denied that the judiciary often had to enforce authoritarian, racist laws, but it also cannot be said that the judiciary was simply a puppet of the regime.

What seems to be the case is that a large portion of Afrikaner intellectuals and statesmen sincerely considered themselves part of the Western, broadly "liberal-democratic" political tradition, but believed that to apply such a tradition unmodified in South Africa would go badly, even disastrously. On such apprehensions, they engaged in authoritarian social engineering. Edgar Brookes suggested that both communism and nationalism view everything in society, including art and science, as a means to achieve some political end. He implored those "who love freedom," liberals, not to do the same in an attempt to defend themselves from the onslaught of authoritarianism. South Africa, Brookes argued, should be served by education, literature, art, music, and science in their own right, and not merely as part of a grand political project (Brookes 1956, 198). Unfortunately, the ideology of Apartheid subsumed everything in South Africa between 1948 and 1994 in an effort to maintain white supremacy against the perceived inequality of civilization between whites and blacks, with a legacy that continues to this day.

Today, many former supporters of the National and Conservative parties, almost invariably conservative white South Africans, lay part of the blame for South Africa's current corrupt political and sluggish economic state at the feet of liberals who during Apartheid pushed for a non-racial franchise and equal rights. Steve Hofmeyr, a conservative South African singer and media personality, for example, tweeted in Afrikaans on 3 June 2019 that, "The bogus reasonableness of the *verligtes* [the enlightened] is what gave us this dump. They still justify [their actions during Apartheid]. They praise themselves" (Hofmeyr 2019). In an article titled "Critics Who Blame Liberals. Never Had Any Real Answers of Their Own," Kane-Berman (2019b) addressed this type of criticism, saying that South Africa's current malaise is not the result of the white Apartheid government compromising and negotiating with those who sought majority rule, but a result of not doing so earlier. Liberals had been campaigning for a non-racial franchise for decades before 1994, but the white electorate was largely unwilling to budge. Kane-Berman also notes that Apartheid was never going to be economically practicable, hence criticizing liberals for contributing to its demise is misplaced. Liberals in organizations like the IRR consistently marketed a viable liberal alternative to the *status quo*, one that was not adopted to any great extent, especially economically, by either the Apartheid or post-Apartheid governments.

Retaining a non-racial but qualified franchise in the same tradition as the nineteenth-century Cape Colony would likely have been a more-than-sufficient safeguard against a majority running roughshod over Western political traditions, because the qualified franchise required by its nature a level of sophistication and understanding of modern economics and literacy. At some unknowable point in time, if a non-racial qualified franchise were kept intact, the number of black, coloured, and Indian electors on the voting roll would have equaled, and eventually, surpassed, that of the whites, but this

William Schreiner, seated in the center, with a delegation of Cape liberals who went to London in 1909 to plead for Britain to enforce a non-racial franchise on South Africa. John Tengo Jabavu is seated on the left. His son, Davidson, was a co-founder of the Institute of Race Relations in 1929. *Source*: Wikimedia Commons.

process would have been gradual. Indeed, the coloured African Political Organization and the black Transvaal National Natives Union insisted on exactly that before the National Convention met to draft a constitution for South Africa in 1908: qualified franchise and equal rights (Thompson 1961, 214–215, 326).

Instead of going down that route, white Afrikaner and English statesmen sent South Africa down a route of enacting a system of governance that humiliated and oppressed millions, and killed thousands of non-whites, usually black South Africans. Many of Apartheid's victims were indirect, like those of the so-called "People's War" that occurred in the early 1990s between factions associated with the ANC and factions associated with Inkatha. This war claimed tens of thousands of civilian lives, mostly in the Natal Province. The state of anti-liberalism prevalent among many black intellectuals and public policy today should, as a result, not come as a surprise, given how, to the extent that liberalism made any tangible positive changes in the lives of ordinary blacks, it took too long. But South Africa's classical liberals, both black and white, have consistently through it all upheld the values of individual liberty, free markets, and constitutionalism, despite their limited successes. As Kane-Berman wrote when South Africa became a democracy under majority rule:

> It may well be that speaking out for liberal values will become more unpopular, and certainly less glamorous, than it became in the recent past. Liberals must be prepared for this. They should remember that the right of people to be different and to swim against the general tide is the foundation stone of a free society (Kane-Berman 1994, 2).

I've not been able to do justice to many liberals who left a mark in South Africa, including the former Sanlam executive Andreas Wassenaar, Free Market Foundation director Temba Nolutshungu, Liberal Party stalwart Peter Brown, economist Jan Lombard, philosopher and businessman Michael O'Dowd, native representative Margaret Ballinger, academic Temba Sono, and the Schreiner family. William Philip Schreiner, former Cape Colony prime minister, was the only notable white liberal who travelled alongside black South Africans to Britain before the Union of South Africa was established, to ask the British government to ensure that no racial discrimination be allowed in the new country. His sister, the activist Olive Schreiner, also actively tried to lobby the National Convention to respect equal rights. Oliver Deneys Schreiner, William's son, went on to become a judge of appeal in the Supreme Court's Appellate Division, and was known for his principled, liberal dissents from the bench. The End Conscription Campaign, Black Sash, the Civil Rights League, and the Centre for Development and Enterprise, among other liberal organizations, could also not be covered to any great extent if at all. Liberal media such the now-defunct *Rand Daily Mail*,[43] *The Individualist*, and *Free Market*, and the existing *Rational Standard*,[44] *Daily Friend*, and *Politicsweb*, were also unfortunately excluded from this article. The depth and breadth of liberalism throughout South Africa's history and today is far deeper and wider, especially in the realm of advocacy of private enterprise over social engineering, than I could render here.

Epilogue: South African Liberalism During 2020–2022

Since my article first appeared in September 2019, the scene has been eventful for South Africa's liberal political and civil society movement.

Civil society

The Institute of Race Relations (IRR),[45] the premier representative of liberalism in South African civil society, had a change in leadership, with Dr. John Endres replacing Dr. Frans Cronje as CEO at the end of 2021.

Endres had his work cut out for him, as from the middle of 2021 the IRR became the subject of intense criticism by former associates. One such event was a letter signed by about 80 former members, representatives, and staff of the IRR. They alleged that in the 1980s—the time of the liberal slideaway (Van Staden 2019, 284–287)—the IRR "underwent a major change in direction" towards a "free-market, small state agenda." This, the co-signatories believe, was incompatible with a "human rights research organization devoted to

---

43. The original *Rand Daily Mail*, referenced here, was a print newspaper with a clear liberal bent between 1902 and 1985. The Times Media Group relaunched it in 2014 as an online paper without an explicit ideological perspective.

44. The author is a co-founder of the *Rational Standard*.

45. Disclosure: As of 1 October 2022, the author began full-time employment at the IRR.

impartial fact-based analysis" (Concerned Citizens 2021). These individuals, revealing themselves as victims of the liberal slideaway, would rather have wanted the IRR to take a stand against climate change and racial inequality, in favor of COVID-19 vaccine mandates, and against firearm rights. To them, "the IRR's current approach betrays the legacy of its founders." Endres alluded to the slideaway, and ably responded to the criticism by writing that the IRR is "regularly accused of being too right-wing by our left-wing detractors, and of being too left-wing by our right-wing critics. We prefer to think of ourselves as holding the sensible middle, and will continue to stand up for liberal ideals, truth and justice, so continuing the institute's long and proud tradition" (Endres 2021a).

John Kane-Berman, CEO of the IRR for 31 years between 1983 and 2014, and the face of South African liberalism during that time, passed away on 27 July 2022 (*Daily Friend* 2022). Kane-Berman saw the IRR through the slideaway and resisted attempts by some of the aforementioned co-signatories to move the Institute in a direction more accommodating of the African National Congress (ANC)'s wealth-destroying policies.

The Free Market Foundation (FMF), too, had intense internal ructions. Leon Louw, a co-founder of the FMF, after much controversy and contention (Van Staden and Hattingh 2021) was dismissed in 2022 by the FMF—or resigned, depending on who one asks (Cohen 2022).

The DA and muscular liberalism

After the Democratic Alliance (DA)'s first-ever electoral decline in the 2019 general elections, the party regrouped, apparently at least, around its liberal principles, leading to the end of Mmusi Maimane's leadership and the resignation of various political functionaries (Al Jazeera 2019). The DA renewed its dormant commitment to colorblind non-racialism, free markets, and federalism. This regrouping did not lead to more votes in the 2021 municipal elections (Van Staden 2021), however, creating the impression that the DA's support might have plateaued around the 20 percent mark.

The DA's involvement in the aftermath of the July 2021 riots proved controversial for the party, both among supporters and detractors. Country-wide riots relating to the imprisonment of former president Jacob Zuma spilled into the largely Indian-descended community of Phoenix in KwaZulu-Natal. There and elsewhere, communities were forced to organize their own, sometimes violent defense against pillaging insurrectionists. In the middle of this defensive action, it appears that opportunistic murders also took place (ostensibly by community members), and that these murders had a racial element to them.

In the aftermath of the riots, the DA condemned the murders (Phungula 2021), and at the same time put up posters in the Phoenix area (in the run-up to the 2021 municipal elections) saying that the party stands with the community. The posters read: "The ANC calls you racists. The DA calls you heroes." These posters were in turn condemned as racist, however the DA defended them as pointing to the ANC government's failure to protect communities, which were then forced to protect themselves (Felix 2021). Despite this initial defense, the DA buckled under pressure and removed the posters (*Eyewitness News* 2021). DA co-founder and liberal stalwart Mike Waters resigned as a DA functionary after the party relented, condemning "the party's grovelling apology" and its "betrayal of the heroes who defended lives during the period of violence and looting." He called for "muscular liberalism" in the face of "sanctimonious wokerati" (Nemakonde and Cotterell 2021).

The posters saga is yet another instance of a phenomenon that South African liberalism has known for some time: Liberal advocacy is not always polite—indeed freedom, whether the freedom to speak one's mind or to defend oneself, is sometimes a contentious business. Arguably the first notable liberal in South Africa was Dr. John Philip, the Scottish director of the London Missionary Society stationed in South Africa between 1818 and 1851. Upon his arrival in South Africa, he was popular among the white inhabitants of the eastern Cape Colony, not least for his liberal convictions. Indeed, he was chosen as their representative in dealing with the British Cape government (Ross 1986, 83). They would turn on him, however, when he began applying his liberal principles consistently to the Khoi, coloureds, and Xhosa living in and around the Colony, and also acted as their representative. Philip became despised among white society (Ross 1986, 111–112). There is also the case of, again arguably, the first notable Afrikaner liberal, Thomas François Burgers, the fourth State President of the Transvaal, between 1872 and 1877. He was received with much fanfare in the Transvaal, not least for his (imperfectly) liberal intellect, vision, and charm (Appelgryn 1979, 4, 7, 9–10). When it became time for him to make practical political work of his liberal convictions, however—in addition to the untimely annexation of the Transvaal by the British—the burghers of the Transvaal turned on him (Appelgryn 1979, 248–249).

Other such examples abound, not only in South Africa's history, but in the stories of many liberal politicians and organizations around the world. People tend to approve of what they read on paper, but when they themselves have to live with the implications of liberty, the pitchforks come out. Or, in an acronym for the modern reader: NIMBY! The DA experienced this in the reaction to the Phoenix saga. Naturally, the liberal position would be to vaunt those who protected themselves, their property, and their communities with force against thuggish aggression. This was accepted in theory by all associated with the DA and liberal politics. But the moment the DA translated this into practice, a chorus of condemnations came about. Suddenly—without any evidence—the DA represented a racist "subtext": it apparently supported genocidal Indians who sought to murder blacks. Often, when liberalism is applied and threatens someone's private interests or, sometimes, just makes them feel somewhat uncomfortable, the support they may have had for liberalism evaporates. Special pleading is a phenomenon we regularly bear witness to, and South Africa is no exception.

The future

South Africa had one of the strictest COVID-19 lockdowns in the world (BBC 2020a), leading to significantly increased unemployment (BBC 2020b)—no doubt contributing to the ensuing July 2021 riots. Coupled with this severe economic downturn has been a renewed bout of rolling blackouts by the State power utility (Bloomberg 2022). Both the lockdown and blackouts are a result of governmentalization (Katzenellenbogen 2021).

On the hopeful side, even the President, Cyril Ramaphosa, admitted in a 25 July 2022 statement about the persistent electricity crisis that overregulation and red tape were the proximate causes of the failure to bring online additional power capacity (Ramaphosa 2022). It appears to be dawning upon many that liberal economics is the only avenue for South Africa out of its economic malaise. In December 2021, a proposed amendment to the Constitution to remove the unqualified right to receive compensation when property is expropriated by the government was defeated. This occurred primarily due to a dispute between the ANC and Economic Freedom Fighters on the scope of the amendment (Gerber 2021). However it was arguably liberal civil society that generated the environment of public opinion that made the amendment contentious in the first place. Despite these modest victories, liberals in politics and civil society continue to have their work cut out for them.

The next general election, in 2024, is gearing up to be a historic post-Apartheid event, with most notable opposition parties united around a core set of liberal values. Some believe these parties will be able to form a national coalition which, for the first time since 1994, could lead to a government that excludes the ANC (Endres 2021b). If such a government materializes and succeeds in righting South Africa's course, it will in no small part be due to policies that prioritize freedom of enterprise, personal liberty, and constitutionalism. Liberalism in South Africa is set to have an interesting decade.

References

African News Agency. 2019. We Are Coming for What Is Ours, Says ANC's Ace Magashule. *Independent Online* (Cape Town), May 18.

Al Jazeera. 2019. South Africa's Mmusi Maimane Quits as Democratic Alliance Leader. Al Jazeera (Doha), October 23.

Appelgryn, Marthinus Stephanus. 1979. *Thomas Francois Burgers: Staatspresident 1872–1877*. Pretoria: HAUM.

Barnard, S. L., and A. H. Marais. 1982. *Die Verenigde Party: Die Groot Eksperiment*. Durban: Butterworths.

BBC. 2020a. Coronavirus: South Africa Eases Strict Lockdown as Cases Drop. BBC (London), September 17.

BBC. 2020b. Coronavirus Lockdown Costs South Africa Millions of Jobs. BBC (London), September 29.

Berger, Mike. 2018. Race and the DA. *Politicsweb* (Johannesburg), April 3.

Berger, Peter L., and Bobby Godsell. 1988. *A Future South Africa: Visions, Strategies and Realities*. Cape Town: Human & Rousseau and Tafelberg.

Bickford-Smith, Vivian. 1995. South African Urban History, Racial Segregation and the Unique Case of Cape Town? *Journal of Southern African Studies* 21(1): 63–78.

Biko, Steve. 1987 [1970]. Black Souls in White Skins? In *I Write What I Like*, ed. Aelred

Stubbs, 19–26. Oxford: Heinemann.

Black Sash. 1956. Introducing Our Group. *The Black Sash* (Women's Defence of the Constitution League, Johannesburg) 1(1): 1–2.

Black Sash. 2017. History of the Black Sash. Black Sash (Cape Town).

Blanchard, James U. 1979. Introduction. In *In Search of Liberty*, by Fred Macaskill. New York: Books in Focus.

Bloom, Jack. 1994. Liberal Values and Practical Politics. In *The New Liberals*, ed. John Kane-Berman, 3–10. Johannesburg: Institute of Race Relations.

Bloomberg. 2022. Eskom Nears Record for Worst Year of Load Shedding Ever—and There's Still 6 Months to Go. *BusinessTech* (Centurion, South Africa), July 2.

Bloor, Garreth. 2019. South Africa: A New Assault on Economic Liberty. *Library of Economics and Liberty* (Liberty Fund, Carmel, Ind.), January 1.

Blundell, John. 1985. Ciskei's Independent Way. *Reason*, April 1.

Bond, Patrick. 2015. 'Spend on the Poor, Not Flaky Projects.' *Business Report* (Cape Town), October 28.

Brand South Africa. 2014. A Guide to South African Political Parties. July 21. Department of Communications (Johannesburg).

Brookes, Edgar H. 1956. South Africa: The Possibilities in an Impossible Situation. *African Affairs* 55(220): 188–200.

Brookes, Edgar H., and J. B. MacAulay. 1958. *Civil Liberty in South Africa*. Cape Town: Oxford University Press.

Business Day. 1987. Economy Booms as Controls Are Scrapped. *Business Day* (Johannesburg), March 27.

BusinessTech. 2019. South Africa's Unemployment Rate Climbs to 27.6%. *BusinessTech* (Lyttleton, South Africa), May 14.

Byrne, Errol. 1990. *The First Liberal: Rheinallt Jones*. Johannesburg: Angel Press.

Caldwell, Don. 1989. *South Africa: The New Revolution*. Johannesburg: Free Market Foundation.

Cape Times. 1980. Benefits of Free Enterprise. *Cape Times* (Cape Town), November 24.

Cardo, Michael. 2012. The Liberal Tradition in South Africa: Past and Present. *Focus* (Helen Suzman Foundation, Johannesburg) 65: 16–20.

Carter, Gwendolyn. 1958. *The Politics of Inequality: South Africa since 1948*. New York: Frederick A. Praeger.

Cele, S'thembile. 2019. 'Shut Up': Mmusi Maimane Puts His Foot Down on BEE Debate. *City Press* (Johannesburg), February 10.

Cele, S'thembile, and Juniour Khumalo. 2019. DA Ramps Up Black Numbers. *City Press* (Johannesburg), March 17.

Centre for Development and Enterprise (CDE). 2017. Spotlight On: Minimum Wage—A Dozen Questions about the National Minimum Wage. February 2. Centre for Development and Enterprise (Johannesburg).

Chaskalson, Arthur. 2003. From Wickedness to Equality: The Moral Transformation of South African Law. *International Journal of Constitutional Law* 1(4): 590–609.

Citizen. 1987. Peace in SA if Demands Are Met. *The Citizen* (Johannesburg), December 3.

Clarion. 1976. A Major Step Towards Free Enterprise. *Clarion* (Cape Town), November.

Cloete, Karl. 2011. Modern Capitalists Have a Lust for Slavery—NUMSA. *Politicsweb* (Johannesburg), February 9.

Cohen, Tim. 2022. Free Market Foundation President Leon Louw Resigns Following Organisational Fracture. *Daily Maverick* (Cape Town), July 22.

Coleman, Peter. 2000. From Fellow Travelling to Political Correctness. In *Political Correctness in South Africa*, eds. Rainer Erkens and John Kane-Berman, 5–19. Johannesburg: Institute of Race Relations.

Concerned Citizens. 2021. IRR's Current Approach Betrays the Legacy of Its Founders and Does a Disservice to the People of South Africa. *Daily Maverick* (Cape Town), September 17.

Cronin, Jeremy. 2019. No excuse for Zille's hatchet-job analysis of stature capture. *News24* (Cape Town), August 14.

Cronjé, Frans. 2019a. Avoiding an 'Unsurvivable' Political Event. *Daily Friend* (Institute of Race Relations, Johannesburg), May 4.

Cronjé, Frans. 2019b. Soft-ANC Has Failed and the DA Must Go Back to Liberalism. *Daily Friend* (Institute of Race Relations, Johannesburg), May 11.

Cronje, Jan. 2014. 'Stellenbosch Mafia' Controls SA—Malema. *Independent Online* (Cape Town), March 16.

Daily Friend. 2022. In Memoriam: John Kane-Berman 1946–2022. *Daily Friend* (Johannesburg), July 28.

Daily News. 1976. Free Economy Is Their Aim. *Daily News* (Durban), January 9.

Davies, John. 1996. The State and the South African University System Under Apartheid. *Comparative Education* 32(3): 319–332.

Deane, John. 2001. A Brief Account of the J. H. Hofmeyr Memorial Trust in Natal 1949–2000. *Natalia* (Natal Society, Pietermaritzburg, South Africa) 31: 58–63.

De Kiewiet, Cornelis W. 1955. Fears and Pressures in the Union of South Africa. *Virginia Quarterly Review* 31(1): 27–45.

Democratic Alliance. 2000. The DA's Principles. Democratic Alliance (Cape Town).

Dhlamini, Mpiyakhe. 2017. Remembering the Mahlabatini Declaration of Faith. *Rational Standard* (Johannesburg), October 6.

Douglas, Colin. 1994. Liberals on the Campuses of the Future. In *The New Liberals*, ed. John Kane-Berman, 11–19. Johannesburg: Institute of Race Relations.

Dubow, Saul. 2014. Uncovering the Historic Strands of Egalitarian Liberalism in South Africa. *Theoria: A Journal of Social and Political Theory* 61(140): 7–24.

Dubow, Saul. 2019. South Africa's Racist Founding Father Was Also a Human Rights Pioneer. *New York Times*, May 18.

Duncan, Marion, and Richard Paris. 1981. Sky Couriers 'Shot Down' by SAA. *The Star* (Johannesburg), May 7.

Du Toit, Andre. 1988. Understanding Rights Discourses and Ideological Conflicts in South Africa. In *Essays on Law and Social Practice in South Africa*, ed. Hugh Corder, 237–265. Cape Town: Juta.

Economist. 2013. The Longer Walk to Equality. *The Economist*, December 6.

eNCA. 2018. Close Down SAA, Says Free Market Foundation. eNews Channel Africa (Johannesburg), June 28.

Endres, John. 2021a. IRR Holds the Liberal Line Against the Left. *Business Day* (Johannesburg), September 21.

Endres, John. 2021b. The Buffalo and the Wild Dogs. *Daily Friend* (Johannesburg), November 3.

eProperty News. 2018. Nedbank Partners with Khaya Lam to Make Property Ownership a Reality for More South Africa. November 3. eProperty News (Johannesburg).

Erkens, Rainer. 2000. Drinking in Bad Company at the Wrong End of the Bar. In *Political Correctness in South Africa*, eds. Rainer Erkens and John Kane-Berman, 1–3. Johannesburg: Institute of Race Relations.

Esterhuyse, Willem P. 1986. *Anton Rupert: Advocate of Hope*. Cape Town: Tafelberg.

Eyewitness News. 2021. DA Removing Controversial 'Heroes' Posters in Phoenix. *Eyewitness News* (Johannesburg), October 7.

Feldberg, Meyer, Kate Jowell, and Stephen Mulholland, eds. 1976. *Milton Friedman in South Africa*. Cape Town: Graduate School of Business, University of Cape Town.

Felix, Jason. 2021. Elections 2021: DA Defends Posters Placed in Phoenix Telling Residents 'The ANC Called You Racists.' *News24* (Cape Town), October 5.

Financial Mail. 1980. Leon Louw: Doing More by Doing Less. *Financial Mail* (Johannesburg) November 28.

Franks, Peter E. 2014. The Crisis of the South African Public Service. *Focus* (Helen Suzman Foundation, Johannesburg) 74: 48–56.

Free Market Foundation (FMF). 1976. Sosialisme of Vryheid? *The Individualist* (Johannesburg) 11: 7.

Free Market Foundation (FMF). 1996. FMF Evidence to the Constitutional Court in Certification of the New Constitutional Text. Constitutional Court of South Africa (Johannesburg).

Free Market Foundation (FMF). 2018. Ruperts Quietly Get on With Land Reform, Offering Township Title-Deeds. *BizNews* (London), November 22.

Gerber, Jan. 2021. National Assembly Fails to Pass Constitutional Amendment to Allow Land Expropriation Without Compensation. *News24* (Cape Town), December 7.

Gernetzky, Karl. 2019. SAA's Vuyani Jarana the Second SOE Chief to Quit in Two Weeks. *Business Day* (Johannesburg), June 2.

Giliomee, Hermann. 2008. Ethnic Business and Economic Empowerment: The Afrikaner Case, 1915–1970. *South African Journal of Economics* 76(4): 165–188.

Gon, Sara. 2019. 'Disadvantage' Is the Best Proxy for Disadvantage. *Politicsweb* (Johannesburg), February 19.

Green, Michael. 2004. *Around and About: Memoirs of a South African Newspaperman*. Claremont, South Africa: David Philip.

Gurzynski, Z. S. A. 1981. Free Markets and the State. *Free Market* (Free Market Foundation, Johannesburg) 5: 23–25.

Head, Tom. 2019. Julius Malema Turns Heads After Claiming SA "Is Worse Than Zimbabwe." *The South African* (Blue Sky Publications, Cape Town), March 22.

Herman, Paul. 2018. 'We Will Not Allow Smash-and-Grab Interventions'—Ramaphosa on Land Expropriation Without Compensation. *News24* (Cape Town), February 20.

Hetherington, Ian J. 1985. *The Development of Small Business in South Africa*. Self-published.

Hofmeyr, Steve. 2019. "Die kastige redelikheid…." Twitter.com/steve_hofmeyr, June 3.

Hughes, Timothy P. D. 1994. *Political Liberalism in South Africa in the 1980s and the Formation of the Democratic Party*. M.A. diss., University of Cape Town.

Hutt, William H. 1964. *The Economics of the Colour Bar*. London: Andre Deutsch.

Hutt, William H. 1975. South Africa's Salvation in Classic Liberalism. In *Individual Freedom: Selected Works of William H. Hutt*, eds. Svetozar Pejovich and David Klingaman, 53–74. Westport, Conn.: Greenwood Press.

Institute of Race Relations. 2018. Race Relations in South Africa: Reasons for Hope 2018—Holding the Line. March. Institute of Race Relations (Johannesburg).

Investment House. 2016. What Is BBBEE? *Entrepreneur Magazine* (Johannesburg), August 23.

Johnson, R. W. 2011. The Future of the Liberal Tradition in SA. *Politicsweb* (Johannesburg), August 18.

Johnson, R. W. 2019. Strange Days in the DA. *Politicsweb* (Johannesburg), May 22.

Kane-Berman, John. 1994. Welcoming Address. In *The New Liberals*, ed. John Kane-Berman, 1–2. Johannesburg: Institute of Race Relations.

Kane-Berman, John. 2002. The Case for a Liberal Strategy. *Fast Facts* (Institute of Race Relations, Johannesburg), September: 2–7.

Kane-Berman, John. 2017. *Between Two Fires: Holding the Liberal Centre in South African Politics*. Johannesburg: Jonathan Ball.

Kane-Berman, John. 2018. The Rise and Fall of the Torch Commando. *Politicsweb* (Johannesburg), July 30.

Kane-Berman, John. 2019a. Ninety Years Old and Still Going Strong. *Daily Friend* (Institute of Race Relations, Johannesburg), April 23.

Kane-Berman, John. 2019b. Critics Who Blame Liberals Never Had Any Real Answers of Their Own. *Daily Friend* (Institute of Race Relations, Johannesburg), May 5.

Kane-Berman, John. 2019c. Email correspondence with Martin van Staden, September 3.

Kantor, Brian S., and Henry F. Kenny. 1976. The Poverty of Neo-Marxism: The Case of South Africa. *Journal of Southern African Studies* 3(1): 20–40.

Katzenellenbogen, Jonathan. 2021. Why is South Africa's Growth Rate So Feeble? *Daily Friend* (Johannesburg), March 3.

Keniston, William H. 2010. *Richard Turner's Contribution to a Socialist Political Culture in South Africa (1968–1978)*. M.A. diss., University of the Western Cape.

Kennedy, Stan. 1987. Leon Louw—The Driving Force for a Free-Market Society. *The Star* (Johannesburg), December 28.

Kenny, Andrew. 2019. Election Lessons for Liberals. *Daily Friend* (Institute of Race Relations, Johannesburg), May 11.

Kruger, Daniel W. 1960. *South African Parties and Policies, 1910–1960: A Select Source Book*. Cape Town: Human & Rousseau.

Lachmann, Ludwig M. 1956. *Capital and Its Structure*. London: Bell and Sons.

Lachmann, Ludwig M. 1976. FMF Interview—Prof. LM Lachmann [interview by Marc Swanepoel]. *The Individualist* (Free Market Foundation, Johannesburg) 8: 1–2.

Lachmann, Ludwig M. 1986. *The Market as an Economic Process*. New York: Basil Blackwell.

Lagaradien, Ismail. 2019. There Is Much More to Helen Zille's Shift to the Right. *Daily Maverick* (Cape Town), July 30.

Laissez-Fair [pseud.]. 1987. Mining in South Africa and Private Enterprise. *South African Journal on Human Rights* 3: 167–176.

Lavin, Deborah. 1965. The Dilemma of Christian-National Education in South Africa. *The World Today* 21(10): 428–438.

Lawson, Kerianne. 2013. Leon Louw. Working paper, December 17.

Lazar, John. 1988. The Role of the South African Bureau of Racial Affairs (SABRA) in the Formulation of Apartheid Ideology, 1948–1961. In *Societies of Southern Africa in the 19th and 20th Centuries*, vol. 14, 96–109. London: Institute of Commonwealth Studies, University of London.

Leach, Daniel F. 1990. Monopoly Power and the State. In *Liberty and Prosperity: Essays in Limiting Government and Freeing Enterprise in South Africa*, eds. Frank Vorhies and Richard J. Grant, 92–108. Cape Town: Juta.

Leng, Claudio. 2019. DA Roasted for Boasting About 'Constitutional Blacks' on Party List. *Briefly* (Cape Town), March 30.

Leon, Tony. 1998. *Hope and Fear: Reflections of a Democrat*. Johannesburg: Jonathan Ball.

Leon, Tony. 2019. The Need for A Liberal Party in A Time of Peril. Presented at the Friedrich Naumann Foundation (Johannesburg), August 1.

Lewsen, Phyllis. 1987. Liberals in Politics and Administration, 1936–1948. In *Democratic Liberalism in South Africa: Its History and Prospect*, eds. Jeffrey Butler, Richard Elphick, and David Welsh, 98–115. Middletown, Conn.: Wesleyan University Press.

Louw, Leon M. 1978. Executive Director's Annual Report. Free Market Foundation Congress (Johannesburg).

Louw, Leon M. 1981. Free Market—the Solution. *Free Market* (Free Market Foundation, Johannesburg) 5: 2.

Louw, Leon M. 2011. Leon Louw on Sinking South Africa—and How Free-Market Thinking Can Help Recover Prosperity [interview by Anthony Wile]. TheDailyBell.com, November 20.

Louw, Leon M., and Frances Kendall. 1986. *South Africa: The Solution*. Bisho, South Africa: Amagi Publications.

Lubisi, Cassius. 2019. Director-General Cassius Lubisi Announces 2019 National Orders Recipients. April 2. South African Government (Pretoria).

Macaskill, Fred. 1979. *In Search of Liberty*. New York: Books in Focus.

Madlingozi, Tshepo. 2006. Legal Academics and Progressive Politics in South Africa: Moving Beyond the Ivory Tower. *Pulp Fictions* (University of Pretoria) 2: 5–30.

Maimane, Mmusi. 2018a. To Be Free, Africa Must Be Liberated From Its Liberators. November 30. Democratic Alliance (Cape Town).

Maimane, Mmusi. 2018b. Building an African Liberal Agenda. April 7. Democratic Alliance (Cape Town).

Malan, M. P. A. 1964. *Die Nasionale Party van Suid-Afrika 1914–1964: Sy Stryd en sy Prestasies.* Elsiesrivier, South Africa: Nasionale Handelsdrukkery.

Mandela, Nelson. 1964. Statement to the Pretoria Supreme Court, April 20.

Marshall, Geoffrey. 1957. *Parliamentary Sovereignty and the Commonwealth.* Oxford: Clarendon Press.

May, Henry J. 1955. *The South African Constitution.* Cape Town and Johannesburg: Juta.

McGregor, Maurice. 1990. Preface. In *The First Liberal: Rheinallt Jones,* by Errol Byrne. Johannesburg: Angel Press.

Mhlanga, Oswald. 2017. Impacts of Deregulation on the Airline Industry in South Africa: A Review of the Literature. *African Journal of Hospitality, Tourism and Leisure* (Johannesburg) 6(3): 1–14.

Michigan State University African Studies Center. 2005. South Africa: Overcoming Apartheid, Building Democracy—The Black Sash. Michigan State University (East Lansing, Mich.).

Mngadi, Mxolisi. 2017. Mmusi Maimane: Zille's Views on Colonialism are Inconsistent with the DA's Values. *Mail & Guardian* (Johannesburg), March 20.

Morris, Michael. 2019a. Institute of Race Relations' Endurance a Testament to Founders. *Business Day* (Johannesburg), May 6.

Morris, Michael. 2019b. John Harris's Bomb. *Daily Friend* (Institute of Race Relations, Johannesburg), July 24.

Nattrass, Nicoli, and Jeremy Seekings. 2018. Labour Market Reform is Needed for Inclusive Growth. October. Centre for Development and Enterprise (Johannesburg).

Nemakonde, Vhahangwele, and Gareth Cotterell. 2021. Mike Waters Quits DA Post, Slams Party's 'Grovelling Apology' Over Phoenix Posters. *The Citizen* (Johannesburg), October 11.

News24. 2011. Numsa: SAIRR Hostile Towards ANC. *News24* (Cape Town), January 26.

News24. 2017. DA and Zille Reach Settlement. *News24* (Cape Town), June 13.

Ngobese, Sihle. 2019. Young, Black, Conservative: The Politics of Liberty and Identity in South Africa. Presented at the University of Cape Town, April 10.

Ngubane, Jordan K. 1954. African Viewpoint: Liberalism Encounters Heavy Weather. *Indian Opinion* (Durban), April 16.

Ngubane, Jordan K. 1963–1964. Lembede and Africanism. Working manuscript.

Ngubane, Jordan K. 1964. Interview by Gwendolyn M. Carter, March 5.

Ngubane, Jordan K. 1980. Why I Came Back. *Sunday Tribune* (Durban), July 6.

Nkanjeni, Unathi. 2019. Floyd Shivambu Calls Tito Mboweni's Growth Plan 'Imperialism in Action'. *The Sowetan* (Johannesburg), August 30.

Nolutshungu, Temba A. 2000. Political Correctness and the Black Intelligentsia. In *Political Correctness in South Africa,* eds. Rainer Erkens and John Kane-Berman, 20–27. Johannesburg: Institute of Race Relations.

Norton, R. 1978. Most City Blacks Are Leftists—Surveys. *The Star* (Johannesburg), August.

Nthai, Seth A. 1998. A Bill of Rights for South Africa: An Historical Overview. *Consultus* (General Council of the Bar of South Africa, Johannesburg) 11(2): 142–147.

Ntsane, Stephen. 1994. Is Liberalism Acceptable in African Townships? In *The New Liberals,* ed. John Kane-Berman, 21–27. Johannesburg: Institute of Race Relations.

O'Dowd, Michael C. 1996. *The O'Dowd Thesis and the Triumph of Democratic Capitalism.* Johannesburg: Free Market Foundation.

O'Malley, Kierin. 1988. South African Liberal Economics and the Question of Power. *Reality* (Reality Publications, Pietermartizburg, South Africa) 4: 5–6.

O'Malley, Kierin. 1994. The Fundamentals of Liberalism in South Africa Today. In *The New Liberals*, ed. John Kane-Berman, 29–42. Johannesburg: Institute of Race Relations.

Overy, Neil. 2002. *'These Difficult Days': Mission Church Reactions to Bantu Education in South Africa, 1949–56*. Ph.D. diss., University of London.

Paton, Alan. 2011 [1962]. Non-Racial Democracy: The Policies of the Liberal Party of South Africa. *Politicsweb* (Johannesburg), September 6.

Pereira, Paul. 1994. Summing Up. In *The New Liberals*, ed. John Kane-Berman, 61–65. Johannesburg: Institute of Race Relations.

Pereira, Paul. 2015. Back Yourself to Try Freedom. Presented to the Democratic Alliance Johannesburg City Councilor Workshop, November 15.

Phungula, Willem. 2021. DA Leaders Condemn Phoenix Murders. *Daily News* (Durban), August 3.

Pretoria News. 1987. Meeting of Minds the Key, Says Slabbert. *Pretoria News*, May 11.

Ramaphosa, Cyril. 2022. Address by President Cyril Ramaphosa on Actions to Address the Electricity Crisis, Union Buildings, Tshwane. *The Presidency* (Pretoria), July 25.

Reekie, W. Duncan. 1990. Privatisation and the Distribution of Wealth. In *Liberty and Prosperity: Essays in Limiting Government and Freeing Enterprise in South Africa*, eds. Frank Vorhies and Richard J. Grant, 110–131. Cape Town: Juta.

Rhoodie, N. J., and H. I. Venter. 1959. *Apartheid: A Socio-Historical Exposition of the Origin and Development of the Apartheid Idea*. Cape Town: Hollandsch-Afrikaansche Uitgevers Maatshappij.

Rich, Paul B. 1987. The Appeals of Tuskegee: James Henderson, Lovedale, and the Fortunes of South African Liberalism, 1906–1930. *International Journal of African Historical Studies* 20(2): 271–292.

Ritchie, Gemma. 2018. Mantashe Releases Mining Character of Compromises. *Mail & Guardian* (Johannesburg), September 27.

Robertson, Don. 1975. New Champions of Free Market. *Sunday Express* (Johannesburg), September 14.

Robertson, Janet. 1971. *Liberalism in South Africa, 1948–1963*. Oxford: Clarendon Press.

Roodt, Marius. 2018. Economic Empowerment for the Disadvantaged: A Better Way to Empower South Africa's Poor. July. Institute of Race Relations (Johannesburg).

Ross, Andrew. 1986. *John Philip (1775–1851): Missions, Race and Politics in South Africa*. Aberdeen, UK: Aberdeen University Press.

Saunders, Stephen G. 2008. Toward Bridging the Gap Between Theory and Empirical Reality. *South African Journal of Economics* 76(4): 738–748.

Sayyid, Salma. 2019. Connecting the Networks: Putting the Kochs into Race Relations. April 8. Afro-Middle East Centre (Johannesburg).

Segal, Vivienne. 1977. Blacks Must Identify with System. *The Citizen* (Johannesburg), March

10.

Shandler, David. 1991. *Structural Crisis and Liberalism: A History of the Progressive Federal Party, 1981–1989*. M.A. diss., University of Cape Town.

Smith, Carin. 2018. R100 000 Bet on SAA's Future. *Mail & Guardian* (Johannesburg), June 5.

South African History Online. 2011. Black Sash. March 30. South African History Online (Cape Town).

South African History Online. 2012a. Liberal Party of South Africa (LPSA). May 10. South African History Online (Cape Town).

South African History Online. 2012b. States of Emergency in South Africa: The 1960s and 1980s. March 14. South African History Online (Cape Town).

Sowetan. 1987. Loosening the Chains. *The Sowetan* (Johannesburg), January 1.

Spector, J. Brooks. 2013. SAIRR: There's a New Sheriff in Town and He's Moving Beyond Only Race. *Daily Maverick* (Cape Town), October 8.

Spence, J. E. 1965. The Origins of Extra-Parliamentary Opposition in South Africa. *Government and Opposition* 1(1): 55–84.

Sun. 1987. Leon Louw of the Free Market Foundation. *The Sun* (South Africa), June.

Sunter, Clem. 1992. *The New Century: Quest for the High Road*. Cape Town: Human & Rousseau.

Sunter, Clem. 1993. *Pretoria Will Provide, and Other Myths*. Cape Town: Tafelberg and Human & Rousseau.

Suzman, Helen. 1998. Foreword. In *Hope and Fear: Reflections of a Democrat*, by Tony Leon. Johannesburg: Jonathan Ball.

Swanepoel, Marc. 1975. Introducing the South African Free Market Foundation. *The Individualist* (Free Market Foundation, Johannesburg) 1: 1–2.

Swanepoel, Marc. 1976a. Disaster Diary. *The Individualist* (Free Market Foundation, Johannesburg) 10: 4–5.

Swanepoel, Marc. 1976b. Statement of Principles. *The Individualist* (Johannesburg) 11: 1.

Swanepoel, Marc. 1976c. FMF Meeting a Great Success. *The Individualist* (Free Market Foundation, Johannesburg) 9: 6.

Swart, Ray. 1991. *Progressive Odyssey: Towards a Democratic South Africa*. Cape Town: Human & Rousseau.

Thompson, Leonard M. 1961. *The Unification of South Africa 1902–1910*. Oxford: Clarendon Press.

TimesLive. 2019. CEO Who Pledged Cash for Charity If He Could Not Fix SAA Resigns. *TimesLive* (Johannesburg), June 3.

To the Point. 1977. Keep Free Enterprise Free. *To the Point* (South Africa), March 25.

Trewhela, Paul. 2017. The Complexities of Liberalism in South Africa. *Politicsweb* (Johannesburg), December 11.

University of the Witwatersrand. 2011. Records of the South African Institute of Race Relations Part II. University of the Witwatersrand (Johannesburg).

Van den Berghe, Pierre L., ed. 1979. *The Liberal Dilemma in South Africa*. London: Croom Helm.

Van der Westhuizen, Christi. 2018. The DA's White, Liberal Establishment Has to Face the Facts. April 12. Democracy Works Foundation (Johannesburg).

Van Onselen, Gareth. 2019. Vote for the DA, At Your Own Risk. *Politicsweb* (Johannesburg), April 25.

Van Staden, Martin. 2018. In Final Plea, Economists Implore South Africa to Abandon Expropriation Plan. December 6. Foundation for Economic Education (Atlanta).

Van Staden, Martin. 2019. The Politics of Race and Property in South Africa. In *Igniting Liberty: Voices for Freedom Around the World*, eds. Adam Barsouk and Martin van Staden, 271–300. Floyd, Va.: Champion Books.

Van Staden, Martin. 2021. Why A Smaller, More Liberal DA is Not (Necessarily) A Problem. *Rational Standard* (Cape Town), November 4.

Van Staden, Martin, and Chris Hattingh. 2021. Multipronged Battle for Control of Free Market Foundation Unfolds by People with Unjustified Entitlement Complex. *Daily Maverick* (Cape Town), October 31.

Vavi, Zwelinzima. 2019. We Reject Mboweni's Treasury Paper—SAFTU. *Politicsweb* (Johannesburg), August 30.

Vorhies, Frank. 1990. From Liberty to Prosperity in South Africa. In *Liberty and Prosperity: Essays in Limiting Government and Freeing Enterprise in South Africa*, eds. Frank Vorhies and Richard J. Grant, 16–29. Cape Town: Juta.

Wacks, Raymond. 1984. Judges and Injustice. *South African Law Journal* 101(2): 266–285.

Webb, C. de B. 1979. Edgar Harry Brookes 1897–1979. *Natalia* (Natal Society, Pietermaritzburg, South Africa) 9: 39–42.

Welsh, David. 1998. Introduction. In *Hope and Fear: Reflections of a Democrat*, by Tony Leon. Johannesburg: Jonathan Ball.

Wentzel, Jill. 1995. *The Liberal Slideaway*. Johannesburg: Institute of Race Relations.

Winde, Alan. 2019. Clean Government in the Western Cape Shows the Way for the Rest of South Africa. *Daily Maverick* (Cape Town), May 8.

Witness. 1981. New Professor Attacks 'Indifference to Economics.' *The Witness* (Pietermaritzburg, South Africa), November 5.

Zille, Helen. 1981. Afrikaners Warned to 'Maintain Values.' *Rand Daily Mail* (Johannesburg), May.

Zille, Helen. 2013. Foreword. In *Tax, Lies, and Red Tape: Confessions of an Unreconstructed Neoliberal Fundamentalist*, by Dawie Roodt. Cape Town: Zebra Press.

Zille, Helen. 2017. From the Inside: Lessons from Singapore. *Daily Maverick* (Cape Town), March 20.

Zille, Helen. 2019. Dit Was My Fout. *Rapport* (Johannesburg), May 26.

Cases Cited

Collins v. Minister of the Interior and Another 1957 (1) SA 552 (A).

This chapter first appeared as an Econ Journal Watch article in May 2017.
It has been revised slightly and has the addition of a "Postscript" at the end.

Classical Liberalism in China: Some History and Prospects

Xingyuan Feng, Weisen Li, and Evan W. Osborne[1]

Classical liberal economic ideas such as respect for property, competition, freedom of contract, and the rule of law, along with the associated institutions, have played an important role in Western history as well as in other countries, especially from the eighteenth century (North et al. 2009; Hayek 1978). In China the rise of such legal and social institutions has been credited with the immense economic progress of the last four decades (Feng et al. 2015; Coase and Wang 2012).

Although market institutions stretch back many centuries in China (von Glahn 2016), much of the twentieth century was marked by admiration and adoption of uncompromising communism, including Maoism. While other countries in that part of the world prospered after World War II based on free markets and the gradual institutionalization of the rule of law, China suffered three decades of both political and economic catastrophe after 1949. Much of the modern Chinese 'economic miracle,' i.e., rapid, stable, and continuing economic growth since the late 1970s, is also substantially traceable to the implementation of liberal reforms (Feng et al. 2015). The reforms instituted much of the structure of a functioning price system, a relatively stable currency, meaningful property rights, increased competition, increased enforcement of contract and liability law, and reasonably steady economic policy (cf. Eucken 1952). The gradual replacement of state-directed production and resource-allocation decisions with spontaneous-order processes opened the door to participation and hence prosperity for ordinary Chinese

---

1. The authors would like to thank Ning Wang and two anonymous referees for valuable comments. All remaining errors are ours alone.

people, including those who had been historically relegated to the bottom of the social ladder. The reforms opened the way for pioneers, and in the words of Ronald Coase and Ning Wang, the "pioneers were not state-owned enterprises, the privileged actors and the jewels of socialism, but the disadvantaged and marginalized" (2012, 45). There are few if any observers who fail to significantly credit substantial economic liberalization for the Chinese miracle, just as with the broader East Asian miracle before it. And yet abundant literature in China and elsewhere gives paramount credit to the so-called "Chinese model," in which government is credited with steering economic activities while maintaining political control over society (Zhang 2016; 2012; Pan 2007). This paper traces the development and current position of classical liberalism in China, with a focus on Chinese economic thought.

Classical liberalism in modern Chinese society

The Chinese characters for *freedom* or *liberty* are 自由 (Mandarin pronunciation: *zìyóu*), and the two characters combined can be roughly translated as 'emanating from the self.' The first written record of the term appeared in a poem anonymously written in roughly 200 CE, whose title is translated into English among other ways as "An Ancient Poem Written for the Wife of Jiao Zhongqing" (in Barnstone and Chou 2005, 45–56). The term was used therein by a mother to criticize her daughter-in-law, and had a negative connotation akin to 'self-willed, and therefore disrespectful.' Its modern usage grew along with the urgency to acquire the national capacity to resist Western colonial efforts. Figure 1 presents usage frequency for 1800–2008 from Google Ngrams, a database containing the frequency of specific *n*-grams—*n*-grams being phrases of particular lengths in words (lengths in characters, in the Chinese case)—found in the pages of all books in a variety of languages that Google has digitized.[2] The figure depicts the proportion of all Chinese 2-grams in a given year, as a three-year moving average, that the specific 2-gram *zìyóu* makes up. The figure indicates that the prevalence of *zìyóu* increased dramatically in the late nineteenth and early twentieth centuries, i.e., the late Qing Dynasty and early Republican period. This happened as the overall amount of publication in China grew dramatically during this

---

2. For example, 'comparative advantage' is a 2-gram, and 'division of labor' a 3-gram.

time, both because of debates over how to modernize and because of the abandonment of the difficult classical written Chinese for writing that resembled spoken Chinese (*báihuà*, 白话). During this interval the term was rapidly acquiring the meaning of the English word *liberty*.

Figure 1. Prevalence of 自由 ('freedom') in Chinese books, 1800–2008

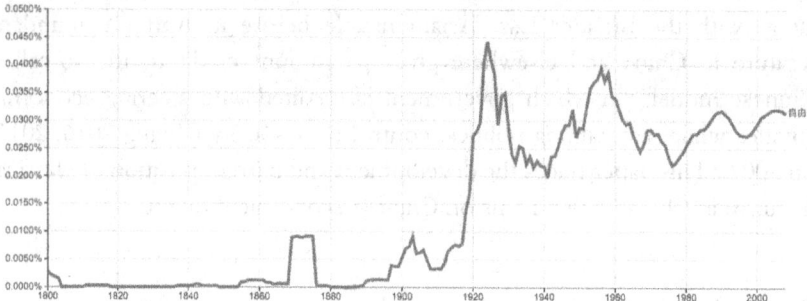

Source: Google Books Ngram Viewer.

In modern Chinese, *zìyóu zhǔyì* (自由主义) translates alternatively as 'liberalism' or 'libertarianism.' But during the Maoist era in both scholarship and in politics, zìyóu zhǔyì was seen as the dominant ideology of capitalist countries and thus as decadent. That view surely was a function of the Marxist vision of bourgeois liberalism as the final stage of capitalism. Mao Zedong himself in 1969, at the height of the Cultural Revolution, republished in a selection of his works a 1937 essay called "Against Liberalism" ("Fǎnduì zìyóu zhǔyì," "反对自由主义"). It criticized non-obedience to the communist party leader as such corrupt "liberalism" (Mao 1969). This loaded usage has, unfortunately, influenced the way some Chinese see the term 自由主义 ever since.

Since 1949 China has been a one-party state, and the Communist Party of China (CCP) has supposedly been building, depending on the current political line, a communist or socialist country. Currently, to accommodate the explosion in market activity since 1978, its system is described by the CCP as "socialism with Chinese characteristics" ("zhōngguó tèsè shèhuì zhǔyì," "中国特色社会主义"). Chinese social-science and historical scholarship is still laden with articles describing social phenomena from an orthodox Marxist (though less often Maoist these days) perspective. The general public and even many at senior levels of the CCP do not take such beliefs seriously.

However, if 'socialism' is taken to signify vague notions of equality of income distribution and social position, it is widely accepted in China, as to a lesser extent it is in Europe and the United States. In China, objections to inequality certainly long predate the twentieth century and its imported ideologies. Even Confucius identified a similar mentality among successful Chinese political rulers.[3]

But thorough understanding of liberalism, let alone support for liberal views, is still rare in today's China. The former is in fact confined to a small number of Chinese intellectuals. Many Chinese do have some sense of the merits in such terms as freedom, democracy, legal equality, and especially justice and the rule of law. Even leading political figures have discussed the importance of the rule of law (*fǎzhì*, 法治). But since the liberal heritage is weak, few people have a deep understanding of such ideas. Instead, people are likely to associate the terms with the good governance, prosperity, and cleaner natural environment they believe to be found in Western countries. To live in such a country, many believe, is to live in a place where opportunities for people like them are greater and where security and happiness are much easier to achieve. The CCP became concerned enough about the spread of such admiration for the terms of liberalism that on November 19, 2012, in the report of the 18th Party Congress, the CCP's proclamation of so-called "socialist core values" included a number of such liberal terms, so they could be framed as justifying its political illiberalism. Through various propaganda mechanisms these values have subsequently been promoted across the country. Note that the attraction of these values is in contrast to a widespread Chinese disquiet about the immediate introduction of democracy in the sense of cleanly counted, competitive elections. China has been an authoritarian country for more than 2,000 years. It has no democratic traditions, a general skepticism of common, less-educated people having a significant say in

---

3. Confucius says to Qiu, in the *Analects*: "The gentleman detests those who, rather than saying outright that they want something, can be counted on to offer a plausible pretext instead. What I have heard is that the head of the state or a noble family worries not about underpopulation but about uneven distribution, not about poverty but about instability. Where there is even distribution there is no such thing as poverty, where there is harmony there is no such thing as underpopulation and where there is stability there is no such thing as overturning. It is for this reason that when distant subjects are unsubmissive one cultivates one's moral quality in order to attract them, and once they have come one makes them content."

national affairs, and a fear of the spread of separatist thinking and even the outbreak of civil war, not a rare event in Chinese history.

Since 1978, economic thought in China, apart from some Marxist redoubts, has in contrast come to resemble that in much of the rest of the world. The Chinese government through its state statistics bureau collects data with the goal of monitoring and as necessary improving Chinese macroeconomic performance. The People's Bank of China, the country's central bank, in some activities operates on substantially the same principles as central banks in developed countries. Perhaps the Chinese are prepared for the distinct ideas of classical liberalism. But liberalism is not seen by many as a significant, distinctive school of thought there, let alone a particularly valuable one. Other modern ideas in contrast have been widely absorbed in the Chinese collective consciousness, for example modernization (*xiàndàihuà*, 现代化), or environmentalism (*huánbǎo*, 环保). Yet many of liberalism's principles have antecedents in Chinese thought, and after Western quasi-colonialism began in the mid-nineteenth century, several liberal texts were among the larger set of books enthusiastically translated into Chinese.

Elements of liberalism in ancient Chinese thought

Chinese political thought long took an absolute ruler for granted, and so political philosophy emphasized advice to that sovereign on how to rule in order to promote the general welfare and prevent revolt. But there certainly is in the Chinese philosophical and historical corpus significant thinking on economic matters. To be sure, there is a tradition of disdain for commercial activity, sometimes paired with advice on how to cultivate individual rectitude. During the Warring States period (475–221 BCE), the *Book of Lord Shang*, a record of the thoughts of a contemporaneous chief minister, told of his distinguishing between farming, a fundamental activity (*běn yè*, 本业), and the derivative, secondary activity of commerce (*mò yè*, 末业). The Confucianist philosopher Mencius (c. 372–289 BCE) sometimes and the Legalist Han Feizi (c. 280–233 BCE) usually took a dim view of commerce—the former because it was corrupting of human nature, and the latter because concentration of wealth in the hands of a few merchants posed a threat to the state. Han Feizi did speak of self-interest inducing win-win exchanges, and both Mencius and before him Mozi (c. 468–391 BCE) wrote of the foolishness of war. Mozi also particularly emphasized the importance of at least a simulacrum of the rule of law, arguing for the importance of the moral equality of all individuals regardless of social status (Osborne 2012).

There is also a record of advocacy for a liberal economic order, not least in the text known as the *Guanzi*. Long attributed to a seventh-century BCE pre-Chinese-unification minister in the state of Qi named Guan Zhong, the text generally concerns philosophical matters, but there is economic wisdom to be found in it as well. For liberal economic values, two sections are of interest. In one, the author anticipates and even extends ex ante the eighteenth century argument of A. R. J. Turgot and Adam Smith that rates of return will tend to equalize across activities: "Town and country compete for inhabitants; families and public storehouses compete for goods; gold and grain compete for value; countryside and court compete for power" (quoted in von Glahn 2016, 78 n.94; our translation).

Another theme in the *Guanzi* is the economic role of merchants being truly fundamental and not merely derivative (note the contrast with the later, skeptical depiction of mercantile activity outlined above):

> Merchants observe outbreaks of dearth and starvation, scrutinize changes in the fortunes of states, study the patterns of the four seasons, and take notice of what goods are produced in each place. With this knowledge of prices in the marketplace, they gather up their stock of goods, load them on oxcarts and horses, and circulate throughout the four directions. Having reckoned what is abundant and what is scarce and calculated what is precious and what is worthless, they exchange what they possess for what they lack, buying cheap and selling dear… Marvelous and fantastic things arrive in timely fashion; rare and unusual goods readily gather. Day and night thus engaged, merchants tutor their sons and brothers, speaking the language of profit, teaching them the virtue of timeliness, and training them how to recognize the value of goods. (quoted in von Glahn 2016, 78)

The importance of scattered, costly information—strongly hinted at in the above passage from the *Guanzi*—was not laid out until the early modern era in the West.

Taoism, philosophical tracts of which have been traced back to the fourth century BCE, also modestly overlaps with classical liberal values. An undercurrent of the Taoist view of the world is that things are what they are for a reason. Strands of Taoist thought also advocate unhindered individual creativity. In that sense it resembles a bit modern ideas of spontaneous order. Indeed, Tan Min (2014, 90) notes that François Quesnay referred to China as a country where government was "built upon the basis of the natural laws." In 1767's *Despotisme de la Chine*, Quesnay rebutted Montesquieu's criticism in *The Spirit of the Laws* of Chinese "despotism" (ibid., 91).

During the Han dynasty, the writer Sima Qian (c. 145–86 BCE), in a volume that later became part of his *Records of the Grand Historian of China* (Sima 1961), devoted attention to the various distinct regional economies of which he was aware, and to those who were financially successful in them. Sima discussed both the role of merchants and of prices in eliciting goods to be produced, or moved from where they are less desired to where they are more desired. He also argued private incentives were sufficient to do most of what it made sense to do:

> Society obviously must have farmers before it can eat; foresters, fishermen, miners, etc., before it can make use of natural resources; craftsmen before it can have manufactured goods; and merchants before they can be distributed. But once these exist, what need is there for government directives, mobilizations of labor, or periodic assemblies? Each man has only to be left to utilize his own abilities and exert his strength to obtain what he wishes. Thus, when a commodity is very cheap, it invites a rise in price; when it is very expensive, it invites a reduction. When each person works away at his own occupation and the lights in his own business then, like water flowing downward, goods will naturally flow forth ceaselessly day and night without having been summoned, and the people will produce commodities without having been asked. (Sima 1961, 477)

Adam Smith could not have said it better himself, and in the 1990s there was an exchange of articles contending over whether Sima Qian anticipated much of what Smith introduced to Western thought (Young 1996; McCormick 1999).

Subsequently in the same work, Sima contended:

> These, then, were examples of outstanding and unusually wealthy men. None of them enjoyed any titles or fiefs, gifts, or salaries from the government, nor did they play tricks with the law or commit any crimes

> to acquire their fortunes. They simply guessed what course conditions were going to take and acted accordingly, kept a sharp eye out for the opportunities of the times, and so were able to capture a fat profit. (Sima 1961, 498)

While *Records* has long been considered a classic, this particular insight left little trace in later Chinese writings on economics, so that when Smith himself was finally translated into Chinese his insights were thought to be revolutionary.

The degree to which actual policy conformed to the recommendations of liberalism fluctuated greatly. As far back as the Warring States period there was an identifiable class of merchants, but they worked with rulers, to "assist them in gathering and centralizing control over economic resources" (von Glahn, 2016 46)—different in methods but not in fundamental goals from the mercantilist corporations, guilds, and other institutions that would be roundly criticized by Smith. Yet the merchant Bai Gui (c. 463–385 BCE) was recruited to serve as a political leader in the state of Wei and was able to achieve significant reductions in customs duties and bureaucratic complexity (Hu 1988). Sometimes even a change of emperor within a dynasty could make a significant difference. The Taoist second-century-BCE Han emperor Wen (202–157 BCE) is generally held to have ruled very liberally, reducing taxes, reforming the criminal law and largely introducing the exam system for choosing bureaucratic officials that would be used until 1905. But his successor's successor and grandson, the emperor Wu (156–87 BCE) reimposed centralized rule with state direction of economic activity. Evidence indicates that during his rule the urban population of China declined, a number of Chinese cities de-complexified, and agriculture significantly displaced mercantile commerce (Yamada 2000).

Several times subsequently, economic policy changed direction between liberal and illiberal regimes. It seemed to rulers that controlling prices in the very short term made things better for the poor, but of course also caused quantities supplied to dry up. Freedom for merchants was associated with vibrant economies and prosperity for those officially connected to trade networks, but it also generated seemingly dangerous declines in the uniformity of income. In addition, the Confucian legacy of disdain for the commercial life and lauding of family and hierarchy periodically fueled changes toward less liberalism. But to speak approximately, as in literature and the arts, the

Song dynasty (960–1279 CE) was in terms of material prosperity a golden age, and a liberal one to boot. Philosophically, while there was nothing directly resembling the fuller package of Western economic liberalism, during this time neo-Confucian scholars such as Zhu Xi (1130–1200) indirectly promoted limited government by reviving the Confucian tradition of calling rulers to account for lack of individual rectitude. That practices of self-cultivation are both essential to ruling justly and accessible to people of any station has been a long tradition in Chinese thought. But after the collapse of the Song dynasty and the following century of subsequent Mongol rule, the first Ming emperor after taking power in 1368 sought to restore the autarkic villages lionized by Mencius and subsequent neo-Confucian philosophers.

In later centuries, enough data exist to document several episodes of prolonged economic stagnation: both an unnamed depression and the Kangxi depression between the 1630s to the 1690s (Atwell 1999), and the Daoguang depression from the 1820s to the 1840s (von Glahn 2016), the former two straddling the period during which the Ming dynasty fell. While the second stagnation occurred while the authority of the final dynasty, the Manchu Qing, was still strong, it was followed by the roughly 70 years in which contact with Western militaries in possession of mass-produced weaponry ultimately ended the imperial system—but not before provoking intense interest in Western ideas.

Thus there were many examples scattered over the centuries of individual ideas also found in classical liberalism, as one would expect of a civilization with as long a history and as much complexity as China. But there was no coherent philosophy of classical liberalism in the sense of other Chinese schools of thought such as Legalism and Confucianism. That would soon change.

China faces the West and its political economy

During the nineteenth century, a sequence of increasingly alarming events gradually caused a belief to grow inside China that it was now demonstrably behind the countries of the West, which were no longer so distant from Chinese consciousness. The Chinese military was defeated in two 'Opium Wars'—first by Britain in 1839–1842 and then by primarily Britain and France during 1856–1860. At the end of the second war the two so-called Summer Palaces in the Beijing area were both looted and burned, after the Chinese government had executed several British captives. The second Opium War was enveloped by the purely domestic but far more catastrophic Taiping rebellion from 1850–1864, in which millions died. As the second half of the century unfolded, the Qing Government had to make repeated concessions to British, French, Japanese, Russian, German, and American powers with regard first to war reparations and later the granting of privileges such as the right to construct railways, and to establish colonies in Shanghai and elsewhere. Particularly motivating was the Chinese loss to Japan in the brief Sino-Japanese War of 1894–1895, after a much smaller Japan had successfully incorporated Western technology and military strategy on its own within 40 years after initial (also hostile) Western contact.

By this time, China already had a long tradition of translation, especially of Sanskrit Buddhist texts and, starting in the late sixteenth century, of the Latin texts of Jesuits, who were then well ensconced in a few places in China. From 1723, when the Jesuits were expelled, to the loss in the first Opium War, translation effectively stopped. But by 1880 the translation of scientific texts resumed and then expanded, in part because Westerners were then teaching religious, scientific, and social-scientific Western knowledge through formal schools. In addition, there was now increasing Chinese emigration to the countries of the Western Hemisphere, and some of these Chinese went abroad specifically to master Western languages and ideas.

One of the most influential of these latter was Yan Fu (1854–1921), the single most important introducer of liberal ideas in China, who was educated in England at a naval school established in 1866 by the Qing but where most of the teachers were Westerners. Between 1877 and 1879 he lived in England, where he was thoroughly exposed to English-language Western texts. After the Treaty of Shimonoseki that ended the war with Japan, he began to translate many works containing what he saw as the knowledge that was key to Western strength, knowledge that had been absorbed by Japan. While there were many strains of thought contending in the contemporary West, including liberalism, Darwinian evolution, pragmatism, and Marxism, looking back it is striking how important Yan thought that liberal thinking was and liberal thinkers were in explaining Western power. In addition to *The Wealth of Nations*, Yan translated Thomas Huxley's *Evolution and Ethics* (the title of which he chose to translate as *Tiānyǎnlùn*, or 《天演论》, meaning *Theory of Evolution*), Herbert Spencer's *The Study of Sociology*, John Stuart Mill's *On Liberty* (his translation of the title being *Qúnjǐquánjièlùn*, or 《群己权界论》, *On the Boundary Between the Self and the Group*) and *A System of Logic*, Edward Jenks's *A History of Politics*, Montesquieu's *The Spirit of the Laws*, and William Stanley Jevons's *A Primer of Logic* (all collected in Yan 2014).

Some have argued that the spirit of liberalism did not transfer entirely to Yan's Chinese translations (as his altered titles suggest). In particular, the West had long situated the individual in society differently. Thus, it is said that Yan failed to accurately translate or convey Mill's conception of why free competition in the realms of ideas and social organization in particular was beneficial to society (Huang 2008). That all his translations took the form of the then-standard but soon-to-be-obsolete classical Chinese may have made the problem worse. Yan also faced the problem in all his translations of how to translate particular English terms that had no parallel in late nineteenth-century China, among them *the economy* and *economics*. He considered using the Chinese-character translations that had been adopted several decades prior in Japan, such as *jīngjì* or 经济 for *the economy* and this combined with *xué* or 学 for *economics*. Indeed, these are the terms used in modern Chinese. But Yan thought that this translation mistakenly connoted the effective exercise of control over all national questions. He thus chose a translation arguably better for the time, *jìxué* or 计学. This term had a meaning that suggested calculation, "the relations among different economic actors," and "the management of finances at the household or firm level" (Osborne 2017, 298).

Nonetheless, through Yan liberal economics became part of the mix of ideas in China after 1895, a period that included the fall of the imperial system in 1911–1912. Chang Yü-Fa (2000) describes four main strands of Western socioeconomic thought that received significant support in China during this time: liberalism, anarchism, socialist-inspired redesign of society, and women's rights. To this could be added the issue of ethnic-minority rights.[4] Before the 1911 installation of Sun Yat-sen as the president of China, all of these debates were set against the basic question of whether the best way forward

---

4. Women's rights and ethnic-minority rights are not necessarily inconsistent with liberalism, anarchism, or socialism, but this was a time when the internal dialogue was over what the single key was to Western power. Some people argued for classical liberalism, others for other ideas.

was mere reform (*gǎigé*, 改革) or outright revolution (*géming*, 革命). Yan in particular believed that in placing the individual above society, and rights above obligations, in some respects Western liberalism was unsuited for the Chinese.

The debate played out in the 'new culture movement' of the 1910s and 1920s, which featured fierce debate over whether China needed total Westernization or preservation of Chinese tradition. The appeal to embrace democracy and science was particularly spearheaded by Chen Duxiu in his journal *The New Youth* (*Xīn Qīngnián*, 《新青年》), published from 1915–1922. During this time, intellectuals who had undergone a classical education, most famously Lu Xun, led a revolt against Chinese tradition, including Confucianism and classical written Chinese.

And so ideas did battle in China from roughly 1895, when Japan decisively defeated China after a brief war, until the later Japanese invasion of China in 1937. Throughout, there was little meaningful print censorship. Sun Yat-sen himself, while traveling extensively in North America and Europe before 1911 looking for support for his revolution, had been exposed to and was favorably impressed by various schools of socialist thought. As late as 1938, Guo Dali and Wang Yanan could successfully translate Karl Marx's *Capital*, despite several years of civil war and now once again war with Japan. Eugen Böhm-Bawerk's *Marx and the Close of his System* was also published in translation in 1936. And so debate was still vigorous, periodicals came and went, and the battle was done in that arena and in various books.

But meanwhile, politics was continuously chaotic. By the 1920s the liberal cause had been substantially damaged by a transfer of territorial concessions in China from Germany to Japan in the Treaty of Versailles, even though China and Japan had been victorious allies during the war. The CCP was founded in a meeting in Shanghai in 1921 which included Chen Duxiu, who had turned *New Youth* toward Marxism after Russia's October revolution, and Mao Zedong. After Sun Yat-sen had been installed as president, the child emperor Pu Yi abdicated in 1912, but then the generalissimo Yuan Shikai became president, and soon after that pronounced himself emperor before dying in 1916. China fell into warlordism in the 1920s, and 1927 saw both Chiang Kai-shek's campaign against warlords in the north and the adoption of armed struggle by the CCP.

Amidst the domestic chaos and the competition with other ideas, the constituency for political and economic liberalism was now considerably diminished. Even so, several liberal and Enlightenment texts were translated in the 1930s, including David Ricardo's *On the Principles of Political Economy and Taxation* (1931) and Immanuel Kant's *Critique of Pure Reason* (1931) and *Critique of Practical Reason* (1936). The two Marxist scholars Guo Dali and Wang Yanan translated *The Wealth of Nations* into modern (not classical) Chinese in 1931 as preparation for translating *Capital.*

So at the time of the Japanese invasion of the rest of China in 1937—Manchuria having been seized in 1931—liberalism was alive but in retreat in an environment of competing ideas. But there was still a thirst for *the* idea that would 'save' China. The CCP had now been in rebellion for roughly a decade. State management of the economy, as propounded in Sun Yat-sen's *Fundamentals of National Reconstruction* (Sun 1953/1924), if not outright state production, was the leading school of economic thought in China during the 1920s and 1930s, as it was in many countries in the West. But freedom of expression, largely intact through this period, would disappear after the victory of the CCP in China's Civil War.

Liberal ideas in the communist era

1949–1978

From a platform on Tiananmen Square, Mao Zedong proclaimed the founding of the People's Republic of China on October 1, 1949. At that point, the Chinese government gradually moved to adopt the standard communist model of complete state media control, both broadcast and press. After a relatively open first few years, expression became a monologue and not a conversation. In addition, state propaganda, including the content of the daily papers, was used to organize themes for mass meetings. Mao did launch the "Hundred Flowers" campaign for freer expression in May 1956. But by 1957, street demonstrations and strikes were breaking out in several large Chinese cities. The criticism of the CCP was frequently vehement and occasionally violent. In May 1957 Mao issued a communiqué to party leaders specifically urging that people be permitted to speak freely, but only with an eye to identifying CCP enemies and punishing them later. The sweeping of the identified dissidents into prison began weeks later and was completed within months (Dikötter 2013).

Obviously, in such an environment no alternative to prevailing communist orthodoxy, let alone liberalism, could play any role in the Chinese public conversation. Yet a number of landmark liberal texts were published by the state press. Why? To serve as educational 'internal reading material' (*nèibù dúwù*, 内部读物) for leadership elites. Mill's *On Liberty* (1959), Hayek's *The Road to Serfdom* (1962), Böhm-Bawerk's *Capital and Interest* (1959) and *Positive Theory of Capital* (1964), Jean-Baptiste Say's *A Treatise on Political Economy* (1963), and *The Wealth of Nations* (Smith 1972/1931, including a new orthodox Marxist introduction by Wang Yanan) were all published or republished during this time. In each case, the strictures of Marxist ideology meant that the works had to be fit into the corresponding 'scientific' history. This led to two possibilities: Either they were examples of corrupt bourgeois liberalism, sometimes called 'reactionary reference materials' (*fǎnmian cáiliào*, 反面材料, or *fǎndòng cái liào*, 反动材料) or of primitive political economy which eventually flowered into the mature work of Marx and his successors including Mao.[5] In either case these publications were not widely available to the general public.

Liberal publishing, 1978–2017

In 1976 Mao died, and shortly thereafter the Gang of Four were arrested, with their trial concluding in 1980. In the interim Deng Xiaoping took and cemented power, and along with other new senior leadership he sought to reform the Chinese economy pragmatically—in whatever way would develop the country most thoroughly and rapidly. Soon after, censorship of the press and publication became less stringent. As a result, important works of liberalism could, and still can today, be (re-)translated and published in China. Indeed, with works out of copyright there are often multiple editions circulating at the same time. In addition, numerous publishers are issuing their own series of substantial Western works more generally, and classical liberal titles are often included. For example, the firm Commercial Press has

---

5. In his preface to the 1962 edition of *The Road to Serfdom*, Teng Weizao wrote: "Although he regards himself as an 'impartial author,' he is in fact a loyal servant in defending the capitalist system. Hayek has ingrained hatred against socialism and any kind of aggressive tendencies" (1962, 1, our translation).

been publishing a series of Chinese translations of classical academic works since 1981. Among the works in the series at least touching on classical-liberal values are Smith's *The Theory of Moral Sentiments* (1997), David Hume's *An Enquiry Concerning Human Understanding* (1981) and *An Enquiry Concerning the Principles of Morals* (2001), Ricardo's *On the Principles of Political Economy and Taxation* (1981), Mill's *Principles of Political Economy* (1991), Karl Popper's *The Open Society and its Enemies* (1999), and Hayek's *The Road to Serfdom* (1997). Across all editions, *The Road to Serfdom* has sold particularly well, and in intellectual circles has become somewhat influential. Public choice is represented as well with, for example, translated work of Geoffrey Brennan and James M. Buchanan (2004).

To be sure, in the realm of economic policy, the most influential Western economists have generally been of the neoclassical orientation. On the one hand, Milton Friedman was invited to China in the early 1980s to consult with Chinese officials on macroeconomic policy; on the other, the more dominant voices in those early years were figures like James Tobin and János Kornai, who advocated varying degrees of state intervention (Gewirtz 2017).

Yet outside government, some people with views easily described as classical liberal have had influence through their widely read public commentary. One is the Hong Kong native Steven N. S. Cheung, a top institutional and political economist. After a very successful academic career in the United States, he returned to Hong Kong in 1982 and participated in the crafting of early Chinese reforms (see Cheung 1986). For many years after that, he wrote regular columns in the *Hong Kong Economic Journal* and elsewhere, which have been highly influential with some segments of the Chinese public. In these columns, he made such liberal ideas as basic price theory clear to his readership through often-clever storytelling. Another influential market-oriented economist is Zhang Weiying, who has shown special interest in 'Austrian' economics in recent years. He has written books on entrepreneurship and how markets work. His book *The Logic of the Market* (Zhang 2010; 2015a) is designed to explain to a general readership some basic principles of the operation of markets. His recent textbook *Principles of Economics* (*Jīngjìxué Yuánlǐ*, 《经济学原理》, 2015b) combines standard modern economic theory with Austrian views.

Yet while not as stifling as during the Mao years, the pressures of what we might call 'political correctness with Chinese characteristics' continue. When dealing with any politically sensitive topic, publishers or translators frequently include remarks indicating that the book is being translated foremost for the purpose of academic exchange. And sometimes liberal texts have content that directly criticizes socialism, which is major component of the ideology that supports the Communist Party's monopoly on power. And so occasionally even content from the original work itself must be removed. A good example of such self-censorship is a Chinese translation of Ludwig von Mises's *Socialism* (2008). The translators and publisher based on their own judgment chose to remove a number of criticisms of socialism in order to get it published, and the publisher still had to wait three years until the ideological climate was appropriate. But even in the face of the need to self-censor in this fashion, liberal thinking is unmistakably present. Notably, there was only one line removed from the 1997 translation of *The Road to Serfdom*, and it was the very first one: the famous dedication "to the socialists of all parties."

The room to advocate liberalism in today's China

Academia

In Chinese universities today, the economic curriculum is a strange mix of classes on Marxism, which are required for all students, and classes that would look familiar to any Western college student, often using American textbooks and filled with models of aggregate supply and aggregate demand, indifference-curve equilibria, and so on. Thus, certainly by Chinese historical standards the modern economics presented there is little more interventionist than in the West. But Marxism is included on the entrance exams to begin both undergraduate and graduate study, and a Chinese college student must take a certain amount of Marxist economics, history and philosophy. As noted above, Marxist institutes also exist in many Chinese universities, and classical liberal political economy is often introduced there as obsolete thinking. Yet many economics professors at Chinese universities publish in the world's leading economics journals. There is currently little coursework organized around either classical liberal authors or themes. People have built scholarly networks to study and propagate liberal thought, but recently these networks have come under some pressure, as discussed below.

Networks and associations

There is some space in today's China for liberal groups, networks, and associations that may not have any official association with academia, although less since 2019. The two best known have been the Cathay Institute for Public Affairs (CIPA) and the Chinese Hayek Society (CHS). The CIPA was founded in 2002, and its membership included many of the leading Chinese classical liberal scholars, including Liu Junning, Mao Shoulong, Yao Zhongqiu, Xia Yeliang, Wang Jianxun, Mo Zhihong, and Zhu Haijiu.[6] It was sufficiently effective to have won the 2011 Templeton Freedom Award for Excellence in Promoting Liberty. Prior to COVID-19, several times a year it held conferences or other public events that presented research on liberal thought or analyzed public policy from a liberal perspective. It has also provided a structure for Chinese scholars sympathetic to liberalism to engage in exchange with similar scholars from outside China. The CHS was a network of fluctuating membership consisting of both in-country and overseas contributors. Alas, recent trends in official ideology have become unfavorable to these groups, and both organizations have ended their work, though some members have decided their activities will continue in reorganized form. Such behavior, in which the structures through which ideas are promoted are shut down but the propagators of those ideas are usually free to re-organize and continue until they next cross the line—unless they cross too many lines, as has happened with, for example, Liu Xiaobo, who received the Nobel Peace Prize for 2010 while in prison before later dying there in 2017.

A previous, similar organization was a forum for intellectual exchange run by the Unirule Finance and Economics Research Center (Tiānzé jīngjì yánjiūsuǒ, 北京天则经济研究所). It was a very influential non-governmental think tank, with top classical liberal economists such as Mao Yushi, Zhang Shuguang, and Sheng Hong, and the leading historian Wu Si among its members. It was well-known as a center of research on institutional economics and its application to China. It has received both funding from various Western foundations and domestic donations, and currently it depends mainly upon revenues generated internally. (This organization's closure is discussed in the postscript.)

---

6. One of the authors of this article (Feng) was a member of CIPA.

As we write, a still-existing example of an influential liberalism-inspired informal network is one organized by Wang Ying, someone with an extensive history both as an entrepreneur and a government official. In reading groups that both meet in person and gather online, she encourages Chinese entrepreneurs to become both familiar and comfortable with the idea of continuous, undirected social change, and to see themselves as key agents in that process.

To the extent that such people are admired by the public and respected by government officials, their cultivation may be key to the success of enhancing the role of liberalism in the Chinese conversation. As a whole, these informal groups, like groups organized around many causes, fade and then grow as political pressures wax and wane. At the moment, they do not necessarily seek to engage in widespread public persuasion of the sort that might occur in an election campaign. Rather, they try to make a difference by exposing potential key players in China's possible futures to the ideas of classical liberalism.

Political pressure

After 1978, as indeed throughout much of Chinese history, sympathy for liberal policies has risen and fallen in Chinese leadership circles. In the first decade, the enthusiasm of Deng Xiaoping for economic liberalism in particular undeniably grew in tandem with Chinese prosperity. China's leader Hu Yaobang had liberal economic sympathies, and perhaps liberal political sympathies by the standards of the early post-Mao era. In the latter half of the 1980s Zhao Ziyang was guardedly active in this role for political liberalism, but any official lionizing of this thinking ended with the brief, liberal-oriented 1989 protest movement, which was launched by Hu's death and whose violent termination also ended Zhao's career.

Today, some Chinese intellectuals sympathetic to classical liberalism also function as opinion leaders and seek to change current policy. And yet, such influence as they have is mainly indirect. Sometimes, as we have seen, their advocacy of freedom today or tomorrow and their exposure of illiberalism in the recent past draw the glare of the authorities. And, sometimes, they are as a result removed from specific positions of influence that are subject to the dictates of the authorities.[7]

---

7. The aforementioned Zhang Weiying was removed after twelve years as dean of the

The experience of Mao Yushi is illustrative. Mao is a trained engineer who graduated from Shanghai Jiaotong University in 1950. Since then he has been a breakthrough thinker and has been punished by the authorities for things he says and writes. In 1958 he was purged as a rightist while working for a state railway agency. He became a largely self-taught economist in the 1970s, and since then has advocated for liberal economic values. His best-selling introductory economics book *The Economics of Everyday Life* (*Shēnghuó zhōng de jīng jì xué*, 《生活中的经济学》; Mao 2004), which emphasizes the role of freely adjusting prices in moving resources to where they are more valued at the margin, the norms and culture of markets, and other liberal themes, continues to be a popular text. Along with Zhang Weiying's *The Logic of the Market* (Zhang 2010; 2015a), which also incorporates many liberal and Hayekian insights on the role of knowledge and competition, it perhaps performs a similar role in China as Thomas Sowell's *Basic Economics* (2014) does for American readers. But Mao also attracted attention with a series of essays in which he criticized excessive state power and advocated for a more open society (e.g., Mao 2008). In 2010, he was prevented from traveling to Norway to see the imprisoned Liu Xiaobo receive his Nobel peace prize in absentia. The next year, Mao (2011) ignited the anger of China's small but inordinately influential community of Maoist devotees by releasing an essay called "Returning Mao Zedong to Human Form" ("Bǎ Mao Zedong huànyuán chéng rén," "把毛泽东还原成人"), in which he documented the human toll of Mao Zedong's (no relation) rule; the essay is no longer available in China. He won the Cato Institute's Milton Friedman Prize for Advancing Liberty in 2012, but his website was shut down in 2017, and both his influential Weibo account and Wechat public channel were closed recently. (Mao's fate is also discussed in the postscript.) Other classical liberal figures have also recently had their Internet communication sites shut down, among them scholars such as Sheng Hong and Wu Si.

So the space for vigorous advocacy of classical liberal ideas may be shrinking, and this is troubling because the need for further liberalization is pressing. Coase and Wang (2012) emphasize, with good reason, the immense freeing-up of talent and drive in the post-Mao era. But substantial political

---

Guanghua School of Management, the business school at Beijing University, in 2010. His economic and political liberalism are generally thought to have played a major role in his removal.

control of resource use remains, and with China's growing prosperity the corruption flowing from this control has grown dramatically. Further, in some respects official CCP ideology has in recent years turned more collectivist, and more hostile to economic freedom and the instability that naturally comes with it. Classical-liberal ideas are as necessary now as at any time since the late 1970s. Where liberals can network and speak, especially speak so that others not so familiar with classical-liberal ideas can listen, it will be important for them to do so.

Summary and prospects

Beginning in 1978 China began what at that time was the most dramatic reshaping of an almost totally planned economy to date. Since then its standard of living has grown dramatically. While at the outset confined to a few experimental zones, reform has taken hold to the extent that employment at large state-owned factories has shrunk dramatically as a share of the total, even as private enterprises of all sizes have formed to fill the gap (Ma 2015). Liberal policies deserve much of the credit for this historic transformation.

This paper has offered an account of the history and current position of the classical-liberal values that promote economic and political competition in China. Built on some foundation of indigenous economic liberalism, the arrival of specifically Western liberal thinking was greeted enthusiastically in the late nineteenth century, although other imported ideologies were probably more appealing by 1930. But since reforms began in 1978, liberal texts, combined with recent Chinese interpretations of economic liberalism, have once again become widely available in China. There is plenty of raw material to generate discussions on the pragmatic and moral virtues of economic liberty. In the new China such discussions are not rare, whether online or offline. The Chinese have many eras of economic dynamism and minimal government economic intervention in their history, and the success of ethnic Chinese overseas is well known.

But the story with regard to political liberalism is very different. China is a one-party state, and while there is considerably more vitality in the marketplace for economic ideas than there was in the late 1970s, there are clear limits. The level of permissiveness rises and falls, but it is always difficult to publish translations or to own works with arguments about sensitive topics such as liberty or constitutionalism. CCP directives induce self-censorship by major commercial publishers and groupthink among academics, although such directives seldom explicitly restrict purely economic texts, whether meant for college classrooms or the general public, including ones oriented toward liberalism. And the censorship process is idiosyncratic. Some foreign books are allowed in, but content is deleted or modified directly by translators fearful of stricter censorship. Only a small number of books are banned outright, and often those directly implicate the CCP or its leaders (e.g., Yang 2012). Any writings that call into question the legitimacy of one-party rule or the conduct of officials present or past who have not fallen into disfavor are completely unacceptable.

That people might attribute, and political leaders might opportunistically ascribe, Chinese economic success to political illiberalism (as opposed to economic liberalism) is a worrying prospect for friends of China, including scholars, who might themselves be seduced by this myth or by the temptation to serve it (Holz 2007; Cowen 2017). Foreigners and Chinese alike ought to nourish the small but flourishing classical-liberal networks there.

Fortunately, survey research by Jennifer Pan and Yiqing Xu (2017) suggests that there is a constituency in China that believes simultaneously in economic liberalism, political liberalism, and even social libertarianism. Perhaps unsurprisingly, these views are more common among those who perceive themselves as having done well under reform. While Pan and Xu do not estimate the size of this constituency, levels of individual economic success and economic development in the region where respondents live seem to be positively associated with the prevalence of these beliefs. Those who have benefited from economic liberalization thus may offer a ready base from which to build greater support for comprehensive liberalism. The link between liberal policies and enhancement of opportunities should be stressed. And so we conjecture that entrepreneurs, particularly those who can avoid excessive entanglement with government, must be in the vanguard of remaking China. For now, liberal ideas are alive and liberals are active. But even as public disagreement over some issues, especially the environment, has grown—with the grudging tolerance of the authorities—there has been a corresponding trend toward limits on anyone who takes too far any criticism that might threaten one-party rule, although it is not so often that such offenders are exiled, imprisoned, or murdered. Despite the strong hand classical liberals have to play, whether they will win in a game in which the deck is stacked remains to be seen.

Postscript

There has been some change in the Chinese government attitude toward economic liberalism overall since our article appeared in 2017, although not as much as is sometimes argued. Xi Jinping, who took office as national leader in 2012, is often said to be a skeptic of continuing market reforms. Yet, to commemorate the famous trip Deng Xiaoping took in 1991 to praise the early achievements of economic reform in the southeast, Xi in 2018 in the same place made a speech indicating his commitment to reform and openness overall. In fact, some reforms have continued. In any event their previous extent has been too substantial to undo without courting public opposition. According to data in Tables 4.3–4.10 of National Bureau of Statistics of China (various years), between 1989 and 2019 the number employed in urban areas who either work in private firms or are self-employed has risen from 25 to over 90 percent. Chinese are now substantially employed, fed, housed, and clothed through market processes, and this will not be substantially undone. Market forces even play a significant role, not without controversy, in health care. Many economists in China understand market mechanisms well enough, and some of them believe in those mechanisms. In 2021, as coal prices soared, the government gave utilities with plants not less but more pricing freedom for the power they produced, and the problem abated. There have also been continued moves to further liberalize portfolio investment flows into and out of the country, and to give foreign financial firms more freedom to operate.

However, the government is more committed to making sure that strategically important industries, as defined by the CCP, operate as the government wishes. In high technology, natural resources, finance, and other activities, the government, if not necessarily producing goods outright, insists that large companies toe the government line. The approach resembles to some extent what is said to be the model employed by other countries in northeast Asia during their postwar miracles, although the capacity for corruption, and the degree of social control exercised by the Chinese government, using new surveillance technology, are atrocious in today's China. The government now requires all domestic institutions of any size, including private companies, to have departments to monitor their ideological conformity. This increasing control has been exacerbated by rising Western skepticism of the CCP in the wake of the crackdown on Hong Kong that began in 2019, its aggressive behavior with respect to its neighbors, and its concealing of the early stages of the COVID-19 epidemic that spread around the globe after first exploding in the Chinese city of Wuhan. In response, in all activities with domestic-security implications real or imagined, the Chinese government is now aggressively implementing "decoupling," that is, eliminating economic engagement with Western powers that could threaten the CCP's ability to act as it wishes. Most conspicuously, it is thus seeking to become self-sufficient in high technology, following Western and especially U.S. measures against Chinese technology companies such as Huawei.

Still, economic liberalization since the late 1970s, though plagued by corruption, has been substantial. While every young person must learn Marxist economic pieties, including in postsecondary education, Western textbooks that substantially praise the virtues of markets are widely used in universities. The classical-liberal texts translated into Chinese mentioned in the article can still be purchased by the general public, and while Mao Yushi and the Unirule organization have been silenced, the latter after official de-registration by the CCP in 2019, other less-trenchant authors mentioned in the text, along with others, still engage in a cautious advocacy of further liberalization. While no longer a dean, Zhang Weiying remains a publicly active professor at the same university. While their activities have been constrained to some degree, economic liberals are not imprisoned or exiled. The substantial although far-from-complete marketization of what was once Mao Zedong's completely economically illiberal experiment will stay, no matter who rules, because the domestic opposition to their repeal would be too terrible for the CCP.

However, entranced by geopolitical dreams and fearing domestic political unrest, the CCP has since our article turned even more to the commanding-heights model, in which the state deeply influences anything involving its perceived interests. The CCP has exerted control by seeking price stability, e.g., its so-far misbegotten attempts to first control a housing bubble and then control its popping. It has reoriented economic activity toward increasing its international influence, e.g., via its long-term "Belt and Road" initiative to secure resource supplies from and promote Chinese firms in developing countries in Asia and Africa. And it is hampering creative destruction that might generate political unrest, for example through its crackdown on the previously rapidly growing private-tutoring industry. It has also cancelled the giant Shanghai IPO of Alibaba founder Ma Yun's potentially financially revolutionary Ant Group, which would have put Ma's financial resources behind a network to connect individual lenders with individual borrowers, enabling a major alternative to the state-dominated banking system. Such increasing economic illiberalism, born more of desire for political control rather than of any old-fashioned enthusiasm for import substitution, indicates that the CCP, while asserting a strong hand in certain industries, also fears the broader social instability generated by certain kinds of liberalization. At the margin, it sees these new, and growing, restrictions as substantially more valuable to its own interests than continued improvement in the common people's standard of living, despite the fact that the latter itself is a means for protecting Chinese power. Given that by the mid-2010s the Chinese economy already was possibly entering an era of lower growth (Lin, Morgan, and Wan 2018), the combination of a strong government and its obsessions with preserving its monopoly of power may make for troubling times ahead for the Chinese people.

References

Atwell, William S. 1990. A Seventeenth-Century 'General Crisis' in East Asia? *Modern Asia Studies* 24(4): 661–682.

Barnstone, Tony, and Chou Ping, eds. 2005. *The Anchor Book of Chinese Poetry*. New York: Random House.

Böhm-Bawerk, Eugen von. 1936. 《马克思主义体系的崩溃》 [*The Collapse of the Marxist System*]. Shanghai: Commercial Press.

Böhm-Bawerk, Eugen von. 1959. 《资本与利息》 [*Capital and Interest*], trans. Kunzeng He and Dechao Gao. Beijing: Commercial Press.

Böhm-Bawerk, Eugen von. 1964. 《资本实证论》 [*The Positive Theory of Capital*], trans. Duan Chen. Beijing: Commercial Press.

Brennan, Geoffrey, and James M. Buchanan. 2004. *Constitutional Economics* [in Chinese], trans. Keli Feng, et al. Beijing: China Social Sciences Press.

Chang Yü-Fa. 2000. 《近代中国民主政治发展史》 [*The Recent History of the Development of China's Democratic Politics*]. Taipei: Dongda Books.

Cheung, Steven N. S. 1986. *Will China Go Capitalist? An Economic Analysis of Property Rights and Institutional Change*, 2nd rev. ed. London: Institute of Economic Affairs.

Coase, Ronald H., and Ning Wang. 2012. *How China Became Capitalist*. Basingstoke, UK:

Palgrave Macmillan.

Confucius. 2009. *The Analects*, trans. Bojun Yang and Din Cheuk Lau. Taipei: Lianji Publishing Company.

Cowen, Tyler. 2017. Between Authoritarianism and Human Capital. *Cato Online Forum* (Cato Institute, Washington, D.C.), March.

Dikötter, Frank. 2013. *The Tragedy of Liberation: A History of the Chinese Revolution 1945–1957*. New York: Bloomsbury.

Eucken, Walter. 1952. *Grundsätze der Wirtschaftspolitik*. Tübingen, Germany: J. C. B. Mohr (Paul Siebeck).

Feng, Xingyuan, Christer Ljungwall, and Guangwen He. 2015. *The Ecology of Chinese Private Enterprises*. Singapore: World Scientific.

Gewirtz, Julian. 2017. *Unlikely Partners: Chinese Reformers, Western Economists, and the Making of Global China*. Cambridge, Mass.: Harvard University Press.

Hayek, Friedrich A. 1962. 《通往奴役的道路》 [*The Road to Serfdom*], trans. Teng Weizao and Zhu Zongfeng. Beijing: Commercial Press.

Hayek, Friedrich A. 1978. *The Constitution of Liberty*. Chicago: University of Chicago Press.

Hayek, Friedrich A. 1997. 《通往奴役之路》 [*The Road to Serfdom*], trans. Mingyi Wang, Xingyuan Feng, et al. Beijing: China Social Sciences Press.

Holz, Carsten A. 2007. Have China Scholars All Been Bought? *Far Eastern Economic Review* 170(3): 36–40.

Hu Jichuang. 1988. *A Concise History of Chinese Economic Thought*. Beijing: Foreign Languages Press.

Huang, Max Ko-Wu. 2008. *The Meaning of Freedom: Yan Fu and the Origins of Chinese Liberalism*. Hong Kong: Chinese University Press.

Hume, David. 1981. 《人类理解研究》 [*An Enquiry Concerning Human Understanding*], trans. Wenyun Guan. Beijing: Commercial Press.

Hume, David. 2001. 《道德原则研究》 [*An Enquiry Concerning the Principles of Morals*], trans. Xiaoping Zeng. Beijing: Commercial Press.

Kant, Immanuel. 1931. 《纯粹理性批判》 [*Critique of Pure Reason*], trans. Renyuan Hu. Shanghai: Commercial Press.

Kant, Immanuel. 1936. 《实践理性批判》 [*Critique of Practical Reason*], trans. Mingding Zhang. Shanghai: Commercial Press.

Ma, Hong. 2015. Job Creation and Job Destruction in China During 1998–2007. *Journal of Comparative Economics* 43(4): 1085–1100.

Mao Yushi. 2004. 《生活中的经济学》 [*The Economics of Everyday Life*]. Guangzhou: Jinan University Press.

Mao Yushi. 2008. 人民的利益，国家的利益，政治家的利益 [The People's Interest, the National Interest, and Politicians' Interest]. *Epoch Times*, July 22.

Mao Yushi. 2011. 把毛泽东还原成人 [Returning Mao Zedong to Human Form: Reflections from Reading the Book "The Fall-Down of the Red Sun"]. *China Review Net*, April 26.

Mao Zedong. 1969. 反对自由主义 [Against Liberalism]. In 《毛泽东全集1917–1949》 [*Selected Works of Mao Zedong 1917–1949*], vol. 2, 359–361. Beijing: People's Press.

Marx, Karl. 1938. 《资本论》 [*Capital*], trans. Guo Dali and Wang Yanan. Shanghai: Reading Life Publishing.

McCormick, Ken. 1999. Sima Qian and Adam Smith. *Pacific Economic Review* 4(1): 85–87.

Mill, John Stuart. 1959. 《论自由》 [*On Liberty*], trans. Baokui Xu. Beijing: Commercial Press.

Mill, John Stuart. 1991. 《政治经济学原理》 [*Principles of Political Economy, With Some of Their Applications to Social Philosophy*], trans. Rongqian Zhao et al. Beijing: Commercial Press.

Mises, Ludwig von. 2008. 《社会主义》 [*Socialism: An Economic and Sociological Analysis*], trans. Jianmin Wang, Keli Feng, and Shuyi Cui. Beijing: Commercial Press.

North, Douglass C., John Joseph Wallis, and Barry R. Weingast. 2009. *Violence and Social Orders: A Conceptual Framework for Interpreting Recorded Human History*. Cambridge, UK: Cambridge University Press.

Osborne, Evan W. 2012. China's First Liberal. *Independent Review* 16(4): 533–551.

Osborne, Evan W. 2017. A Revolutionary's Evolution: The View Over Time of The Wealth of Nations in China. *Adam Smith Review* 9: 295–319.

Pan, Jennifer, and Yiqing Xu. 2017 (forthcoming). China's Ideological Spectrum. *Journal of Politics*.

Pan Wei. 2007. The Chinese Model of Development. Presented at Foreign Policy Center (London), October 11.

Popper, Karl. 1999. 《开放社会及其敌人》 [*The Open Society and Its Enemies*], trans. Heng Lu et al. Beijing: China Social Sciences Press.

Ricardo, David. 1931. 《政治经济学及赋税之原理》 [*On the Principles of Political Economy and Taxation*], trans. Guo Dali and Wang Yanan. Shanghai: Divine Land State Glory Press.

Ricardo, David. 1981. 《政治经济学及赋税之原理》 (《大卫·里卡多全集》) [*On the Principles of Political Economy and Taxation (The Works and Correspondence of David Ricardo, vol. I)*], ed. Piero Sraffa, trans. Guo Dali and Wang Yanan. Beijing: Commercial Press.

Say, Jean-Baptiste. 1963. 《政治经济学概论》 [*A Treatise on Political Economy*], trans. Fusheng Chen and Zhenhua Chen. Beijing: Commercial Press.

Sima Qian. 1961. *Records of the Grand Historian*, trans. Burton Watson. New York: Columbia University Press.

Smith, Adam. 1931. 《國富論》 [*An Inquiry into the Nature and Causes of the Wealth of Nations*], trans. Guo Dali and Wang Yanan. Shanghai: Shenzhou Light of the Nation Publishing.

Smith, Adam. 1972 [1931]. 《国富论》 [*An Inquiry into the Nature and Causes of the Wealth of Nations*], trans. Guo Dali and Wang Yanan. Beijing: Commercial Press.

Smith, Adam. 1997. 《道德情操论》 [*The Theory of Moral Sentiments*], trans. Ziqiang Jiang, Beiyu Qin, Chongdi Zhu, and Kaizhang Shen. Beijing: Commercial Press.

Sowell, Thomas. 2014. *Basic Economics: A Common Sense Guide to the Economy*, 9th ed. New York: Basic Books.

Sun Yat-sen. 1953 [1924]. *Fundamentals of National Reconstruction*. Taipei: Sino-American Publishing Company.

Tan Min. 2014. The Chinese Origin of Physiocratic Economics. In *The History of Ancient*

Chinese Economic Thought, eds. Cheng Lin, Terry Peach, and Wang Fong, 82–98. London: Routledge.

Teng Weizao. 1962. Preface to 通往奴役的道路 [*The Road to Serfdom*] by Friedrich A. Hayek. Beijing: Commercial Press.

Von Glahn, Richard. 2016. *The Economic History of China: From Antiquity to the Nineteenth Century*. Cambridge, UK: Cambridge University Press.

Yamada Katsuyoshi. 2000. *Kahei no Chūgoku kodaishi* [*Ancient Chinese Monetary History*]. Tokyo: Asahi Shinbunsha.

Yan Fu. 2014. 《严复全集》 [*Collected Works of Yan Fu*]. Fuzhou: Fujian Educational Publishing.

Yang Jisheng. 2012. *Tombstone: The Great Chinese Famine, 1958–1962*, ed. Edward Friedman, Guo Jian, and Stacy Mosher, trans. Stacy Mosher and Guo Jian. New York: Farrar, Straus and Giroux.

Young, Leslie. 1996. The Tao of Markets: Sima Qian and Adam Smith. *Pacific Economic Review* 1(2): 137–145.

Zhang Weiwei. 2012. *The China Wave: Rise of a Civilizational State*. Hackensack, N.J.: World Century.

Zhang Weiwei. 2016. *The China Horizon: Glory and Dream of a Civilizational State*. Hackensack, N.J.: World Century.

Zhang Weiying. 2010. 《市场的逻辑》 [*The Logic of the Market*]. Shanghai: Shanghai People's Press.

Zhang Weiying. 2015a. *The Logic of the Market: An Insider's View of Chinese Economic Reform*, trans. Matthew Dale. Washington, D.C.: Cato Institute.

Zhang Weiying. 2015b. 《经济学原理》 [*Principles of Economics*]. Nanning: Guangxi Normal University Press.

This chapter first appeared as an Econ Journal Watch article in January 2016. It has not been revised except for the addition of an "Epilogue" at the end.

Liberalism in Korea

Young Back Choi and Yong J. Yoon[1]

Liberalism in Korea came from the West, and all political outlooks sometimes called 'liberalism' are present there. Some of those outlooks are more paternalistic or communitarian, and those are construed as compatible with some traditional political views in Korea. But classical liberalism, which, hereafter, is what we signify in using the term *liberalism*, is without antecedent in Korea before the turn of the 20th century.[2] Today, liberals there are relatively small in number and are mostly, but not exclusively, economists. Yet they do seem to have attained a critical mass in recent years. The aim of the essay is to trace the evolution of liberalism in Korea. Before we discuss its recent development, we provide a brief historical discussion. Korea's history illustrates the difficulties of liberalism in the face of totalitarian threats of all varieties.

Pre-modern Korea (before 1850)

The dominant political views in pre-modern Korea reflected monarchical absolutism and rigid social stratification. The last dynasty of Korea, Chosun (which spanned the years from 1392 to 1910), adopted Confucianism as the state ideology in order to combat the previous era's rampant superstition and corruption. Since 206 BCE, Confucianism had been the ruling ideology of various dynasties in China, including the Ming dynasty (1368–1644). Acting in the name of Confucianism, the literati had tried to limit the arbitrary rule of the king through a system of censorship. In Korea, the centralized

---

1. We benefited much from helpful suggestions by anonymous referees.
2. American-style 'liberalism' that promotes the welfare state is referred to in South Korea by an appropriate term, namely, *progressivism*.

bureaucracy of Chosun operated by a set of codes, notably the Great Ming Code, supplemented by the Code of Administration. Confucians also tried to introduce orderliness into society by education in morality and etiquette, with emphasis on maintaining proper social relations through loyalty, fealty, filial piety, chastity (for women), respect for the elderly, and so forth. Individual conduct was to be guided by Confucian principles and the traditional decorum. Confucians did not view the issue of natural rights of individuals or personal liberty within the bound of just laws as relevant.

Society was divided into distinct hierarchical classes—king and royal families, the gentry (Yang-ban), the middle classes (Joong-In), the commoners (Pyung-Min), and the slaves (No). Only members of the gentry could become government officials, rewarded by pay and/or fiefdom. The middle classes served in various respected technical capacities, as physicians, clerks, translators, artisans, craftsmen, et cetera. They also could become merchants, who were less respected. Commoners would usually become farmers or peasants. The slaves were properties, to be bought and sold.

After a period of cultural flowering in the early decades of the dynastic founding,[3] the Chosun dynasty gradually declined as a result of wars, heavy taxation, and forced labor. It is estimated that by the middle of the 19th century, more than 50 percent of the Korean population was serfs or slaves.[4]

The satirist Park Ji-Won traveled to China (Qing) in 1780 and was struck by how much better off Chinese were than Koreans. What he witnessed in Beijing confirmed his view that Korea was backward because of its contempt for trade and industry and its system of rigid social stratification. He argued that Koreans should open their eyes and learn from the Chinese. He dreamed of a more prosperous Korea where trade and industry were esteemed and the social stratification was done away with so that people could interact as equals. Unfortunately, his ideas attracted few followers, as they were rather exceptional for the time.

It sometimes has been claimed that elements of Confucianism are an antecedent of liberalism in pre-modern Korea. We disagree. It is a mistake to

---

3. Cultural achievements during the period include the invention of the Korean alphabet, printing books using movable metallic type, and publication of encyclopedias.
4. Even so, Tullock (2012) suggests that the political system of the Chosun dynasty, which lasted 600 years with a dense population and a reasonable standard of living (in comparison with other countries at the time), may have some features worth studying.

conflate Confucius's observations on human nature and personal ethics with his political philosophy. Confucius's observations on human nature are often very apt; he should be regarded as one of the greatest humanists in history. But the political philosophy of Confucius and his followers conceived the reign of the Duke of Zhou (before 1046 BCE) as the ideal. In this ideal state the king is wise and benevolent, ministers and government officials just and decorous, and the common folks respectful and industrious. There is little room for individual rights or freedom of thought and action.[5]

Another way to illustrate the relationship of Confucianism to modern political systems is to review the variety of reactions of Confucians when East Asian countries encountered the superior power of the West. There were three types or forms of reaction: (1) insistence on adhering to Confucianism and rejecting the ways of the West; (2) retaining Confucianism as a political philosophy, while adopting Western technologies; and (3) abandoning Confucianism as the ruling political ideology (that is, radically restructuring the political structure) and adopting the ways of the West. The first two forms of reaction failed. Japan successfully adopted the third type of reaction, and other late-comers in Asia have subsequently adopted it as well. But, abandoning Confucian political ideology is of course not inconsistent with retaining many of the Confucian elements of personal ethics.[6]

First transitional period (1850–1905)

During the 19th century, Korea was encircled by foreign powers, but it was also a vassal state of China (Qing dynasty). Western powers such as Tsarist Russia, France, Britain, the German Empire, and the United States all tried to pry Korea away from China and obtain privileged concessions. Japan, with a successful crash program of modernization under way, eventually elbowed out others.

A significant development coming in 1869 was the formation of the Party

---

5. Of all the ancient thinkers of East Asia, only Lao-tzu can be construed as being an antecedent to liberalism, or even libertarianism. But his teaching in its original form, which appears to strike at the underpinnings of feudalism, was never popular in China, nor was it in Korea.

6. Kim (1999) thinks the cultural legacy of Confucianism still too much hinders the social development of Korea.

for Opening ("Gae-Hwa-Dang"). One of the principal actors, Park Gyu-Soo, was a grandson of Park Ji-Won. Unlike his grandfather, he had a successful career as a government official and rose to become the Chief Magistrate of Seoul and the Minister of Justice. He and like-minded intellectuals reflected on the state of China, which had fallen victim to Western imperialistic aggressions, discussed the reasons why the Western nations became strong, and what needed to be done for Korea to avoid a fate similar to that of China. Over time, they recruited young and ambitious adherents from the gentry. They were particularly keen on learning lessons from the modernization programs under way in Japan and China.

In 1875, about twenty years after Commodore Perry's gunboat diplomacy jolted Japan into a modernization program, Japan itself used gunboat diplomacy to force Korea to open up. In the late 1870s and the early 1880s Korea's Queen Min sent overseas missions to report on advances in Japan, China, and the United States. Duly impressed by what they saw, the emissaries agreed on the urgency of reforms. But there developed two factions, divided over on the nature of reforms Korea needed. The 'moderate reformers' wanted a Chinese-style reform of adopting Western technologies and industries while retaining the traditional social structure. The 'radical reformers' thought the Chinese-style reform was not sufficient; they wanted thorough-going sociopolitical reform in the manner of Japan. The moderate faction sought support from China, and the radical faction sought support from Japan.[7]

Delegates to Japan met and were influenced by Fukuzawa Yukichi, the great advocate of Japan's modernization. He argued that the West became powerful because the nations had liberal institutions, fostering individualism, free exchange of ideas, education, and competition. He argued that Japan should adopt the liberal institutions of the West in order to become powerful enough to resist the Western nations' demand for unequal treaties. He translated the term *liberalism* as 「自有主義」, a term since used in Japan, Korea, and China. Fukuzawa shared his views on the necessity of political reforms with Korean delegates and continued to provide moral support for Korean reformists.

---

7. The factions influenced by reports of the missions to the United States were to play a role later as the Party of Independence in the last days of Chosun.

Fukuzawa, however, had doubts that Koreans were culturally ready for a successful reform. It would be a mistake to classify Fukuzawa as a liberal; he was also a nationalist, and for him liberalism was a means of building a rich nation with a strong military. He believed that if Korea could not reform successfully, and thus would fall into the hands of Western imperialists, Japan might as well pre-empt them and colonize Korea. Thus, he justified Japanese colonization of Korea.

In 1884, the radical reformers, with a promise of Japanese military assistance, led a bloody putsch to eliminate the rival factions and impose a reform fashioned after the Meiji Restoration. However, the radical faction was quashed in three days by Queen Min, with the help of Chinese troops. The coup failed because it was carried out in haste without securing enough supporters, plus the radicals were naïve in trusting the good intentions of the Japanese who, after a successful crash program of modernization, were gearing up to secure control over Korea.

In 1894–1895, Japan fought China for control of Korea, obtaining cessions of territory (including Taiwan) and a rich indemnity, among other things. Japan then fought Russia (1904–1905) over control of Korea and Manchuria and shocked the world by destroying Russian fleets. Thus, Japan established herself firmly as an imperial power with an undisputed claim over Korea. Japan relegated Korea to a protectorate in 1905. Soon, Korea became a colony of Japan.

During this turbulent period, in 1896, was formed the short-lived but significant—from the point of view of the development of political thought in Korea—Party of Independence ("Dok-Rip-Hyup-Hoe"). Key figures of the Party included Min Young Hwan, Yoon Chi-Ho, Yoo Gil-Joon, Yi Sang-Jae, Ahn Chang-Ho, and Seo Jae-Pil.

Seo Jae-Pil was recruited from the United States by Yoon Chi-Ho to be the editor of *Independent Times* ("*Dok-Rip-Shin-Moon*"). Seo Jae-Pil returned to Korea with a new name, Philip Jaisohn. He had fled to the United States after the failed coup of 1884, in which he was one of the principal actors. In absentia he was found guilty of treason, and his family had been exterminated in the old Korean practice of collective punishment. During his stay in the United States, Seo studied to become a physician, and he learned much about the American political system from a retired federal judge (who was a brother-in-law of Seo's landlord).

In his speeches and writings, Seo admitted the mistake of naively trusting the benign intentions of the Japanese for Korean development. Seo emphasized that the core of Korean reform should be the establishment of a system in which freedom of action and individual responsibility are emphasized and individual merits are respected, instead of relying on familial ties and factionalism, which lead to corruption and inefficiency.

The Party of Independence tried to push political reforms: Korea should become an independent constitutional monarchy, run by the democratically elected parliament; Korea should stop selling various economic rights to foreigners for little in return;[8] foreign technologies should be utilized in agriculture and industry to increase productivity; and Korean markets should be protected, to allow infant industries to take root and grow.

The principals of the Party had been either emissaries to the U.S. or exposed to the West in schools founded by American missionaries. Whereas earlier reformers, whether moderate or radical, had been influenced by Japanese or Chinese reformers, the principals of the Independence Party were influenced by what they learned about the United States. They advocated a democratic political system, emphasizing individual liberty and responsibility as keys in the political system.[9] The Independents began to gain popular support.

However, the Party incurred the wrath of both Korean royalists and the Japanese colonizers. The Party and the newspaper could not survive the joint attacks of the royalists and the Japanese military. Active members of the Party

---

8. For example, rights to build railroad or trams, rights to gold and coal mines, rights to harvest timber, and rights to collect custom, sold to Russians, French, Japanese, and Americans.

9. Those who had a chance to travel to the United States were most impressed not only by the degree of industrial development, but by the governmental structure based on the liberal Constitution. At the same time, many were deeply troubled by racism they personally experienced and witnessed toward blacks and Asians. For example, Lee Sang Jae (as a secretary to the Korean ambassador to the U.S.) was stoned by a boy in New York. Yoo Gil Joon had been beaten up for no reason by schoolmates when he attended school in Boston. Philip Jaisohn could not make a living as an M.D., nor as a lecturer at a medical school (the present-day George Washington University), because of racism by patients and students. Some noted that even American missionaries were condescending toward Asians. Their experience of racism, however, was counterbalanced by the liberality and kindness shown by other Americans they met. Most importantly, they correctly identified democratic republicanism based on individual liberty as the true source of what was admirable in America.

were soon harassed and imprisoned. They were tortured for subversion by the royalists, and they were also forced to acquiesce to the Japanese takeover of Korea—some did, while others refused and suffered greatly.

One of the popular speakers at the Party's rallies, Syngman Rhee, was arrested, tortured and sentenced to death. In 1904, after five years of imprisonment, however, he was given an amnesty and released from the prison with the help of Min Young Hwan. He was given an amnesty in part because of his command of English, which he had improved by reading an English Bible while in jail.[10] Rhee was sent to the United States on a secret mission to convey the Korean king's letter to President Theodore Roosevelt, beseeching him to honor the Treaty of Amity between the two countries and help prevent the Japanese colonization of Korea. The United States government refused to receive the letter.[11]

Just before his release, Rhee finished a handwritten book manuscript, *The Spirit of Independence* ("*Dok-Rip-Jung-Shin*"). It was hand-copied and circulated among friends.[12] In the book, he reviewed the American and French revolutions and the failed reform attempts in Korea. Then he laid out his vision for Korea: a constitutional monarchy in which self-reliant individuals with inviolable human rights enjoy the fruits of their labor through free exchange of goods and ideas, and a society governed by the rule of law, undergirded by Christian values which accord dignity to individuals and the determination to fight injustice. Rhee's visions for Korea were obviously influenced by the founding principles of the United States and Christianity.

---

10. While imprisoned Rhee had also converted many inmates to Christianity, including Lee Sang-Jae.

11. Min Young-Hwan did not know that President Roosevelt had already made a secret pact with the Japanese that the United States would not interfere with Japan's control of Korea in exchange for Japan's acquiescence of the American control of the Philippines. Min committed suicide in 1905 when he could not prevent the treaty in which Japan took away the sovereignty of Korea.

12. Pieces of the pamphlet were published in the *Independent Times*. Rhee published it as a book in Los Angeles in 1910.

Second transitional period (1905–1945)[13]

Japan was a quick student of Western imperialism and soon became imperialist in its own right. Through a combination of military aggression and diplomatic duplicity, in 1910 Japan formally annexed Korea as its first overseas colonial acquisition.[14] To secure complete control of Korea, Japan ruled Korea with an iron fist and forced Mikadoism upon Koreans.[15] Koreans were made second-class citizens, denied political voice and strongly discriminated against. Japanese expatriates, given preferential treatments and subsidies, came to dominate the Korean economy. The Japanese oppression drove a large number of Koreans to emigrate to Manchuria and far eastern Russia.

The brutal and discriminatory Japanese rule awakened nationalist senti-ments and an aspiration for national independence among many Koreans. In March 1919 a nationwide nonviolent demonstration calling for independence met with bloody suppression.[16] People were machine-gunned, bayoneted, imprisoned, and tortured. Christians were gathered inside churches and burned alive. The international community abhorred the brutality of Japanese

---

13. The purpose of this section is to trace the rise of Korean national independence movements, influenced by socialism, communism, fascism, and liberalism, in reaction to Japanese colonial rule. An anonymous referee suggests that the paper neglects positive roles Japanese colonial rule may have played in the future development of South Korea, as suggested by Kohli (1994), Kimura (1993), and Cha (2004). We think those who advance the thesis that Japanese colonialism was instrumental in the economic development since the mid-1960s are wrong; it is like arguing that a man who had been bullied by a thug has grown up because of all the bullying he received. Given the limited space, we simply refer to Haggard et al. (1997), who offer an able critique of the thesis.

14. Japan had wrested Taiwan from Qing China after the Sino-Japanese war in 1895.

15. Mikado (meaning "the royal gate" in Japanese) is an ancient designation of the Japanese emperor. Mikadoism is the cult of emperor worship in Japan. Japanese fascists feverishly promoted Mikadoism, demanding complete loyalty of subjects for national purposes whatever they are, including the subjugation of foreigners (see Kitagawa 1990). Mikadoism is like the cult of the Führer in Nazi Germany. The ferocity with which Japanese soldiers fought and the abandon with which Kamikaze pilots crashed their planes into American targets are difficult to understand unless one recognizes the similarity between the martyrdom sought by Japanese patriots, on the one hand, and the martyrdom sought by the radical Islamic terrorists, on the other.

16. The Declaration of Korean Independence was inspired by President Wilson's principle of national self-determination announced in 1918, even though he had in mind mostly the settlement of boundaries in Eastern European after WWI.

suppression, which was reported by American missionaries, but little if anything was done. Many survivors fled the country, some to establish a provisional government in exile in China, others to wage various forms of militant resistance in Manchuria, China, far eastern Russia, and elsewhere. The battle for independence from the mighty Japanese empire, as it continued, took many forms. Some appealed to human decency and justice, but in the world of power politics that appeal mostly fell on deaf ears.[17] Some fought alongside the Chinese (both Nationalists and Communists) against the Japanese, hoping for eventual victory over the Japanese. Some went abroad (including to Japan) to study. Those who remained in Korea had to survive under Japanese rule. Some decided to undertake education and business as a way of increasing the capability of Koreans, looking toward future independence.

The Japanese colonial government discouraged education and industry among Koreans. What schools the Japanese established in Korea were for Japanese transplants, with only limited admission for Koreans. The Japanese colonial government did its utmost to suppress education among Koreans, even when Koreans wanted to educate themselves at their own expense.[18] Soon the Japanese were all but trying to obliterate the Korean culture, forbidding Korean language from schools and forcing people to adopt Japanese surnames.

Emboldened by the successful colonization of Korea and the establishment of a puppet regime in Manchuria, militarist fascists came to dominate Japanese politics. They soon launched aggressive military campaigns into China, brutalizing the people and committing atrocities, all the while insisting that Japan was only trying to defend its own interests.[19]

---

17. As a member of the Allies, Japan fought Germans in Asia during World War I. As victors, the Japanese were able to exert a diplomatic influence to keep her brutality in Korea invisible.
18. Soongsil University, the first privately founded university in Korea in 1907 (started with the help of American missionaries), was forced to downgrade to a college in 1925. In 1938, Soongsil closed its doors altogether instead of complying with directives to practice Mikadoism.
19. For an example of the fine art of duplicity and disinformation, see Emperor Hirohito's radio message of surrender in August 1945 containing the following passage: "We declared war on America and Britain out of Our sincere desire to ensure Japan's self-preservation and the stabilization of East Asia, it being far from Our thought either to infringe upon the sovereignty of other nations or to embark upon territorial aggrandizement."

After his failed mission in 1904, Syngman Rhee had remained in the United States and pursued education, getting a B.A. at George Washington, an M.A. at Harvard, and a Ph.D. in politics at Princeton in 1910, when Woodrow Wilson was the president of the university. After a brief return as a Christian missionary in colonized Korea, he returned to the United States to seek international assistance in restoring Korean independence, much of the time as the president of the Provisional Government of Korea in exile, which was located in China.

In June 1941, six months before the Japanese attack on Pearl Harbor, Rhee published a book in English, *Japan Inside Out*, warning of an impending Japanese attack on the United States. He documented the pattern of Japanese duplicity and aggression, starting with Korea, to Manchuria, then to China, a pattern surprisingly consistent with the notorious Tanaka Memorial.[20]

In addition to accurately describing the pattern of Japanese aggression and predicting the coming conflict with the United States, Rhee (1941) pointed out one of the central issues a free society faces, namely, pacifism in the face of threats from totalitarianism. In the last chapter, "Democracy vs. Totalitarianism," he argued that individual freedom was incompatible with the totalitarianism of the day—Nazism, fascism, Mikadoism, and Communism. Unfortunately, he observed, few people in a free society were willing to fight for the freedom they enjoyed. Pacifists who argued that free people should not fight even in the face of impending threats from totalitarian regimes, in his view, were like "fifth columnists" of totalitarianism. Pacifism invited slavery under the domination of dictators. If pacifists were truly serious about peace, Rhee suggested, they should preach peace to war-mongering totalitarians such as Hitler and Japanese militarists.

Rhee was in the minority among Korean nationalists in his opposition to totalitarianism. One can see why many Koreans suffering from the Japanese brutality disliked fascism, but many Korean intellectuals, like many intellectuals elsewhere, were attracted to communism as a liberating idea and sought guidance for national liberation from the Soviet Union. Rhee thought

20. The Tanaka Memorial is the alleged plan submitted by the Japanese Prime Minister Tanaka to the Emperor Showa in 1927, laying out a strategy for overseas conquests. Its existence became known when it was published in a Chinese newspaper in 1929. The Japanese and some historians say the document is a sophisticated hoax or forgery, but events through WWII nevertheless make it prophetic.

it was a fatal mistake not to see communism as a variant of totalitarianism.[21]

As Rhee predicted, Japan eventually attacked the United States and opened an all-out war in China, Southeast Asia, and elsewhere in the Pacific region. According to the Cairo Conference declaration at the end of the war, the Japanese colony Korea was to become a free and independent nation in due course. The U.S. Army, however, hastily decided to stop the advancing Russian army by dividing Korea at the 38th parallel. The Russian army was to disarm the Japanese military stationed in the northern half of Korean Peninsula, and the U.S. army was to do the same in the southern half. In place of the Japanese colonial government, Korea came to be ruled by two foreign armies, the Russian in the north and the American in the south. The fateful decision, based on military expediency, laid the ground for the two distinct forms of political structure in Korea.

Division of Korea and ideological battles (1945–1953)

Joseph Stalin established a communist state in the northern half of Korea, in a manner similar to that in the Soviet occupation of Eastern Europe. After the brutality of the occupying Russian Army, Korean communists tried to force communism on people and began to harass landlords, businessmen, non-communist intellectuals, and the religious. An anti-communist uprising in Shin-Ui-Joo in November 1945, the first in the Soviet-occupied territories after WWII, was brutally suppressed. In March 1946, all farmlands in the Soviet-occupied North were confiscated and redistributed to erstwhile landless peasants and tenant farmers. In 1948, the Soviet Union established a communist government in the North, installing Kim Il-Sung as the ruler. During this period about 1.8 million people (mostly landlords, businessmen, intellectuals, and Christians) managed to migrate to the south.

The U.S. military government in the South tried to establish a non-communist state, but the process was not easy. Having lived under an oppressive colonial overlord for thirty-five years, many people were perhaps

---

21. Rhee, serving as the Prime Minister/Foreign Secretary of the provisional government in exile since its inception, had to deal with communists and became highly critical of their hostility toward property, capitalists, intellectuals, religion, and nationalism. Rhee thought them loyal only to international communism, and to Moscow, its puppet master (see Rhee 1923).

not even sure what human dignity and freedom were. There were also many Korean communists from the days of Japanese colonialism. Some went to the North to join the communist state.[22] Others remained in the South and tried to establish a communist state there.[23] They organized nationwide labor strikes, armed revolts, and had violent clashes with the police and anti-communist organizations.

The American military government ended up backing Syngman Rhee as the future leader of the South, a choice consistent with the Truman Doctrine of containing the spread of communism. Rhee presided over the constitutional convention of South Korea. The Constitution declared that South Korea was a republic, in which the political power resides with people, who are free and equal under the law. Subsequently, the 73-year-old Rhee was in 1948 elected the first president of the Republic of Korea. Three years after the liberation of Korea from Japan, therefore, two different governments were established in Korea: the North as a communist state and the South as a liberal democracy. In the South the new government had to face communist armed rebellions. These were put down, but there remained a substantial number of communists in South Korea.[24]

Soviet-backed North Korea—believing that South Korea could be easily taken over with the help of the communists there—invaded the South in June 1950. Within two months, the unprepared South was indeed easily overrun by the North Korean army, and the South Korean government was driven into a small southeastern corner. In the areas now occupied by North Korean forces, local communists often eagerly helped the North Korean Army to control the area, harassing and killing many 'enemies of the revolution.' However, the last-

---

22. For example, the Marxist economist Baek Nam-Woon migrated to the North in 1948, after intense political activities in the South.

23. According to a poll conducted by the U.S. military government, a majority of Koreans preferred socialism to either capitalism or communism (*Dong-A-Il-Bo*, August 13, 1946; see Moon 2015, 182 n.11). We thank an anonymous referee for this reference.

24. There is a parallel between the communists' activities in South Korea in the late 1940s and those of Viet Cong in South Vietnam in the late 1950s. Both South Korean communists and Viet Cong (South Vietnamese communists) were trying to undermine the government and reunite their respective countries under communism. Had Rhee's government not succeeded in suppressing communists and in carrying out a successful land reform in 1948 to create a class of farmers willing to defend their possession of land, the fate of South Korea probably would have been like that of Vietnam.

minute decision by the U.S. to enter the war resulted in the North Korean army being driven back, nearly to the Chinese border. However, Chinese intervention on the side of the North, with deployment of its massive army, drew the war to a stalemate near the line of initial division of Korea within a year of the outbreak of the war.

The Korean War involved some 2.5 million soldiers from 20 nations in combat, plus 18 nations involved in other capacities. Because the back-and-forth ground battles covered almost the entire Korean Peninsula, with intensive aerial bombing, there was massive property damage and great loss of life. The death toll among combatants was 600,000 to 900,000, along with over 2 million civilian deaths and about 1.2 million wounded. South Korea ended up with some 200,000 widows and 100,000 orphans, along with about a million refugees from the North, in addition to about 1.8 million refugees before the War. The total population of South Korea at the time was less than 20 million.

After another two years of protracted trench warfare, an armistice was signed in 1953 and the division of Korea acquired a sense of permanence. North Korea became a belligerent communist country, daily professing her desire to take over the South. South Korea became an outpost of the Cold War, with strong anti-communist laws (Park 2007, 108). The Korean Peninsula became highly militarized, with combined standing armies of about 1.6 million strong facing each other across the 2.5-mile-wide and 160-mile-long Demilitarized Zone (DMZ).

What has happened since in North Korea is a sad story. Kim Il-Sung became the unchallenged leader of North Korea by purging his rivals from the South and communist expatriates from China and Russia. Taking the credit for the successful reconstruction of North Korea (downplaying the substantial help from Chinese, Russians, and East Europeans), Kim Il-Sung began to build a totalitarian state based on a caste system, anchored on a cult of hero worship of himself.[25] The North Korean population was controlled through

---

25. Kim Il-Sung became, in all but name, king, his immediate family members, the royalty, and his loyal comrades and their family members, barons, or the "Special" caste. They constitute the ruling inner circle of North Korea. The kingship has in due course become hereditary. The rest of the population is divided into three hereditary castes, based on their perceived degree of loyalty to Kim Il-Sung—"Core," "Wavering," and "Hostile." Inmates in concentration camps undergird the caste system. The caste system thus created is an amalgam

constant surveillance, brainwashing, and punishment, including torture, banishment to a concentration camp, or death by a firing squad. Freedom was obliterated, and only the visibly sincerest devotions to the ruler would ensure survival. With the ambition of conquering the South by force, Kim devoted substantial resources to the outsized military and the armament industry. The standard of living for the rest of population steadily declined to the point of forcing people to eat only two meals a day by the early 1980s.

After the dissolution of Soviet Union and the fall of communism in Eastern Europe, the North Korean economy collapsed completely. Hundreds of thousands of people died of starvation in the 1990s, and millions more suffer today from chronic malnutrition. The countryside came to be filled with orphan-beggars scavenging dumpsters and foraging the mountains. More than half a million desperate people crossed the Chinese border at the risk of being shot by the border guards, arrested and tortured, or captured by Chinese human traffickers.[26] Today, nearly everyone in North Korea lives in constant fear of being branded disloyal and suffering grave consequences, and North Korea is one of the poorest countries in the world.

The developmental state (1953–1987)

The 1953 armistice was only a temporary ceasefire. South Korea was still being threatened by the hostile enemy in the north. President Rhee, who was an anti-communist to begin with, adopted strong national security laws aimed at the elimination of communist support in South Korea.

Known communists who refused to renounce communism were imprisoned. Anyone suspected of communist sympathy, including the family members of known communists, were put under surveillance and their civil rights were severely curtailed, including banning them from government employment and overseas travel. One may be tempted to liken the heightened anti-communism to that of McCarthyism in the United States, except that Korea's experience reflected the fresh memory of fighting an intensive war against the

---

of the Marxist-Leninist conception of the capitalist class structure and a feudal conception of the heredity of one's social station by bloodlines (see Choi 2015).

26. Some twenty thousand North Korean refugees managed to escape to South Korea, via China, Vietnam, Mongolia, and Russia (see Choi 2015).

communist North, with millions of casualties, the memories of the atrocities committed against their families by communists, and the bitter memories of persecution and expropriation for millions of refugees from the North. The communist threat was much more real.

At the end of the war the surviving South Koreans found themselves among ruins. Cities were teeming with beggars, mostly crippled soldiers or orphans. Many of the hundreds of thousands of refugees from the North built shacks anywhere they could and became squatters. The shortage of food was severe. A major famine was averted only with massive U.S. aid. The U.S. aid also included equipping the army, training of manpower, and higher education, sometimes by providing visits to American universities. South Korean dependence on government-to-government assistance from the United States in the 1950s was extreme.

While South Korea was rebuilding slowly, one of the important tasks of the government became the distribution of resources transferred from the United States. The government soon began to take further charge of the economy. To maximize the real value of imports, the exchange rate was kept artificially high. To keep the balance of trade in check, the government imposed severe restrictions on imports with a tight foreign exchange control, and it encouraged import substitution. Foreign aid and statist domestic policies made a perfect breeding ground for rent-seeking and cronyism.

Complaints of corruption and demands for cleaner government became perennial among South Koreans. Most believed that only if more honest political leaders came to power, the situation would become better; few realized that the economic policies themselves necessarily invited corruption. In the late 1950s there was still no sign of South Korea becoming less dependent on U.S. aid; by contrast, North Korea claimed itself to be a model of Soviet-style economic development and declared an ambition to liberate the poverty-stricken South.[27] Eventually the U.S. government began to cut back on aid.

The combination of dwindling resources, complaints of widespread corruption, and the discovery of election irregularities led to nationwide stu-

---

27. The estimated per capita GDP of South Korea in 1960 was roughly one-twentieth of that of the United States. North Koreans continued to escalate military actions along the DMZ, as well as commando actions through the sea throughout 1960s, taking advantage of the U.S. predicament in the quagmire of Vietnam.

dent protests, and in 1960 to the toppling of President Rhee's government. The democratically elected government subsequently became paralyzed, beset by protests from various interest groups and ideologues. In 1961, General Park Chung-Hee seized power in a coup d'état, aiming to get rid of the widespread corruption and poverty. He imposed martial law, arrested corrupt government officials and businessmen, and revised the Constitution. General Park became President Park through an election in 1963.

After a period of trial and error in economic policy, Park became a firm believer in export-led growth. The Korea economy began to grow at a rapid rate. There have been debates over whether the export-led growth policy of Korea is an example of successful dirigisme. Certainly, President Park did much to promote exports—and he did his best to suppress organized labor strikes. But against the backdrop of the then existing regulations inherited from the past, much of Park's measures to promote export can be seen as selectively lifting restrictions on trade.

The life of a nation is more than just earning foreign exchanges through export. Preservation of peace from external and internal enemies is a paramount concern of a nation. The international geopolitical situation in the 1960s was the expansion of communism and the U.S. attempt to contain it.[28] After the mid-1960s, emboldened by the success of the communists in Vietnam and sensing Americans' weakened will to fight, North Korea escalated military provocations. They included the capture of the USS Pueblo near the North Korean territorial water and in 1968 the sending of a commando unit to kill President Park, which almost reached the presidential residence. North Korean provocations continued through the 1970s, including the murder of the First Lady by a communist assassin (he had aimed at President Park and missed) and the killing of two U.S. Army officers by axe-wielding North Korean guards in Pan-Moon-Jom.

Unsure whether the United States was committed to help South Korea, Park became gravely concerned about the national security. He saw the reasons for the demise of South Vietnam as being its penetration by communists and a lack of leadership to combat it. He assumed that he should be the one to provide the leadership to change South Korea—and to that

---

28. South Korea sent combat forces to Vietnam in the late 1960s, with an understanding that the U.S. forces stationed in South Korea would be maintained and certain quid pro quo for South Korea.

end, in fall of 1972 he imposed the *Yushin* constitution, which effectively ended many democratic practices. To affirm anti-communism, he organized the countryside through the "New Village Movement" and announced the "National Creed" ("국민교육헌장") as the national ideology.[29] Park pursued an industrial policy to promote industries deemed necessary for the production of armaments (such as steel, machines, and chemicals) in preparation for the day when South Korea would be unable to obtain weapons from the United States.

Park's industrial promotion may have laid some important bases for later development in steel production, machine making, shipbuilding, and chemicals industries. But in the late 1970s, over-investment in these strategic industries and the resulting crushing debt burdens, amid the worldwide economic downturn, resulted in widespread protests against the *Yushin* constitution and Park's rule of almost two decades. In December 1979 Park was assassinated, by the chief of the Korean Central Intelligence Agency (KCIA).

General Chun Doo-Hwan, chief of the army intelligence, led the investigation into Park's assassination, gained the control of the army, and took steps to seize power. Anti-authoritarian student demonstrations erupted, culminating in an armed revolt in Kwang-Ju during May 1980. It was put down after a bloody confrontation. General Chun became the president in September 1980. Chun ruled with an iron fist, dealing sternly with challengers from the entrenched political-business nexus, political opposition, and the street.

Anti-authoritarian movements went underground and steadily spread, encompassing not only democrats and human rights advocates, but also religionists, unionists, farmers, progressives, socialists, and even pro-North Korean agents. It became increasingly popular, through the 1980s, among college students to study in secret the banned Marxist literature. Quite a few went to Japan to study *Koza-ha*, the Japanese variant of Marxism. Quasi-Marxist ideas such as liberation theology and dependency theory became vogue among the youth.

While President Chun was merciless toward anyone who might challenge

---

29. All schoolchildren, government officials, and soldiers were required to memorize the creed.

his authority, his rule was marked by many liberalizing reforms, such as lifting the decades-long midnight curfew and overseas travel restrictions. The most notable reforms were economic. Chun's administration inherited severe economic dislocations from President Park's excessive investment in strategic industries and the attendant unserviceable debt to foreign creditors. Knowing that he was rather unpopular politically, Chun wanted to focus his energy on improving the economy. Confessing ignorance in economic matters, he hired as his chief economic advisor Kim Jae-Ik, a career bureaucrat trained in economics. Through Kim, President Chun came to appreciate the merit of liberalizing the economy through such measures as letting the market determine the interest rate and exchange rate and lowering tariffs. Helped by favorable international economic conditions, the South Korean economy boomed, growing at a brisk rate.

Kim Jae-Ik was one of few free-market economists in Korea at the time, says Kim Jin-Hyun (2008). In October 1983, Kim Jae-Ik, along with more than a dozen South Korean cabinet members and high-ranking officials accompanying President Chun in a state visit to Burma, was killed in a bomb explosion. The bombing was ordered by Kim Jong-Il, the son of the North Korean ruler Kim Il-Sung, to assassinate President Chun—but Chun escaped death because his arrival had been unexpectedly delayed by 30 minutes. It was a troubled time. Only a month before, the Soviet Union had shot down the Korean Airline Boeing 747 as it strayed into Russian airspace, killing all 269 passengers and crew aboard.

South Korea is often touted as an example of successful economic development combined with a transition to democracy. Before we discuss its 1980s movement to democracy in the next section, we should address its economic development, which is much debated. There is no doubt that, from abject poverty, the Korean economy was transformed in about twenty years, beginning in the early 1960s. What is disputed is the reason why.

At one pole, some at the World Bank have argued that South Korea developed because its development policies were in conformance with market forces; at the other pole, it is argued that South Korea developed because of its industrial policies (see Amsden 1992; Chang 2002; Jwa and Yoon 2011). We believe that neither of these extreme views can well explain the uneven process of Korean economic development. For example, Jungho Yoo (2011) argues that the main reason for South Korean development was the access to the vast world market through export, but the export boom started unintentionally, through devaluations, before the government deliberately began to promote exports. The South Korean government in the mid-1960s recognized the benefit of export earnings, and it tried to provide additional incentives to encourage exports.[30]

The additional incentives had two aspects. One was to undo or neutralize the distortions inherited from the past, which had the net effect of neutralizing some of the existing distortions. The other was to provide extra incentives for select industries or businesses to achieve targets set by the government, which has led to misallocation of resources, cronyism, and corruption. The second aspect became more transparent in the late 1970s when the growth rate declined substantially as a result of promoting heavy and chemical industries. Also, it should be noted that by allocating credit to those industries, the government ended up suppressing light industries.

One cannot but compare the development trajectories of South Korea, which deliberately promoted heavy industry, and of Taiwan, which did not. Taiwan's economic development does not compare unfavorably to that of South Korea. All Asian countries that did not hinder exports and that removed institutional barriers against exports enjoyed a high rate of growth, whether or not they promoted industrial policies. In the late 1970s, as it was deliberately promoting certain industries at the expense of others, South Korea actually fared less well than other Asian countries. In addition, the tradition of cronyism became a basis for social discord that was to adversely impact the transition to democracy.

Transition to democracy (1988–present)

In 1985 President Chun lifted restrictions on politicians—some had been under house arrest—permitting them to organize political parties for the scheduled election of the legislature. He intended the election to meet the popular demand for democratization, while retaining the control of the legislature through machination, in preparation for handing over the rein of the government to his chosen successor. However, President Chun and his advisors had grossly underestimated the popular demand for democracy and

---

30. Choi (1994) argues that the ruling party acted as if they were residual claimants.

a regime change—the opposition parties took nearly half the seats of the legislature. The pro-democratic movement grew stronger and became more violent with the passage of time, demanding a direct election of the next president.[31]

In June 1987, as the political situation seemed to be getting out of control, Roh Tae-Woo, a former general and the designated successor of President Chun, made a surprising announcement that he would agree to a revision of the constitution to allow a direct presidential election. President Chun did not insist on an orchestrated transfer of power to insure his safety; instead, he acquiesced to Roh's willingness to take a chance in election. It looked as if Roh simply yielded to the mounting popular pressure and, given the unpopularity of the ruling party, he would surely lose the election. However, Roh ended up winning the election, with only a third of the votes, because opposition factions could not agree to field a unified candidate and ended up splitting their votes three ways.[32] This was how South Korea managed a peaceful transition to democracy.

The South Korean transition to democracy has been successful thus far. Since President Chun stuck to his agreement to serve only one term (seven years in his case) in 1987, six Presidents have served the constitutionally limited five-year single term and yielded power to democratically elected successors. By 2015, per capita GDP (nominal) reached $28,338. South Korea is not yet ranked among the rich countries, but she has come a long way, from abject poverty as late as the early 1960s, and from a dictatorship as late as the mid-1980s to a full-blown democracy.

The decade following the advent of democracy in South Korea was eventful. In November 1987, the Korean Air Flight 858 blew up over the Indian Ocean, killing all 119 on board. Kim Jong-Il of North Korea orchestrated the terrorist act in a failed attempt to disrupt the 1988 Summer Olympics, which were hosted in Seoul. The Games allowed South Korea to showcase its economic development to the world, especially to the socialist countries as they were falling apart.[33] In 1991, South Korea, along with North

---

31. At the time, the President was to be elected indirectly by the Electoral College.

32. The opposition votes went to 'the three Kims': Kim Young-Sam, Kim Dae-Jung, and Kim Jong-Pil. The first two Kims subsequently became Presidents in succession.

33. Not to be outdone by South Korea, Kim Jong-Il and Pyongyang hosted at great cost the World Festival of Youth and Students, a socialist counterpart of Olympics, in 1989. The

Korea, was admitted as a member of the UN.[34] In the early 1990s South Korea normalized relationships with Russia and China. The economy grew briskly through the mid-1990s, and in 1996 South Korea became a member of the OECD.

In 1997 South Korea was embroiled in the financial crisis that swept through Asia and had to seek a bailout from international financial institutions such as the IMF and World Bank.[35] After some painful adjustments the South Korean economy roared back, and the international loans (some $30 billion in U.S. dollars) were paid off ahead of the schedule. In 2002, South Korea co-hosted the World Cup with Japan. Also, a number of reforms have been adopted to reduce the possibility of a military coup,[36] as well as financial transparency, in part to root out corruption.

Significant changes in politics also have taken place since the transition to democracy. The left has emerged from underground and has come to dominate South Korean politics, as evidenced by the back-to-back elections of Presidents Kim Dae-Jung (1998–2002) and Roh Moo-Hyun (2003–2007). National security laws have been emaciated in the name of protecting human rights, to the point where several pro-North Korean activists and their sympathizers have been elected lawmakers. Since 2005 several motions in the legislature to condemn the human rights violations in North Korea have been blocked by pro-North lawmakers.[37]

In the name of protecting freedom of speech, all manner of disorderly and violent demonstrations and illegal occupations of public spaces have been tolerated. Leftists have staged a number of nationwide anti-American rallies, demanding the withdrawal of the U.S. military forces stationed in South

---

financial help pledged by other socialist countries did not come through because they were themselves falling apart; in fact, socialism was collapsing. It goes without saying that the extravagance further ruined the finance of an already bankrupt North Korea (see Choi 2015).

34. The South Korean diplomat Ban Ki-Moon has served as the Secretary General of the UN since 2007.

35. It was a result of the combination of decades-long cronyism and the hasty liberalization of the financial sector to meet the requirements of joining the OECD (see Choi 2000).

36. One of the most important was disbanding of the Ha-Na-Hoe, a powerful and not-so-secret club of army officers. Chun Doo-Hwan and Roh Tae-Woo were members of the club when Chun seized power.

37. In 2013 the UN established a commission to investigate North Korean human rights violations. The following year the commission filed its report, charging North Korea with crimes against humanity (United Nations Human Rights Council 2014).

Korea.[38] In the name of preventing the collapse of the North Korean regime, and avoiding the astronomical costs of re-unification by absorption in the style of the German re-unification of 1990, South Korea under Kim Dae-Jung and Roh Moo-Hyun transferred a massive amount of cash and food aid to North Korea, this despite the North's belligerence and continued development of nuclear weapons.[39]

Also significant has been the domination of the left in the media and the schools, especially K–12. Major textbooks in social sciences in high schools are completely silent on the nature of market competition and the value of freedom (Kim 2015). Instead, the textbooks promote progressive and socialist values—that inequality is socially unjust, that the rich got rich at the expense of the poor, that businesses practice unfair and shady tactics to get rich, that the pursuit of income is unethical, that globalization is an imperialist tactic to dominate and exploit the weak and poor, that individualism is bad, that collectivism is good, that competition is cutthroat and excessive, and that government should redress all sorts of 'social injustices.'

The transition to democracy was based on the constitutional revision of 1987, containing the provision for the direct election of the president.[40] But what passed with little notice in the midst of political hoopla was the constitutional provision for "economic democracy," at the insistence of the opposition parties, to which the ruling party acquiesced. This constitutional provision for "economic democracy"—Article 119, Section 2—provides the basis for the discretionary power of government to intervene in the economy for so-called balanced growth, equitable distribution, and fair competition. Section 2 (which contradicts Section 1 on matters of economic freedom) was to become a Pandora's box, to the delight of the subsequent democratically

---

38. Occasions used for anti-American rallies include the 2002 rallies protesting the death of two school girls by the U.S. Army tank in a traffic accident and the unfair legal status of the U.S. forces stationed in Korea and 2008 rallies against U.S. imported beef on the suspicion of 'mad cow disease.'

39. Hwang Jang-Yop (2010), a high-ranking defector from North Korea, asserts that if not for the massive aid from South Korea, the North Korean regime would have collapsed in the late 1990s.

40. Nine revisions of the constitution since the Inaugural Constitution of 1948 represent a lack of political consensus in South Korea, where political actors have been all too willing to rewrite the constitution for their convenience.

elected governments.[41]

In some ways, the democratically elected governments have continued the process of liberalization started under President Chun, especially in the area of international trade. For example, the proliferation of 'free trade agreements' also appears to indicate increasing liberalization of the economy.[42] Additional liberalizing reforms were made in the aftermath of the 1997 financial crisis, to meet the conditions for World Bank bailouts.

But on the whole, government regulation of the economy has become more intrusive and pervasive, in pursuance of so-called economic democracy, social justice, and so on. There has been a marked increase in government-provided benefits to all sorts of groups. One example is the Economic and Social Development Commission established in the aftermath of the financial crisis of 1997 as a presidential advisory body. Its Korean title more clearly reveals the corporatist nature of the commission: we translate it as "Labor-Business-Government Committee on Economic and Social Development." Another example is the quasi-private Commission for Balanced Growth, founded in 2010 to insure "harmony and parity" among large, small, and medium firms.

The successive democratically elected governments have not only expanded welfare provisions that were introduced earlier, such as health insurance and income guarantees, but also created many new programs. For example, since 1988 the South Korean government has provided substantial funding to various civic groups.[43] In the 2000s, most municipalities have begun offering free meals in schools through the 6th grade, in some cases through the 9th grade. Since 2013 the government has paid subsidies for

---

41. Article 119 of the Ninth Constitution of 1987 consists of the following: (1) The economic order of the Republic of Korea shall be based on the respect for the freedom and creativity of individuals and businesses; (2) The state can regulate and adjust the economy to promote the balanced growth and stability of the national economy, to maintain a proper distribution of income, to prevent monopolization of the market and abuses of economic power, and to promote economic democracy through harmonizing the interests of economic actors (authors' translation). Section 1 was a carryover from previous constitutions. Section 2 greatly expanded on previous constitutions' concerns for economic stability and market monopolization, and it clearly contradicts Section 1.

42. South Korea has 'free trade agreements' with the U.S., the European Union, Canada, China, Vietnam, and New Zealand, among others.

43. Civic groups are mostly left-leaning activist organizations and lobbyists. It goes without saying that a lion's share of government funding has gone to the leftist groups.

raising pre-school children whether or not they are sent to daycare or kindergarten.[44] These are just a few examples of the growing governmentalization of social affairs.

The power of the South Korean presidency is almost kingly. Since the transition to democracy, the legislature is supposed to counterbalance the powerful presidency to help preserve freedom. But popularity-seeking lawmakers seem to have something else in mind, passing at a torrential rate all manner of laws to promote their own interests, dispensing handouts for political expediency, or granting privileges to favored groups. Onerous burdens and arbitrary restrictions have been imposed on certain targeted groups, especially *jae-bol*—big businesses.[45] In all these, of course, the lawmakers who wield the arbitrary power of government never fail to recite the mantra of fairness and economic democracy. The relatively high level of corruption in South Korea shows that there is much room for abuse.[46] Also, indiscriminate redistribution schemes and over-regulation of the economy have resulted in slow growth and high unemployment, especially among the young.[47]

Liberalism taking root

The gradual realization in the 1980s and 1990s that democracy is not the panacea that many leftists thought it would be has created a yearning for a more secure freedom from the arbitrary rule of government, whether or not

---

44. The subsidy for daycare costs was initially meant to assist working mothers, but most non-working mothers insisted on equal treatment and got comparable benefits. In nationwide demonstrations during 2011, college students demanded that their tuition be cut in half. They seemingly did not care whether the tuition cut would be made up by government subsidy, or if colleges and universities simply would be forced to cut tuition.

45. It is unfortunate that big businesses in Korea, so used to cronyism, are dispensing large sums of money to various anti-business activist groups. Now, in an unrestrained democracy, such pressure groups wield great power. The practice is nothing short of bribery. In the short run, businesses buy respite from the social gadflies. But as the ancient Chinese thinker Han Feitzu said, it is like trying to chase away flies with a piece of meat; over time, there will be more flies (Choi 1989).

46. Even though many South Koreans feel that things are much better than before, the 2014 Corruption Perceptions Index from Transparency International places South Korea only 43rd out of 176 countries.

47. The result is the lowest birth rate among the OECD nations at 1.19 children per woman.

democratic.

That realization had been a worldwide phenomenon. In 1979 Margaret Thatcher became the prime minister of the United Kingdom on the promise of curing the 'sick man of Europe' by liberalization and privatization. In 1981 Ronald Reagan became the president of the United States on the promise of rolling back the state.[48] The trend culminated in the dissolution of the Soviet Union and its self-proclaimed socialist utopia in 1991. But any realizations concerning the excesses of government's role in social affairs came belatedly in South Korea, because the primary concern there before 1988 had been getting rid of authoritarianism.[49] Only after the transition to democracy did South Koreans begin to sense the oppressive nature of the collectivist state in various guises and realize that the 'anti-authoritarian movement' contained many disparate and contradictory strands.

The period of the 1980s and the 1990s in Korea was marked by raging ideological battles, with progressives and socialists pitted against conservatives and liberals.[50] The former, riding on the triumphal wave of democratization, tended to be hostile to market forces; they advocated greater state intervention in the economy, in the name of social justice. In the latter coalition, the conservatives were generally pro-business—and, often, in favor of government intervention on behalf of business. Most conservatives did not distinguish between being pro-business and being pro-market; very few saw that the two were not the same.

One of the very few was Kim Jin-Hyun, who was appointed the leader of the newly founded Korean Economic Research Institute (KERI). KERI was launched by the powerful Federation of Korean Industries (FKI) as an affiliate organization in 1981.[51] Kim faced opposition from FKI when he showed interest in promoting the idea of a free-market economy, because most members of the FKI—captains of industry—did not care at all for

---

48. Stockman (2013) argues that the promise to roll back the state was not kept.
49. Most active anti-authoritarians curiously overlooked the despotism just across the DMZ.
50. In the Korean context, a liberal is person who is opposed to the expansive governmentalization of social affairs, including communism and progressivism. Liberalism in Korea is not confused with the "American liberalism," because the latter is properly called Progressivism.
51. KERI's first President was Chung Ju-Young, the founder of Hyundai, and its first vice-president was the economist Shin Tae-Hwan.

free markets. For them cronyism (or mercantilism) was the norm.[52] But, Kim persisted. He managed to publish in 1984 his own translation of *Anti-Capitalist Mentality* by Ludwig von Mises.[53] Subsequently, in the late 1980s and the early 1990s, he commissioned translations of *Liberalism* by Mises, *Competition and Entrepreneurship* by Israel Kirzner, and *The Economics and the Ethics of Constitutional Order* by James Buchanan, among other books.

Kim Jin-Hyun's project of translating works by free-market thinkers had the effect of introducing liberalism to a few Korean economists who would not otherwise have become familiar with it. One of them was a researcher at KERI, Gong Byung-Ho. In 1997 Gong managed to establish the Center for Free Enterprise (CFE) as an entity separate from the Korean Economic Research Institute (KERI).[54] Though it was a small operation, the energetic and enterprising Gong expanded the efforts at translation, in few years many important works of liberalism had been published in Korean, from authors including Friedrich Hayek, Frederic Bastiat, Ayn Rand, Milton Friedman, Thomas Sowell, Henry Hazlitt, Bruno Leoni, Murray Rothbard, and Richard Epstein. The translators, such as Gong Byung-Ho, Ahn Jae-Wook, Min Kyung-Gook, Kim Chung-Ho, Kang Gi-Choon, Lee Sang-Ho, Kim Yi-Sok, and Yoon Yong-Joon, along with the CFE's own economists Choi Seung-No and Kwon Hyuk-Chul, constituted the bulk of a still small number of free-market economists in Korea.[55] The project provided an important opportunity for the liberal economists to associate.

The significance of the CFE's translation project in recruiting and training free-market economists can only be appreciated in light of the development and composition of the economics profession in Korea, which by and large

---

52. In the early 1980s Kim Jin-Hyun became interested in the ideas of the compatibility between a free-market economy and morality espoused by Michael Novak of the American Enterprise Institute and invited Novak to Korea (see Kim 2008).

53. Kim (2008) recounts how the publication needed the blessing of Kim Jae-Ik, then the Chief Economic Secretary to President Chun.

54. The establishment of the CFE as an independent entity would not have been possible without the help of Son Byung-Doo, the vice-president of KERI in 1996 and the vice-chairman of FKI in 1997, and the blessing of the then-chairman of FKI, Choi Jong-Hyun of the SK Group. Choi studied economics at the University of Chicago and was greatly interested in free markets (see Kim 2007; Bok 2013, 70).

55. Translators from other disciplines include Joh Young-Il, Shin Joong-Sup, Park Hyo-Jong, and others. The CFE also commissioned numerous books oriented toward liberalism by Korean authors.

follows the neoclassical synthesis prevalent in the United States. The Korean Economic Association (KEA) was founded in 1952 during the Korean War by some 30 economists.[56] In the 1950s the massive U.S. aid after the Korean War allowed a few Japan-trained economists (both in academia and in government) a chance to visit American universities and get some retooling. In 1960s a few South Koreans began to study economics in the U.S. and to earn doctorates from American universities. With the rapidly developing South Korean economy in the late 1960s and 1970s, economists came to be valued highly as consultants on policy and as communicators, both with international organizations and the populace at home. The growing demand for economists in academia and in government was met by an increasing number of Koreans studying abroad, mostly in the United States but also in Germany and Japan.[57]

By the early 1990s economists with Ph.D.s from American universities came to constitute the majority of almost 1,900 members of the KEA (see Choi 1996). The race for better credentials was a big factor in seeking a degree from overseas, especially the United States. Reflecting the source of the members' training, the Korean economics profession became a clone of that of the United States, which is by and large dominated by the neoclassical synthesis. Given the pervasive involvement of government in all areas of society in Korea, the majority of economists, regardless of their training, tend to become pragmatic, workaday economists, whether they are in academia or in government.

That is why a free-market thinker such as Kim Jin-Hyun was rare in the early 1980s. Perhaps it helped that Kim was not a professional economist (though his fellow liberal thinker Kim Jae-Ik was, with a Ph.D. from Stanford University).[58] But his efforts to make known the merit of free-market economics bore fruit by influencing Gong Byung-Ho, the eventual founder of the CFE, and in the subsequent growth in the number of people interested in liberalism in Korea. There is no question that CFE drew much inspiration from liberal think tanks and institutes overseas, especially the Institute of

---

56. The founding members were non-Marxist economists trained in Japan during the colonial period. Shin Tae-Hwan, who studied economics at the Tokyo College of Commerce (present day Hitotsubashi University), became the first President (see Shin 1983).
57. Later, Korean universities began to produce Ph.D.s, but these tended to be valued less than a foreign degree. A Ph.D. from an elite American university carried the most prestige.
58. Kim Jin-Hyun's undergraduate training was in politics and diplomacy.

Economic Affairs, the Cato Institute, the Heritage Foundation, the Center for Study of Public Choice, and the Ludwig von Mises Institute.

Even those rare souls who had independently discovered the virtues of liberal economic policies must have been encouraged by the growing number of free-market economists associated with the CFE.[59] These independent thinkers include the novelist Bok Geo-Il, who started to advocate openly a free-market economy in the early 1980s, and Min Kyung-Gook, a graduate of Freiburg University and the foremost Korean evangelist for Hayek's work since the early 1990s. Today, Bok and Min have become leading members of the growing network of liberal thinkers in Korea, regularly contributing to popular newspapers and making TV appearances.

The growing confidence of Korean liberals is expressed in a collection of intellectual biographies, *Why I Became A Liberal* (Bok 2013). Twenty-one Korean liberals describe in that volume why and how they became liberal. The majority of contributors are economists with an advanced degree from abroad;[60] the rest include a philosopher, a political scientist, a novelist, etc., who are nevertheless familiar with economics. Their initiation into liberalism was varied, including life experience, research, books, professors, colleagues, and even fathers-in-law. Their critical inspirations were invariably classical liberals of the West. They cited as their major influences the following thinkers: Mises, Hayek, Friedman, Buchanan, Kirzner, Rothbard, Adam Smith, Walter Eucken, Karl Popper, Ronald Coase, Gordon Tullock, Douglass North, Mancur Olson, Gary Becker, Armen Alchian, Samuel Brittan, Randall Holcombe, and so on. Most often cited are Mises, Hayek, Friedman, and Buchanan. Some of the twenty-one Korean liberals, however, testify that they drew much of their inspiration for liberalism from other Korean liberals, such as Lee Yong-Wook (cited by Kim I-Sok), Gong Byung-Ho (cited by Kim Chung-Ho, Shin Joong-Sup, Ahn Jae-Wook, and Choi Seung-No), Min Kyung-Gook (cited by Ahn Jae-Wook), and Lee Seung-Chul

---

59. Kim I-Sok was introduced to Mises and Hayek by a professor at Young-Nam University, Lee Yong-Wook, in the mid-1980s. Professor Lee had earned his Ph.D. from Seoul National University for his research on Piero Sraffa (Bok 2013, 175–176).

60. Not all of the contributors state where they studied when they were introduced to liberalism, but it is interesting to note, in this relatively small sample, that two of them studied at the University of Freiburg, two at George Mason University, two at Ohio State University (where the faculty carried on the free-market tradition of the University of Chicago), and one at New York University (under Israel Kirzner and Mario Rizzo).

(cited by Kim Jung-Ho). This is an indication that Korean liberals have gone beyond the stage of merely importing Western ideas. Liberalism has begun to take root in Korea.

The deepening Korean roots of liberalism are even more clearly seen in a recently published book, *Thirty-Three Books That Awakened Me* (Song and Bok 2014). In that book, thirty-three Korean liberals each cite one book that was most important for them personally. Among the books mentioned are: *The Fatal Conceit* and *The Road to Serfdom* by Hayek; *The Law* by Frederic Bastiat; *Free to Choose* and *Capitalism and Freedom* by Friedman; *The Anti-Capitalist Mentality* by Mises; *Economics in One Lesson* by Hazlitt; *Competition and Entrepreneurship* by Kirzner; *The Open Society and Its Enemies* by Popper; and *Property and Freedom* by Richard Pipes. But there is a significant presence of books by Korean liberals (all written in Korean), including: *The Story of Korea* by Lee Young-Hoon (2007); *Nation Building and Enriching the Nation* by Kim Young-Il (2004); *The Shadow of China on the Korean Peninsula*, *The Evolution of the Market*, and *Why I Became A Liberal*, all by Bok Geo-Il (2009; 2012; 2013, ed.); *Answer! Liberalism* by Ahn Jae-Wook (2013); *Hayek, A Road to Freedom* by Min Kyung-Gook (2007); *The Miracle Called Individual* by Park Sung-Hyun (2011); *I Sell My Daughter for 100 Won* by Jang Jin-Sung (2008), a poet who defected from North Korea; and *Everyday Economics* by Kim Young-Yong (2009).

An important development in the late 1990s, when South Korea seemed to have been swept away by social democrats and socialists, was the creation of the Korean Hayek Society in 1999 by Min Kyung-Gook and other admirers of Hayek. Its goal was to sustain scholarly exchanges on liberalism. The founding members of the society constituted the bulk of CFE translators and contributing authors. The society holds a monthly seminar and posts online member writings on various issues.

After the initial flurry of translating and commissioning Korean authors to write on relevant topics, the CFE decided in the early 2000s to shift its focus to educating the public.[61] One example is offering a course on the market economy at college campuses. Initially, even free-market economists were skeptical about the prospect of such a course at colleges, given the widespread anti-liberal sentiments among the youth in South Korea. They were pleasantly surprised, however, when the first of such courses bravely

---

61. Gong Byung-Ho left CFE in 2000 to strike out on his own venture.

offered by Professor Chun Sam-Hyun of Soongsil University had all 230 seats filled within 30 minutes of opening for registration. The enrollment in the program steadily increased to some 3,000 students per semester by spring 2007 (Kim 2007, 293). Another success is a continuing education program called Open Society Academy. When the CFE faced financial difficulties and could not continue the program in fall 2006, the alumni of the academy contributed funds to continue the program. Under the current leadership of Hyun Jin-Kwon (since 2014), CFE has redoubled its efforts for popular education through publications, lectures, seminars, and various events. The continued success of the CFE education programs has led to the founding in 2013 of Freedom Factory, a for-profit corporation that offers courses on subjects such as the history of entrepreneurship in Korea. Freedom Factory's founder is Kim Jung-Ho, a former president of CFE (2003–2012).[62]

It seems to us that liberals in South Korea have not only become more self-confident, but they may have reached a critical mass.

December 2022 Epilogue

I.

by Young Back Choi

"Liberalism in Korea" (2016) ended with a cautious optimism about the future of classical liberalism in Korea. This Epilogue, written late 2022, is a further reflection on the status of liberalism in Korea today.

Many events that bolster anti-liberalism have taken place in and around Korea since the early 2015: the Covid-19 pandemic, increasing tensions from chronic international trade imbalances, and an increasingly assertive China, which tries to domineer, especially over neighboring countries.

Also significant was the impeachment of President Park Geun-Hye in December 2016. Pursuing an industrial policy and promoting corporatism, she was no friend of liberalism. Her impeachment was an outcome of campaigns

---

62. The funding of the Freedom Factory came from 731 individual investor-shareholders; see www.freedomfactory.co.kr.

by political opponents denouncing her incompetency and being under the spell of a Svengali. The impeachment demonstrated that a duly elected president can be removed through mobilizing mobs, via social media and staged demonstrations.

Subsequently, Moon Jae-In became the President in May 2017. A series of his policies reveals that he was a committed socialist and climate warrior. The very first thing he did as President was a moratorium on nuclear energy, greatly raising the cost of electricity. Moon's other policies included big fiscal stimuli, greatly expanding public sector jobs, demonizing big business, drastic increases in the minimum wage, substantial increases in welfare benefits, and massively increasing government debt. Throughout his term that ended in May 2022 President Moon exercised discretionary power unhindered. Yet his popularity among his followers was undiminished. The reason is that nearly all commanding heights of Korea—the presidency, legislature, bureaucracy, court, police, military, education, arts, media, religion—are captured by like-minded people on the left and woke-cultural red guards. Politics has become highly factional, and the law is increasingly seen as an instrument of extracting rent for those in power.

In the face of the preponderance of anti-liberalism, liberals in Korea have had only a modicum of success waging an uphill battle.

Some noteworthy developments in classical liberalism in Korea in recent years include the following:

- The Korean Society for Studies of Liberalism (KSSL) has emerged as an important force by absorbing the Korea Hayek Society (KHS) in early 2022. The KSSL has two units—academic and educational. The KHS morphed into the academic unit, holding the scholarly Monthly Forum. In spring 2022 the theme of the Monthly Forum was "Meeting of Economics and Philosophy." In fall 2022, the theme was Austrian Economics. KSSL's educational unit, the Freedom Academy, offers seminars for members and the public. In fall 2021 it offered 14 seminars on the theme of "Korea in Chaos: Liberalism as the Way Out." In spring 2022 it offered 11 seminars on the theme of "Meeting of Economics and Philosophy." In May 2022, the KSSL cosponsored a symposium, "Hayek on Liberty."
- A group of Korean liberals have begun to plan for a graduate school

as a long-term strategy to recapture some of the lost commanding heights.

Korean liberals, just as liberals elsewhere, have no other means than steadily appealing to fellow citizens of the goodness of liberalism—for individual freedom and for shared prosperity. Recurrent crisis and external threats, from North Korea, China and elsewhere, add to the challenges that liberals in Korea face. Even so, I remain cautiously optimistic.

II.

by Yong J. Yoon

This note is a brief statement of liberalism in Korea (South Korea) after early 2016, when our article appeared in *Econ Journal Watch*. The six years since then have been a nightmare for the country and to liberalism in particular. The conservative president Park Geun-Hye was impeached and demoted. After this, in a special election in March 2017, Moon Jae-In was elected by 42 percent support. Moon has been behaving like a communist following the North Korean Labor Party. During his five-year term, he has been trying to destroy liberal democracy in Korea. The process of destruction was stopped, in March 2022, by electing Yoon Suk-Yeol as the president, a conservative party candidate.

In discussing liberalism, I will consider the basic concepts and ideas, and the policies based on liberal democracy. In his inauguration address on May 10, 2022, Yoon emphasized freedom, world citizenship, and economic liberalism. His emphasis on economic freedom supporting political liberalism reminds me of Milton Friedman. No Korean president since the founding president Syngman Rhee (1948) mentioned freedom in their inaugurations. However, what matters is how Yoon will handle the real questions.

Many are optimistic and enthusiastic about Yoon's presidency, but difficulties are looming. The most visible and worrisome is the low approval rating. Yoon has achieved a lot already in the first half year. Yet his approval rate is around 30 percent. Moon used to enjoy 80 percent, while destroying constitutional values and messing up the economy and cancelling atomic power plants. How do we make sense of this? Here are some explanations.

1. Koreans have a new president but not a new government yet.
2. The major public media are controlled by the left and labor. They distort the news by propaganda and incitation.
3. The polls are biased.
4. Ordinary Koreans are confused by the propaganda from the left and cannot make decisions wisely. The left has the cultural hegemony in all areas. They have been following Gramsci's communist strategy for more than 30 years.

Is there hope for classical liberalism in Korea? I can only say this much. It is part of human nature to aspire to become a better person.

References

Ahn, Jae-Wook. 2013. 《응답하라! 자유주의》 [*Answer! Liberalism*]. Seoul: FKI Media.

Amsden, Alice H. 1992. *Asia's Next Giant: South Korea and Late Industrialization*. Oxford: Oxford University Press.

Bok, Geo-Il. 2009. 《한반도에 드리운 중국의 그림자》 [*The Shadow of China on the Korean Peninsula*]. Seoul: Moon-Hak-Gwa-Ji-Sung.

Bok, Geo-Il. 2012. 《시장의 진화》 [*The Evolution of the Market*]. Seoul: Korean Economic Research Institute.

Bok, Geo-Il, ed. 2013. 《나는 왜 자유주의자가 되었나》 [*Why I Became A Liberal*]. Seoul: FKI Media.

Cha, Myung-Soo. 2004. Facts and Myths about Korea's Economic Past. *Australian Economic History Review* 44(3): 278–293.

Chang, Ha-Joon. 2002. *Kicking Away the Ladder: Development Strategy in Historical Perspective*. London: Anthem Press.

Choi, Young Back. 1989. Political Economy of Han Feitzu. *History of Political Economy* 21(2): 367–390.

Choi, Young Back. 1994. Industrial Policy as the Engine of Economic Growth in South Korea: Myth and Reality. In *The Collapse of Development Planning*, ed. Peter J. Boettke, 231–255. New York: New York University Press.

Choi, Young Back. 1996. The Americanization of Economics in Korea. *History of Political Economy* 28(Supp.): 97–122.

Choi, Young Back. 2000. Financial Crisis and Perspectives on Korean Economic Development. In *Asian Financial Crisis: Financial, Structural and International Dimensions*, ed. J. Jay Choi, 357–378. Oxford: JAI/Elsevier.

Choi, Young Back. 2015. Whither North Korea? *Review of Business* 36(1): 130–159.

Haggard, Stephen, David Kang, and Chung-In Moon. 1997. Japanese Colonialism and

Korean Development: A Critique. *World Development* 25(6): 867–888.

Hwang, Jang-Yop. 2010. 《나는 역사의 진리를 보았다》 [*Memoir: I Witnessed the Truth in History*]. Seoul: Shi-Dae-Jung-Shin.

Jang, Jin-Sung. 2008. 《내 딸을 백원에 팝니다》 [*I Sell My Daughter for 100 Won*]. Seoul: Chogabje.

Jwa, Sung-Hee, and Yong Yoon. 2011. Economic Development and Institutions. In *Institutional Economics and National Competitiveness*, ed. Young Back Choi, 217–230. New York: Routledge.

Kim, Chung-Ho. 2007. 자유기업원과 함께한 10 년 [Ten Years with the Center for Free Enterprise]. In 《한국의 자유주의》 [*Liberalism in Korea*], by Bok Geo-Il, et al., 269–318. Center for Free Enterprise.

Kim, Jin-Hyun. 2008. Interview by Kim Chung-Ho. *Shin-Dong-A*, January: 296–305.

Kim, Kyung-Il. 1999. 《공자가 죽어야 나라가 산다》 [*Confucius Must Die, for Korea to Prosper*]. Seoul: Bada.

Kim, So-Mi. 2015. 고교 사회과 교육과정의 편향성 검토 [Biases of High School Textbooks]. *CFE.org* (Center for Free Enterprise, Seoul), October 13.

Kim, Young-Il. 2004. 《건국과 부국》 [*Nation Building and Enriching the Nation*]. Seoul: Center for Free Enterprise.

Kim, Young-Yong. 2009. 《생활속 경제》 [*Everyday Economics*]. Seoul: Center for Free Enterprise.

Kimura, Mitsuhiko. 1993. Standards of Living in Colonial Korea. *Journal of Economic History* 53(3): 629–653.

Kitagawa, Joseph M. 1990. Some Reflections on Japanese Religion and Its Relationship to the Imperial System. *Japanese Journal of Religious Studies* 17(2/3): 129–178.

Kohli, Atul. 1994. Where Do High Growth Political Economies Come From? The Japanese Lineage of Korea's 'Development State.' *World Development* 22(9): 1269–1293.

Lee, Young-Hoon. 2007. 《대한민국 이야기》 [*The Story of Korea*]. Seoul: Ghiparang.

Min, Kyung-Gook. 2007. 《하이에크, 자유의 길》 [*Hayek, A Road to Freedom*]. Seoul: Hanwool Academy.

Moon, Joon-Young. 2015. The Making of the Constitution and the Civil Code in Post-liberation Korea. In *The Spirit of Korean Law: Korean Legal History in Context*, ed. Marie Seong-Hak Kim, 177–201. Leiden, Netherlands: Koninklijke Brill NV.

Park, Hyo-Jong. 2007. 한국의 자유주의는 발전하고 있는가 [Is Liberalism Progressing in Korea?]. In 《한국의 자유주의》 [*Liberalism in Korea*], by Bok Geo-Il, et al., 75–185. Seoul: Center for Free Enterprise.

Park, Sung-Hyun. 2011. 《개인이라 불리는 기적》 [*The Miracle Called Individual*]. Seoul: Deulnet.

Rhee, Syngman. 1910. 《독립정신》 [*The Spirit of Independence*]. Los Angeles: Taedong Sinsokwan.

Rhee, Syngman. 1923. 공산당의 당 부당 [Communist Party: Pro and Con]. *Tae-Pyung-Yang-Jab-Ji*, March.

Rhee, Syngman. 1941. *Japan Inside Out: The Challenge of Today*. New York: Fleming H. Revell Co.

Shin, Tae-Whan. 1983. 50-Year Annals of Korean Economics [in Korean]. In *Searching for Korean Economics*, 13–23. Seoul: Korean Economic Research Institute.

Song, Bok, and Bok Geo-Il, eds. 2014. 《나를 깨운 33한 책》 [*Thirty-Three Books That Awakened Me*]. Seoul: Baek-Nyun-Dong-An.

Stockman, David A. 2013. *The Great Transformation: The Corruption of Capitalism in America.* New York: Public Affairs.

Tullock, Gordon. 2012. 한국판 서문 [Preface to Korean edition]. In 《국민합의의 분석》 [*The Calculus of Consent*] by James M. Buchanan and Gordon Tullock, trans. Soo-Hyun Hwang, ix–xviii. Seoul: Ji-sik-ul-man-du-nun-ji-sik.

United Nations Human Rights Council. 2014. Report of the Detailed Findings of the Commission of Inquiry on Human Rights in the Democratic People's Republic of Korea. A/HRC/25/CRP.1. February 7.

Yoo, Jungho. 2011. The Myth About Korea's Rapid Growth. In *Institutional Economics and National Competitiveness*, ed. Young Back Choi, 154–166. New York: Routledge.

This chapter first appeared as an Econ Journal Watch article in May 2015.
It has not been revised.

The Endangered Classical Liberal Tradition in Lebanon: A General Description and Survey Results

Patrick Mardini[1]

The Lebanese people believe that they live in a free market economy. However, Lebanon is ranked 96th in the Heritage Foundation's 2014 Index of Economic Freedom and 60th in the Economic Freedom of the World Index. Compared to its Arab neighbors, the country is lagging behind Bahrain, Jordan, Kuwait, Oman, Qatar, Saudi Arabia, and the United Arab Emirates.

Economic freedom had been a tradition in Lebanon dating back to the period of the Phoenicians. This tradition reached a peak, under the influence of the 'New Phoenicians,' in the period from independence in 1943 until the beginning of the civil war in 1975 (Gates 1998, 82). Today, however, economic freedom has few prominent advocates.

To the extent that classical liberal ideas still have a home at all in Lebanon today, it is among economics professors, because of the focus of economics on voluntary exchange through markets. Like the rest of the population, though, economics professors usually belong to a religious sect and have a corresponding political bent toward a particular party. Lebanon has 18 recognized sects, including Christian (40.5%), Shia (27%), Sunni (27%), and Druze (5.6%).[2] Some sectors of the government and the economy are known to operate under Christian influence, others under Sunni influence, etc. Some subsidies are known to be directed to Shia interests, others to Druze, others

---

1. I would like to thank Yvonne Khoury for administering the survey.
2. Figures taken from the *CIA World Factbook*, 2014.

to Sunni, etc.

To investigate the extent to which professors of economics hold liberal views, I designed and fielded a survey. The survey is constructed in such a way that some questions elicit the respondent's support of liberal ideas, while other questions concern policies in specific sectors of the economy. The survey aims to see whether professors favor policy reform from an economic conviction (classical liberal, Keynesian, etc.) or from sectarian considerations. It also allows exploration of the ways sectarianism affect policy views and more generally how to identify the characteristics of sectarian economic views.

I start by summarizing the tradition of economic freedom and the history of religious sectarianism in Lebanon. Then I describe the sectarian political framework. Finally, I present and analyze the survey results.

Economic freedom and sectarianism in Lebanon

Lebanon's coastal cities date back to the time of the Phoenicians, who structured their economy around international trade and traveled throughout the Mediterranean from 1550 BCE to 300 BCE. Later, Lebanon was a province in the Roman and Byzantine empires. In Roman times, Beirut (*Berytus*) was a cosmopolitan city and hosted the most important provincial school of law.

Quarrels among Christians during the Byzantine era about the nature of the Christ led to divisions. The followers of Saint Maroun, the Maronites, were accused of monotheism and persecuted, so they took refuge in the mountains and valleys of the north of Lebanon. The rest of the country was Byzantine. The 7th Century saw the rise of the Prophet Muhammad and Islam from Arabia. Regions were divided then unified, smaller kingdoms emerged then disappeared, but these political matters rarely affected the tradition of free trade. The people of Lebanon adopted the Arabic language. Some converted to Shia Islam, mainly in the coastal part of Lebanon, while others remained Christians, mainly in the mountains. Later on, many Shias followed al-Ḥākim, the Fatimid caliph in Cairo, and became Druze. Hence the basic religious divisions in Lebanon are centuries old (Dib 2004).

The various rulers adopted a common strategy for administering Lebanon: The coast was integrated into the empire, while the mountains were largely autonomous as long as feudal lords remitted taxes. Particularly notable was the Druze emir Fakhreddine II (1572–1635), who ruled what was in effect an autonomous principality within the Ottoman Empire. He forged an alliance with the Maronites by delegating tax collection in Christian areas to Maronite feudal lords (Dib 2004). His economic policy was liberal for the time. Fakhreddine signed commercial agreements with the Grand Duke of Tuscany that contributed greatly to the development of silk production in Lebanon. His relations with Italy complemented the Maronites' ties with Europe. François I had signed a trade agreement with Suleiman the Magnificent in 1535, opening the way for cultural and commercial exchange between the Maronites of Lebanon and France. The French invested heavily in the Lebanese silk industry.[3] Beirut was the major port and trade center (Gates 1998, 15). In addition, close ties between French and Lebanese Christians led to a considerable cultural exchange. Ultimately, though, the Ottomans became uncomfortable with Fakhreddine's growing power, and they captured and executed him.

The French influence on Lebanon kept increasing, and Western mercantilist policies transformed the country into an exporter of raw materials and an importer of finished goods (Gates 1989). With the exception of an Egyptian occupation from 1832 to 1840, Lebanon remained within the Ottoman Empire until the empire's breakup following World War I. Lebanon became a French mandate under the League of Nations, as did Syria. Lebanon gained independence in 1943 as the result of a 'National Pact' agreed to by the Christian leader Bechara el-Khoury, who became the first president of the independent republic of Lebanon, and the Sunni leader Riad al-Solh, who became prime minister. Under the National Pact, Christians promised not to seek Western support, and Muslims promised not to merge with Arab countries.

The economic complement to this political agreement between Maronite and Sunni was an economic vision favorable to their businesses. This vision was designed and advocated by the 'New Phoenicians.' This group included figures such as Michel Chiha, a banker, member of Parliament, and brother-in-law of President Al-Khoury; Gabriel Menassa, a jurist; Henri Pharaon, a banker; and Alfred Kettaneh (Gates 1989, 18 n.37; Kaufman 2014, 233).

---

3. The Lebanese economy remained structured around silk exports until 1890, when Chinese and Japanese producers entered the European market.

They were French-educated and some of them cited Montesquieu in their writing (Haykal and Hariri 2012). I do not know if any were familiar with the traditional classical liberal economists. However, Gabriel Menassa was the president of the *Société Libanaise d'Économie Politique*, a free-market think tank. The name of the think tank may have been inspired by the French *Société d'Economie Politique* created by the followers of Jean-Baptiste Say in 1842.

The New Phoenicians were Christians from Beirut, not from the mountains. Their economic views appealed to the Sunni population of the coasts (mainly merchants and traders), who were culturally more like the New Phoenicians than the mountain populations. The New Phoenicians' analysis in favor of economic and social freedom was built on five pillars: First, national peace is better kept with a small government that lacks the ability to intervene in sectarian matters. Second, pluralism, diversity of sects and a variety of cultures and ideologies are an advantage for dealing with both the West and the East and should be preserved in a state allowing liberty and freedom. Third, like the Phoenicians, modern Lebanon should build a wealthy society based on private initiative and free trade. Fourth, the geographic position of the country is at the crossroads of major trade routes linking the East to the West and economic freedom allows Lebanon to take advantage of this position. Finally, governments in this part of the world are corrupt and inefficient and their role should be minimal.

The New Phoenicians had a huge influence on Lebanon's choice of economic system. They pushed for the elimination of all wartime protectionist measures despite the objection of the labor movement and industrialists (Gates 1998, 83). Under their influence, the government removed controls on trade, floated the exchange rate, freed capital movements, dissolved the Syrian-Lebanese customs union, and adopted banking secrecy. The economy entered a period of exceptional growth from the independence until the outbreak of the civil war in 1975 (Gates 1989). Unlike the prior periods of capitalism, which were focused on industrialization and agriculture, this new era witnessed a boom of financial capitalism and the concentration of development in country's financial center, Beirut (ibid.). Politically, these measures detached Lebanon from its Arab neighbors, notably Syria, which went in the opposite direction by adopting socialism. It also created closeness with the West and especially with the United States, which sent Marines to Lebanon in 1958 during a local political crisis.

The devastating civil war that lasted from 1975 to 1990 was a result of the breakdown of the National Pact, as changing demographics and increasing political tensions led Christians to seek assistance from the West and Muslims to seek to merge with Arab countries. The 'Taif Agreement' of 1989 was reached under Saudi mediation and managed to end the civil war using a carrot-and-stick approach. Warlords and sectarian leaders were offered opportunities to become public officials and were allowed to abuse government resources in exchange for peace. Those who refused were crushed by the Syrian army, which had entered Lebanon in 1976.

The Lebanese business tycoon Rafik Hariri, who represented Saudi mediation, became prime minister of Lebanon in 1992 and supervised the country's reconstruction. He was assassinated in February 2005, which triggered internal and external demands for Syrian withdrawal from Lebanon. On March 8, 2005, a huge demonstration was organized by pro-Syrian parties to object to the Syrian army's withdrawal. On March 14, another huge demonstration took place, organized by anti-Syrian parties. Finally, Syrian forces withdrew. Since then, Lebanon's political scene has been divided between the pro-Syrian March 8 Alliance of parties and the anti-Syrian March 14 Alliance of parties.

Without Syrian military force and Saudi mediation, the political system began to suffer from important blockages. Allowing some warlords and sect leaders to loot public resources is the price that the country has since paid for civil peace.

Sectarian politics in Lebanon

Since independence, seats in the Lebanese parliament have been allocated by sect: Sunni candidates run for Sunni seats, Shia candidates run for Shia seats, et cetera. The founders of this system imagined that by preventing direct confrontation between candidates of different sects, sectarian conflicts could be appeased. However, each voter, regardless of sect, is entitled to vote for the all seats of his district. If a majority of voters in a district belong to the same sect, they can decide the winner of not only their sect's seats but also the winners of the other sects' seats. In this case, the majority sect usually has candidates who are on paper members of another sect but whose allegiance is to the leader of the majority sect in the district; when elected, they will join that leader's group in the parliament. By doing this, a sect raids the seat officially allocated to another sect. These raids are not restricted to parliamentary seats. They involve all public sector jobs, they create tensions between sects, and they are the topic that monopolizes most political and economic debate in the country.

The major political parties in Lebanon are sectarian, which is why I may seem to use the term *sect* as a synonym for *party*. But sectarianism is considered in its moderate aspect and refers to a way in which the parties seek to differentiate their ideologies. Political debate is never about the superiority of one's sect or the fallacy of other's sects. No politician will accuse a rival of being an infidel for belonging to another religion. The dispute is not along religious lines; it is about privileges and political patronage. The sectarian political parties cultivate their authority through the government. Each sect is assigned key bureaucratic positions by law or by tradition. These positions include ministries, general directorates, parliament seats and other key positions in the government service. The framework is similar to that described by Anthony Downs (1957) in a multi-party political framework, and it has little to do with the sectarianism associated with religious fundamentalism (studied in, e.g., Epstein and Gang 2007).

Politicians aim to nurture among their own partisans the feeling that other sects are a threat. They also argue that they themselves are the most fit to hold their sects' privileges and powers. They engage in polarizing speech to rally support during electoral campaigns.[4] Therefore, election within the sects usually favors the candidate with the most muscle, the purported defender of the sect's rights, who is supposed to protect his sect against other sects' appetites.

Egil Matsen and Øystein Thøgersen (2010) suggest that if a politician applies extreme measures, he becomes more attractive to his voters and he increases his chance to get reelected. For Lebanese parties, extreme policies consist of attempting to grab the positions of authority traditionally held by rival sects. Grabbing privileges allows a party to increase its authority, in the government and within its own sect. Economic debate is absent from the political scene and is replaced by a debate over sects' privileges and rights.

---

4. As shown by Glazer et al. (1998), Glazer (2002), and Glaeser et al. (2005).

The situation is like *The Lord of the Rings*: Each contending group battles over power, partly because holding the ring gives them power and partly because if it doesn't hold the ring then the rival group does. Moreover, it is very difficult to hold the ring without abusing its power; the ring corrupts.

Given the large diversity of sects, a government can only be formed through a coalition of parties. These types of governments usually create high and enduring deficits and debts.[5] Coalitions in Lebanon are in continual change, and politicians know that they that they may not be in power when the debt is due. Such a situation tends to increase spending and debt.[6] To summarize, politicians from different sects sometimes compete and sometimes collude; they end up sharing the government resources. All factions are interested in the increase of the overall government-privilege pie, which may explain the continuous and unsustainable rise in the size of government. For 2015, Lebanon is expected to have a debt of 148 percent of GDP, a budget deficit of 12 percent and government expenditure of 34 percent of GDP (International Monetary Fund 2014).

Clientelism is deeply rooted in Lebanese policymaking. One trait of this clientelism is the bargain that exists between the political parties and their voters. Voters vote for the party's candidate, and in return they are privileged.[7] Privileges include channeling government resources to those voters and resolving their problems (arranging for the government to hire them, coming to their aid within the judicial system, etc.). Access to entry into government service is generally possible though the sectarian political parties. This kind of clientelism is well described by Herbert Kitschelt (2000) and Luigi Manzetti and Carole Wilson (2007). As recognition for a politician's favor, members of the extended family of the beneficiary, including cousins, uncles, etc., are grateful and typically vote for the politician's party for generations to come.

A second trait of clientelism is the perpetuation of political dynasties. Traditionally, the sons of Lebanese members of Parliament are considered natural candidates for office. It resembles feudalism in the sense that people who voted for the father systematically vote for the son, or daughter or

---

5. *See* Roubini and Sachs (1989a; 1989b); Alesina and Drazen (1991); Howitt and Wintrobe (1995); Tsebelis (1995; 1999).
6. *See* Buchanan and Wagner (1977); Buchanan (1997); Persson and Svensson (1989); Alesina and Tabellini (1990); Aghion and Bolton (1990).
7. See the core voter model elaborated by Cox and McCubbins (1986).

nephew, regardless of competence. This 'personal vote' persists from generation to generation (creating the consequences described in Ames 1995; Cain,
Ferejohn, and Fiorina 1987; Carey and Shugart 1995). A public official has the
incentive to abuse government power and to adopt rent-seeking behavior in
return for personal enrichment, since he knows that the voters will elect him
anyway. His bet is that voters will elect him because of his capacity to protect
them and to favor them, rather than for his honesty or competence. Criticism
of policies is usually taken as criticism of the sect, triggering solidarity within
the sect. And supporters suffer few consequences of their actions, being
protected by their political representatives.[8] Therefore, clientelism is shielded
by sectarianism, and the two go hand in hand.

Background questions

I grew up in Lebanon but did my university studies and started my working
career in France. Upon returning to Lebanon I was startled by the extent and
depth of sectarianism. I am creating an organization, the Lebanese Institute
for Market Studies (LIMS), to promote scientific, market-based economic
reforms that have the potential to serve as a unifying social force in Lebanon.
The institute will produce policy-oriented papers and emphasize quantifying
the financial impact of policy alternatives on families, businesses, and the
economy in general. Topics can vary from standard market-based reforms
such as privatization, free trade, government deficit and debt, financial
liberalization, etc., to novel fields such as monetary systems without a central
bank, sectarian economics, war and economics, and so forth. I expect to
launch LIMS shortly after the publication of this paper containing the results
of the survey, which may be seen as an unofficial first activity of LIMS.

The survey, conducted in English and in Arabic, was sent to professors
teaching in programs that confer economics degrees in public and private
universities.[9] Table 1 provides a list of those universities. Seven of the
universities mentioned in Table 1 had professors' email addresses available on
their websites, which I compiled. For the remaining, one of two options was

---

8. *See* Brusco et al. (2004); Estévez et al. (2002); Lizzeri and Persico (2001); Luttmer (2001).
9. I did not include universities that grant only a degree in business, though admittedly some
of these offer a concentration, major, track, or emphasis in economics.

used: physical surveys were sent directly to faculty members, or the survey was sent to department chairs who were asked to forward it to appropriate faculty members. A total of 214 surveys were sent out and 40 were returned, giving a response rate of 19%. So the survey results should be treated with some caution—even if responses were drawn randomly from the population, sampling error as conventionally measured would be on the order of plus-or-minus 14%.

TABLE 1. University programs conferring economics degrees in Lebanon

University	Faculty/Department	Private or Public	Degree in Economics
American University of Beirut (AUB)	Department of Economics	Private	Bachelor's and Master's
American University of Science and Technology (AUST)	Faculty of Business and Economics	Private	Bachelor's and Master's
Beirut Arab University (BAU)	Department of Economics	Private	Bachelor's, Master's and Ph.D.
Haigazian University	Faculty of Business Administration and Economics	Private	Bachelor's
Islamic University of Lebanon (IUL)	Faculty of Economics and Business Administration	Private	Bachelor's and Master's
Lebanese American University (LAU)	Department of Economics	Private	Bachelor's and Master's
Lebanese University (LU)	Faculty of Economic Science and Business Administration	Public	Bachelor's, Master's and Ph.D.
Notre Dame University–Louaize (NDU)	Faculty of Business Administration and Economics	Private	Bachelor's
Saint Joseph's University (USJ)	Faculty of Economic Sciences	Private	Bachelor's and Master's
University of Balamand (UOB)	Department of Economics	Private	Bachelor's

The survey contains 36 questions, of which 26 are policy-issue questions, nine are background questions and one is an open-ended question about the survey in general. Of the 40 respondents, 31 were Ph.D. holders, with 29 having their doctorate in economics. Thirty-one faculty members work in a private university. Twenty-nine work at an institution where a Master's is the highest degree issued.

Background questions included inquiries about religious and political beliefs:

35. What is your religious affiliation? (Once again, skip any question you are not comfortable answering.
ما هو انتماؤك الديني ؟(الرجاء تخطي أي سؤال لا ترغب بالإجابة عليه)

Druz	Maronite	Muslim Shia	Muslim Sunni	Other Christians	Other Muslims	None of the mentioned
درزي	ماروني	مسلم شيعي	مسلم سني	مسيحي آخر	مسلم آخر	لا شيء من المذكور

36. To which political party have the candidates you've voted for in the past ten years mostly belonged? (Once again, skip any question you are not comfortable answering.)
إلى أي حزب ينتمي معظم الذين صوت لهم في السنوات العشر الماضية؟ (مرة أخرى، تخطي أي سؤال لاترغب بالإجابة عليه)

Future Movement	Free Patriotic Movement	Progressive Socialist Party	Amal Movement	Hezbollah	Lebanese Forces
تيار المستقبل	التيار الوطني الحر	الحزب التقدمي الإشتراكي	حركة أمل	حزب الله	القوات اللبنائية

Tachnak Party	Other 14 march	Other 8 march	Independent Candidates	Did not vote	
حزب الطاشناك	أحزاب أخرى من 14 آذار	أحزاب أخرى من 8 آذار	مرشحين مستقلين	لم أصوت	

Many respondents refrained from answering those questions. Only 24 stated their religious belief and just 12 indicated a political affiliation. These two questions registered the highest rate of abstention. That just 12 people out of 40 respondents were willing to indicate their political affiliation in an anonymous survey tells us something about the culture in Lebanon.[10] Of those who did specify their religious affiliation, 11 were Maronite, six other Christians, four Shia, and three Sunni. Among those acknowledging a political party affiliation, three have voted for candidates belonging to the Free Patriotic Movement, three for Hezbollah, three for other March 8 Alliance parties, two for Other March 14 Alliance parties, and one for the Future Movement. The remaining respondents either did not vote or did not answer the question.

It is surprising that the Future Movement, which is currently the biggest bloc in the Lebanese parliament, garnered only one mention of support among respondents. In addition, none of the respondents said they voted for

---

10. Klein and Stern (2007) surveyed American economists, and 90.9% of their respondents answered the question about their political affiliation. Šťastný (2010) surveyed Czech economists and 72.5% of the respondents answered the question.

any of the Progressive Socialist Party, the Amal Movement, or the Lebanese Forces, which are among the main blocs of the parliament. This is probably due to the low number of people answering the question and to the fact that politics is the source of fierce discord among the Lebanese, leading them to be very discreet about their voting preferences. Such tendency is confirmed when crossing the answers of both the political and religious affiliations. In fact, none of the three Sunni respondents said they had voted for the Sunni-backed Future Movement. Four professors belonging to the Shia tradition disclosed their voting preferences. Two voted for the strongly backed Shia party, Hezbollah, and these two worked at the public university. Of the two remaining professors, who worked for private universities, one voted for Hezbollah's ally and one reported not voting. Finally, eight of the 17 respondents who revealed their Christian affiliation (Maronite and Other Christian) did not vote or did not answer the vote question. The remaining votes were split between the Free Patriotic Movement and Other March 8 Alliance parties (five respondents) on one hand, and the March 14 Alliance (three respondents) on the other. I admit that the 12 survey respondents who disclosed their voting preference provided answers that fail to illustrate my general description of clientistic politics in Lebanon. I conjecture that respondents whose political views differ from the stereotypes may have been more willing to express those views.

Two questions were asked about the respondent's orientation in economic outlook:

33. Who are your favorite economic thinkers? please list, up to three:
من هم المفكرون الاقتصاديون المفضلون لديك؟ (يرجى ذكر ثلاثة على الأكثر)

_____

_____

34. Which of following comes closer to your economic views?
أي من الوجهات الإقتصادية التالية تعتبرها الأقرب إلى وجهة نظرك؟

| Classical liberal | Keynesian | Libertarian | Marxian |
| الكلاسيكية الليبرالية | الكينيزية | التحررية | الماركسية |

other [please specify]:_____
أخرى وجهات

As concerns economic intellectual affiliation, 15 declared themselves Keynesians, nine classical liberals, five libertarians, and one Marxian. The remaining ten did not answer the question. The favorite economic thinker is John Maynard Keynes, cited by seven respondents. Adam Smith, Karl Marx, Milton Friedman, and Friedrich Hayek ranked second, cited four times each. David Ricardo and Joseph Stiglitz were named three times each.

Policy questions

Following the example of Daniel Šťastný (2010), the policy questions used the status quo as the baseline, as in: Should trade barriers (tariffs, quotas, etc.) on imports be increased, kept unchanged, or reduced? An answer thus indicates whether the respondent is for more liberalization. Table 2 presents policy propositions and the distribution of answers.

TABLE 2. Survey propositions and response statistics

	Increased	Kept unchanged	Reduced	Did not answer
1. Government spending to tune the economy should be	25	4	10	1
2. Government spending on the production and maintenance of infrastructure should be	35	2	3	0
3. Trade barriers (tariffs, quotas etc.) on imports should be	4	11	25	0
4. The minimum wage in the public sector should be	19	16	3	2
5. The minimum wage in private sector should be	18	18	3	1
6. Government budget to public schools should be	31	6	3	0
7. Government budget for the Lebanese University should be	29	8	3	0
8. Freedom for additional private companies to enter the electricity sector should be	31	5	2	2
9. Government spending on electricity imports (Turkish power ships for example) should be	12	6	18	4

	Increased	Kept unchanged	Reduced	Did not answer
10. Government production of water dams should be	32	4	3	1
11. Full-time employment of the contract workers and part timers at the government owned *Electricité du Liban* should be	11	13	13	3
12. Privatization in the phone and internet sector should be (OGERO being currently the single most important player)	28	7	5	0
13. Laws to block sexually lewd websites should be	21	7	12	0
14. Laws and decisions to censor "immoral and sectarian artistic productions" (movies, books, magazine, paintings, etc.) should be	17	6	16	1
15. Government control on gambling should be	20	9	10	1
16. Government control and regulation on Mobile services sector should be	16	9	15	0
17. Freedom for additional private companies to enter the Mobile services sector should be	33	6	1	0
18. Government spending in the regions (outside Beirut) should be	33	4	3	0
19. Banque du Liban ownership in Casino du Liban should be	10	15	10	5
20. Banque du Liban subsidized loans (to housing, small entrepreneurs, students, etc.) should be	20	13	6	1
21. Banque du Liban ownership in the Middle East Airlines should be	11	16	10	3
22. The measures taken by Lebanon to grant exclusive rights to the Middle East Airlines (MEA) should be	2	12	23	3
23. Government funds allocated to the Displaced Fund should be	7	11	20	2
24. Government funds allocated to the South Fund should be	9	8	20	3
25. Government funds allocated to the Higher Body of Relief Fund should be	11	6	18	5

	Increased	Kept unchanged	Reduced	Did not answer
26. Controls on refugees and immigration should be	27	3	9	1

Public spending

Respondents clearly favored the should-be-increased response in public spending when it came to fine-tune the economy (25 respondents did so, in answering Q1),[11] to produce and maintain infrastructure (35 did so, in answering Q2), to allocate funds to public schools (31, Q6) and to the public university (29, Q7), to provide water dams (32, Q10), to spend money for development outside of Beirut (33, Q18) and to subsidize loans (20, Q20). Keynesian respondents were almost unanimous about increasing government spending on these issues, and they were backed in their views by about half the self-described classical liberals and libertarians.

Respondents were not in favor of allocating additional budget to the Central Fund for the Displaced or to the Council of the South. The Central Fund for the Displaced is a public fund established to finance the return of people who were forced to leave their homes during the civil war. The Council of the South finances the development of the south of Lebanon, an underdeveloped region that suffered from Israeli occupation. These two entities have very bad reputations.[12] They have been vehicles allowing specific political parties to grab privileges, to operate clientelistic redistribution policies, and to increase their authority in the government and within their own sect. It is remarkable to see[13] that none of the respondents belonging to the sects backing the parties that control these vehicles favored increasing their budget. In addition, the few respondents who favored handing additional resources to the Council of the South and the Central Fund for the Displaced were not of the expected sect; they were simply Keynesians.[14] It seems that economics professors who filled the survey decided about policy reforms

---

11. Figures in parentheses indicate the number of respondents who favored the change in a specific direction.
12. *See* Nazzal (2012), Adwan (2004), and the *Daily Star* (2000).
13. After crossing the results of Q35 with Q23 and Q24.
14. After crossing the results of Q34 with Q23 and Q24.

based on their economic analysis and not on their sectarian beliefs. Again, the survey responses do not illustrate my description of clientistic politics in Lebanon.

While it is well established in the minds of the Lebanese that the above entities are major vehicles for patronage and nepotism, corruption in electricity imports and in the Higher Relief Committee[15] is widely suspected but has yet to be confirmed. The Higher Relief Committee intervenes in order to help people in case of a disaster. The head of the Higher Relief Committee was released from his job from allegations of corruption. The Ministry of Energy and Water started importing electricity produced on Turkish ships stationed in the Mediterranean near the Lebanese shore. Electricity imports were accompanied by scandals related to nepotism and bribes, but no solid proof has yet been provided. Respondents were divided about these two entities. Twelve and 11 respondents, respectively, believe that government spending on electricity imports and the Government funds allocated to the Higher Body of Relief should be increased. However, 18 respondents were in favor of decreasing spending and funding related to those entities.

Employment in the public administrations

Employment in the public administrations is subject to patronage. An employee is hired only after enjoying support by a politician and is expected to return the favor by using his office to serve his political sponsor. Such patronage allows politicians to use these offices to acquire votes. In return, bureaucrats know that they may expect to be protected even if they do their job badly.

Government-owned Electricité du Liban delegates many tasks to contract workers and part-timers. Part-timers have requested full-time employment at Electricité du Liban although they failed the entrance examination. Sixteen respondents favor keeping full-time employment unchanged and ten favor reducing it.

---

15. The committee is currently extensively engaged in supporting Syrian refugees.

Public provision of goods and services

The public sector is a direct provider of energy through state-owned Electricté du Liban, and of landline services and Internet bandwidth through the state-owned company Ogero. The Lebanese central bank is a major shareholder in Middle East Airlines and holds a big share in Casino du Liban. These institutions are protected against competition though statutory monopoly schemes.

Although respondents were in favor of public spending, they were clearly against the government's monopolization of goods and services. The vast majority of respondents wanted to see an increase in the freedom for additional private companies to enter the electricity sector (Q8). They were also for the increase in the privatization of the phone and internet sector (Q12). However, answers were less pointed for the sectors managed by the central bank: there the response selected most often was to keep things unchanged (Q19). The central bank enjoys a good reputation. The current governor was appointed shortly after the strong exchange rate devaluation of the early 1990s and the central bank has since managed to keep the exchange rate of the Lebanese pound stable against the U.S. dollar. The Lebanese financial system, which operates under the supervision of the central bank, did not suffer during the global financial crisis that started in the 2007. The central bank's reputation has therefore been enhanced and the people trust its management.

Monopoly privileges

Mobile phone services are provided by two private companies that are protected though a statutory duopoly scheme. The sector has always been subject to politicians' disputes over who will have the patronage (Gambill 2003). Unlike the public monopolies, which produce economic losses, the private duopoly generates high profits for shareholders and high revenues for the state. Respondents want a change to occur in the sector. The vast majority of respondents favored freedom for additional private companies to enter the sector (Q17). On the other hand, they are divided about government control and regulation should the duopoly be kept.

Regulation

Respondents mainly oppose the increase of trade barriers and exclusive rights for Middle East Airlines. They generally favor freer trade and entry into the market. However, very few think the minimum wage should be decreased.

Immigration

Twenty-seven respondents are in favor of increasing controls on refugees and immigration. Given the current Syrian war, the number of Syrian refugees in Lebanon is now well over one million, and this in a country where the population (prior to the Syrian war) was between four and five million. The huge inflow of refugees and the security threats that came with it may have had an effect on the respondents' answers.

Public morals laws

Respondents show strong religious feelings and conservatism. Half of the respondents are for increased laws to block sexually lewd websites and government control on gambling, and half of the remaining are for keeping the current laws, which are very restrictive, unchanged.

Conservatism did not apply to laws and decisions designed to censor immoral and sectarian artistic productions. The wording "immoral and sectarian" is used in the text of the relevant Lebanese law. It is a vague concept occasionally used by the authorities for cracking down on "disturbing" individuals. Seventeen respondents were in favor of increasing censorship, probably motivated by their moral values. However, 16 respondents were in favor of reducing censorship, probably motivated by concerns about the liberty of expression.

Concluding remarks

Currently, the gap left by the fading of liberal ideas is filled by policies characterized by clientelism, nepotism, and corruption. It is encouraging that economists are sometimes able to reach conclusions across sectarian lines by employing a common framework of analysis. However, in the minds of the respondents there seems to be a dichotomy between the idea of increasing government spending, which they favor, and the fact that the government often cannot be trusted with money, which they acknowledge. Repeated episodes of misdirected spending seem unable to convince economists that high spending is a problem. They continue to hope that the bloated Lebanese public sector can be tamed and made to behave better.

The history of Lebanon from Phoenician times until today has seen periods of high economic liberalization that went together with quick economic development. The classical liberal tradition of the coasts, and the policies of Fakhreddine II and the New Phoenicians, deserve more attention from researchers. So too does the relation between the decline of this tradition and the periods of sectarian tension throughout the history of the country.

References

Adwan, Charles D. 2004. Lebanon's Corruption Dilemma. *The Daily Star* (Beirut), May 19.

Aghion, Philippe, and Patrick Bolton. 1990. Government Domestic Debt and the Risk of Default: A Political-Economic Model of the Strategic Role of Debt. In *Public Debt Management: Theory and History*, eds. Rudiger Dornbusch and Mario Draghi, 315–344. Cambridge, UK: Cambridge University Press.

Alesina, Alberto, and Allan Drazen. 1991. Why Are Stabilizations Delayed? *American Economic Review* 81(5): 1170–1188.

Alesina, Alberto, and Guido Tabellini. 1990. A Positive Theory of Fiscal Deficits and Government Debt. *Review of Economic Studies* 57(3): 403–414.

Ames, Barry. 1995. Electoral Strategy Under Open-List Proportional Representation. *American Journal of Political Science* 39(2): 406–433.

Brusco, Valeria, Marcelo Nazareno, and Susan Carol Stokes. 2004. Vote Buying in Argentina. *Latin American Research Review* 39(2): 66–88.

Buchanan, James M. 1997. The Balanced Budget Amendment: Clarifying the Arguments. *Public Choice* 90: 117–138.

Buchanan, James M., and Richard E. Wagner. 2000 [1977]. *Democracy in Deficit: The Political Legacy of Lord Keynes* (*The Collected Works of James M. Buchanan*, vol. 8). Indianapolis: Liberty Fund.

Cain, Bruce, John Ferejohn, and Morris Fiorina. 1987. *The Personal Vote: Constituency Service and Electoral Independence*. Cambridge, Mass.: Harvard University Press.

Carey, John M., and Matthew Soberg Shugart. 1995. Incentives to Cultivate a Personal Vote: A Rank Ordering of Electoral Formulas. *Electoral Studies* 14(4): 417–439.

Cox, Gary W., and Mathew D. McCubbins. 1986. Electoral Politics as a Redistributive Game. *Journal of Politics* 48(2): 370–389.

Daily Star. 2000. Politicians Want Displaced Fund Used to Win Seats. *The Daily Star* (Beirut), February 9.

Dib, Kamal. 2004. *Warlords and Merchants: The Lebanese Business and Political Establishment.* Reading, UK: Ithaca Press.

Downs, Anthony. 1957. *An Economic Theory of Democracy.* New York: Harper.

Epstein, Gil S., and Ira N. Gang. 2007. Understanding the Development of Fundamentalism. *Public Choice* 132: 257–271.

Estévez, Federico, Beatriz Magaloni, and Alberto Diaz-Cayeros. 2002. A Portfolio Diversification Model of Electoral Investment. Presented at Frontiers in Latin American Political Economy conference, Stanford University (Stanford, Calif.), January.

Gambill, Gary C. 2003. Lebanon's Cell Phone Scandals. *Middle East Intelligence Bulletin* (Middle East Forum, Philadelphia, Pa.), January.

Gates, Carolyn L. 1989. The Historical Role of Political Economy in the Development of Modern Lebanon. *Papers on Lebanon* 10, Centre for Lebanese Studies (Oxford, UK).

Gates, Carolyn L. 1998. *Merchant Republic of Lebanon: Rise of an Open Economy.* London: I. B. Tauris.

Glaeser, Edward L., Giacomo A. M. Ponzetto, and Jesse M. Shapiro. 2005. Strategic Extremism: Why Republicans and Democrats Divide on Religious Values. *Quarterly Journal of Economics* 120(4): 1283–1330.

Glazer, Amihai. 2002. Strategic Positioning and Campaigning. In *Political Extremism and Rationality,* eds. Albert Breton, Gianluigi Galeotti, Pierre Salmon, and Ronald Wintrobe, 105–121. Cambridge, UK: Cambridge University Press.

Glazer, Amihai, Mark Gradstein, and Kai A. Konrad. 1998. The Electoral Politics of Extreme Policies. *Economic Journal* 108(451): 1677–1685.

Haykal, Rayan, and Nizar Hariri. 2012. La pensée économique de Michel Chiha: Variations sur le thème de la liberté. *Travaux et Jours* 86: 43–72.

Howitt, Peter, and Ronald Wintrobe. 1995. The Political Economy of Inaction. *Journal of Public Economics* 56(3): 329–353.

International Monetary Fund. 2014. IMF Executive Board Concludes 2014 Article IV Consultation with Lebanon. Press Release 14/376, July 31. International Monetary Fund (Washington, D.C.).

Kaufman, Asher. 2014. *Reviving Phoenicia: The Search for Identity in Lebanon.* London: I. B. Tauris.

Kitschelt, Herbert. 2000. Linkages Between Citizens and Politicians in Democratic Polities. *Comparative Political Studies* 33(6/7): 845–879.

Klein, Daniel B., and Charlotta Stern. 2007. Is There a Free-Market Economist in the House? The Policy Views of American Economic Association Members. *American Journal of Economics and Sociology* 66(2): 309–334.

Lizzeri, Alessandro, and Nicola Persico. 2001. The Provision of Public Goods Under Alternative Electoral Incentives. *American Economic Review* 91(1): 225–239.

Luttmer, Erzo F. P. 2001. Group Loyalty and the Taste for Redistribution. *Journal of Political Economy* 109(3): 500–528.

Manzetti, Luigi, and Carole J. Wilson. 2007. Why Do Corrupt Governments Maintain Public Support? *Comparative Political Studies* 40(8): 949–970.

Matsen, Egil, and Øystein Thøgersen. 2010. Habit Formation, Strategic Extremism, and Debt Policy. *Public Choice* 145: 165–180.

Nazzal, Mohamed. 2012. The Untouchable Looters of the Lebanese Displaced. *Al-Akhbar* (Beirut), July 28.

Persson, Torsten, and Lars E. O. Svensson. 1989. Why a Stubborn Conservative Would Run a Deficit: Policy with Time-Inconsistent Preferences. *Quarterly Journal of Economics* 104(2): 325–345.

Roubini, Nouriel, and Jeffrey D. Sachs. 1989a. Political and Economic Determinants of Budget Deficits in the Industrial Democracies. *European Economic Review* 33(5): 903–933.

Roubini, Nouriel, and Jeffrey D. Sachs. 1989b. Government Spending and Budget Deficits in the Industrial Countries. *Economic Policy* 4(8): 99–132.

Šťastný, Daniel. 2010. Czech Economists on Economic Policy: A Survey. *Econ Journal Watch* 7(3): 275–287.

Tsebelis, George. 1995. Decision Making in Political Systems: Veto Players in Presidentialism, Parliamentarism, Multicameralism and Multipartyism. *British Journal of Political Science* 25(3): 289–325.

Tsebelis, George. 1999. Veto Players and Law Production in Parliamentary Democracies: An Empirical Analysis. *American Political Science Review* 93(3): 591–608.

About the Authors

Chris Berg is a Senior Fellow at the Institute of Public Affairs. He is the author of *The Libertarian Alternative* (2016), *Liberty, Equality and Democracy* (2015), *Magna Carta: The Tax Revolt That Gave Us Liberty* (with John Roskam, 2015), *In Defence of Freedom of Speech: From Ancient Greece to Andrew Bolt* (2012), and *The Growth of Australia's Regulatory State: Ideology, Accountability, and the Mega-Regulators* (2008).

G. P. Manish is an Assistant Professor of Economics in the Sorrell College of Business, and a member of the Manuel H. Johnson Center of Political Economy, at Troy University. He received his Ph.D. from Suffolk University, and he has published articles in *The Independent Review*, *Review of Austrian Economics*, and *Atlantic Economic Journal*. His areas of interest include development economics and economic history, monetary and business cycle theory, entrepreneurship and price theory, and the history of economic thought.

Shruti Rajagopalan is an Assistant Professor of Economics at Purchase College, State University of New York, and a Fellow at the Classical Liberal Institute at the New York University School of Law. She earned her Ph.D. in economics in 2013 from George Mason University. Her research interests include law and economics, public choice theory, constitutional political economy, and history of economic thought.

Daniel Sutter is the Charles G. Koch Professor of Economics with the Manuel H. Johnson Center for Political Economy at Troy University. He has published over 100 journal articles and book chapters. His research has spanned the areas of public choice, constitutional economics, Austrian economics, environmental economics, and the market for ideas, and covered topics including the constraint of government officials, the transition from authoritarian rule, automobile safety regulation, left bias in the news media and the academy, and the societal impacts of extreme weather.

Lawrence H. White is Professor of Economics at George Mason University. He is a co-editor of *Econ Journal Watch* and is the host of EJW Audio. He previously taught at New York University, the University of Georgia, and the University of Missouri–St. Louis. He is the author of several books, including *The Clash of Economic Ideas: The Great Policy Debates and Experiments of the Last Hundred Years* (2012) and *Better Money: Gold, Fiat or Bitcoin?* (2023). His articles on monetary theory and banking history have appeared in the *American Economic Review*, the *Journal of Economic Literature*, the *Journal of Money, Credit, and Banking*, and other leading journals.

Martin van Staden is Deputy Head of Policy Research at the South African Institute of Race Relations. At the time of writing, he was pursuing a doctorate in law at the University of Pretoria, from where he obtained a Master of Laws (cum laude) in 2020. Martin has been published in various South African and international academic journals, including the *Cato Journal* and *Cosmos + Taxis*, and has written a book, *The Constitution and the Rule of Law: An Introduction*. He serves on the executive committee and board of the Free Market Foundation, is editor in chief of the *Rational Standard*, and served as a member of the African executive of Students For Liberty between 2015 and 2018, and a legal fellow at business group Sakeliga between 2021 and 2022.

Prof. Dr. Xingyuan Feng is Senior Research Fellow, Research Institute of Economic Thought and Economic History, Fudan University. He was a co-founder of Chinese Hayek Society, of Cathay Institute for Public Affairs, and of Forum for Austrian Economists in China, and he is co-editor of Modern Western Thought Series. He received his Ph.D. in economics from the University of Witten/Herdecke, Germany. Xingyuan's main research fields include the Austrian school of economics, institutional economics, new political economy, government finance, and banking and finance. He has authored or co-authored a dozen monographs including *The Political Economy of China's Great Transformation* (2016, Routledge) and *The Ecology of Chinese Private Enterprises* (2015, World Scientific). He is also the co-translator for a Chinese edition of Hayek's *The Road to Serfdom*.

Weisen Li is a Professor in Economics at Fudan University, Shanghai. He was the Deputy-Dean of School of Economics at the University for many years, and currently he is the Director of the Research Institute of Economic Thought and Economic History at Fudan. He holds a B.A. in Economics from Shandong University, a Master's Degree from the Australian National University, and a Ph.D. in Economics from the University of Sydney. Professor Li has interests in the language of economics, ethics, anthropology, jurisprudence, and Austrian economics, particularly Hayek. He has published fifteen books and a range of articles in both Chinese and English. He also translated many English works of institutional economics, game theory, legal theory, and political sciences into Chinese. He is a columnist for the *Wall Street Journal* (Chinese), *Financial Times* (Chinese), and other leading media in China.

Evan Osborne is professor of economics, Wright State University. He reads and writes Chinese, and his current interests include Chinese history from the late Qing to the present. He has done work on ethnic conflict and more general social conflict, and on the economics of art, empirical analysis of litigation, development economics, and various topics in sports economics. He is married and the father of two children.

Young Back Choi is professor of economics at St. John's University in New York. He received his Ph.D. in Economics from the University of Michigan. Professor Choi has published in the areas of entrepreneurship, institutional economics, economic development, income distribution and mobility, and the history of economic thought. His works appeared in numerous professional journals, including *Constitutional Political Economy*, *Kyklos*, *Social Philosophy and Policy*, *History of Political Economy*, *Review of Social Economy*, *Human Systems Management*, and *Review of Austrian Economics*. He is the author of *Paradigms and Conventions: Uncertainty, Decision Making and Entrepreneurship* (University of Michigan Press, 1993). His recent interests include re-examination of Adam Smith.

Yong J. Yoon is an economist at George Mason University and senior research scholar at the Center for Study of Public Choice. He received his Ph.D. degree from Northwestern University's Kellogg Graduate School of Management; he also earned a Ph.D. degree in mathematics. He authored with James Buchanan *The Return to Increasing Returns* (University of Michigan

Press, 1994) and *Individualism and Political Disorder* (Edward Elgar, 2015). His research examines the moral psychology of individualism, moral community, and political disorder. His current interest includes innovations in politics and commerce in East Asia (China, Japan, and Korea) during the transformative period, 1850–present, in response to the Western challenge.

Patrick Mardini is an assistant professor of finance, coordinator of the finance track, and manager of the DBA program at the University of Balamand in Lebanon. He is also the founder of Lebanese Institute for Market Studies, a research institute designed to promote market reforms and policies in Lebanon. He holds a Ph.D. in Economics from Paris Dauphine University. His past employment includes four years at the Paris mutual fund Modèles & Stratégies.

CL Press
A Fraser Institute Project
https://clpress.net/

Professor Daniel Klein (George Mason University, Economics and Mercatus Center) and Dr. Erik Matson (Mercatus Center), directors of the Adam Smith Program at George Mason University, are the editors and directors of CL Press. CL stands at once for classical liberal and conservative liberal.

CL Press is a project of the Fraser Institute (Vancouver, Canada).

People:

- Dan Klein and Erik Matson are the co-editors and executives of the imprint.
- Jane Shaw Stroup is Editorial Advisor, doing especially copy-editing and text preparation.
- An Advisory Board:
    - Jordan Ballor, *Center for Religion, Culture, and Democracy*
    - Donald Boudreaux, *George Mason Univ.*
    - Caroline Breashears, St. *Lawrence Univ.*
    - Ross Emmett, *Arizona State Univ.*
    - Knud Haakonssen, *Univ. of St. Andrews*
    - Björn Hasselgren, *Timbro, Univ. of Uppsala*
    - Karen Horn, *Univ. of Erfurt*
    - Jimena Hurtado, *Univ. de los Andes*
    - Nelson Lund, *George Mason Univ.*
    - Daniel Mahoney, *Assumption Univ.*
    - Deirdre N. McCloskey, *Univ. of Illinois-Chicago*
    - Thomas W. Merrill, *American Univ.*

- James Otteson, *Univ. of Notre Dame*
- Catherine R. Pakaluk, *Catholic Univ. of America*
- Sandra Peart, *Univ. of Richmond*
- Mario Rizzo, *New York Univ.*
- Loren Rotner, *Univ. of Austin*
- Marc Sidwell, *New Culture Forum*
- Emily Skarbek, *Brown Univ.*
- Craig Smith, *Univ. of Glasgow*
- David Walsh, *Catholic Univ. of America*
- Barry Weingast, *Stanford Univ.*
- Richard Whatmore, *Univ. of St. Andrews*
- Lawrence H. White, *George Mason Univ.*
- Amy Willis, *Liberty Fund*
- Bart Wilson, *Chapman Univ.*
- Todd Zywicki, *George Mason Univ.*

Why start CL Press?

CL Press publishes good, low-priced work in intellectual history, political theory, political economy, and moral philosophy. More specifically, CL Press explores and advances discourse in the following areas:

- The intellectual history and meaning of liberalism.
- The relationship between liberalism and conservatism.
- The role of religion in disseminating liberal understandings and institutions including: humankind's ethical universalism, the moral equality of souls, the rule of law, religious liberty, the meaning and virtues of economic life.
- The relationship between religion and economic philosophy.
- The political, social, and economic philosophy of the Scottish Enlightenment, especially Adam Smith.
- The state of classically liberal ideas and policies across the world today.

www.ingramcontent.com/pod-product-compliance
Lightning Source LLC
Chambersburg PA
CBHW011833020426
42335CB00024B/2844